ART-TYPE EDITION

POEMS

By ALFRED LORD TENNYSON

THE WORLD'S
POPULAR CLASSICS

BOOKS, INC.
PUBLISHERS

NEW YORK   BOSTON

MANUFACTURED IN THE UNITED STATES OF AMERICA

CONTENTS

JUVENILIA
- Claribel 1
- Nothing Will Die 1
- All Things Will Die . 3
- Leonine Elegiacs 4
- Supposed Confessions 4
- The Kraken 9
- Song 10
- Lilian 10
- Isabel 11
- Mariana 12
- Mariana in the South . 14
- To ——— 17
- Madeline 18
- Song: The Owl 19
- Second Song to the Same 20
- Recollections of the Arabian Nights 20
- Ode to Memory 24
- Song 28
- A Character 28
- The Poet 29
- The Poet's Mind 31
- The Sea-Fairies 32
- The Deserted House . 33
- The Dying Swan 34
- A Dirge 35
- Love and Death 37
- The Ballad of Oriana 37
- Circumstance 40
- The Merman 40
- The Mermaid 42
- Adeline 43
- Margaret 45
- Rosalind 47
- Eleänore 48

EARLY SONNETS
- To ——— 53
- To J. M. K. 53
- Alexander 54
- Buonaparte 54
- Poland 55
- The Bridesmaid 57
- The Lady of Shalott .. 57
- The Two Voices 62
- The Miller's Daughter 76
- Fatima 82
- Œnone 84
- The Sisters 90
- To ——— 92
- The Palace of Art 92
- Lady Clara Vere de Vere 101
- The May Queen 103
- The Lotos-Eaters 109
- Choric Song 110
- A Dream of Fair Women 114
- The Blackbird 122
- The Death of the Old Year 123
- To J. S. 124
- On a Mourner 126
- England and America in 1782 128
- The Goose 128
- Morte D'Arthur 130
- Dora 137
- Audley Court 141
- Walking to the Mail .. 143
- Edwin Morris 146
- St. Simeon Stylites 150
- The Talking Oak 155

CONTENTS

Love and Duty 164
The Golden Year 166
Ulysses 168
Tithonus 170
Locksley Hall 172
Godiva 180
The Day-Dream 182
Amphion 191
St. Agnes' Eve 193
Sir Galahad 194
Edward Gray 197
Will Waterproof's Lyrical Monologue 198
Lady Clare 205
The Captain 207
The Lord of Burleigh . 209
The Voyage 211
Sir Launcelot and Queen Guinevere .. 214
A Farewell 216
The Beggar Maid 216
The Eagle 217
The Letters 218
The Vision of Sin 219
To ——— 226
To E. L. on His Travels in Greece .. 227
The Poet's Song 228
The Brook 229
Sea Dreams 234
Lucretius 242
Ode on the Death of the Duke of Wellington 249
The Charge of the Light Brigade 256
The Grandmother ... 258
Northern Farmer 263
The Daisy 268
To the Rev. F. D. Maurice 271
Will 273
In the Valley of Cauteretz 273
In the Garden at Swainston 274
The Flower 274
Requiescat 275
The Sailor Boy 275
The Islet 276

CHILD-SONGS
The City Child 277
Minnie and Winnie .. 278
The Spiteful Letter .. 278
Literary Squabbles ... 279
The Victim 280
Wages 282
The Higher Pantheism 282
The Voice and the Peak 283
A Dedication 285

IDYLLS OF THE KING 286

THE VILLAGE WIFE 301

POEMS OF
TENNYSON

JUVENILIA

CLARIBEL

A MELODY

I

WHERE Claribel low-lieth
  The breezes pause and die,
    Letting the rose-leaves fall:
But the solemn oak-tree sigheth,
    Thick-leaved, ambrosial,
  With an ancient melody
  Of an inward agony,
Where Claribel low-lieth.

II

At eve the beetle boometh
  Athwart the thicket lone:
At noon the wild bee hummeth
  About the moss'd headstone;
At midnight the moon cometh
  And looketh down alone.
Her song the lintwhite swelleth,
The clear-voiced mavis dwelleth,
  The callow throstle lispeth,
The slumbrous wave outwelleth,
  The babbling runnel crispeth,
The hollow grot replieth
  Where Claribel low-lieth.

NOTHING WILL DIE

WHEN will the stream be aweary of flowing
    Under my eye?
When will the wind be aweary of blowing
    Over the sky?

When will the clouds be aweary of fleeting?
When will the heart be aweary of beating?
    And nature die?
Never, oh! never, nothing will die;
    The stream flows,
    The wind blows,
    The cloud fleets,
    The heart beats,
      Nothing will die.

Nothing will die;
All things will change
Thro' eternity.
'Tis the world's winter;
Autumn and summer
Are gone long ago;
Earth is dry to the centre,
But spring, a new comer,
A spring rich and strange,
Shall make the winds blow
Round and round,
Thro' and thro',
    Here and there,
      Till the air
And the ground
Shall be fill'd with life anew.

The world was never made;
It will change, but it will not fade.
So let the wind range;
For even and morn
    Ever will be
    Thro' eternity.
Nothing was born;
Nothing will die;
All things will change.

All Things Will Die

Clearly the blue river chimes in its flowing
    Under my eye;
Warmly and broadly the south winds are blowing
    Over the sky.
One after another the white clouds are fleeting;
Every heart this May morning in joyance is beating
    Full merrily;
  Yet all things must die.
  The stream will cease to flow;
  The wind will cease to blow;
  The clouds will cease to fleet;
  The heart will cease to beat;
    For all things must die.
    All things must die.
Spring will come never more.
    Oh! vanity!
Death waits at the door.
See! our friends are all forsaking
The wine and the merrymaking.
We are call'd—we must go.
Laid low, very low,
In the dark we must lie.
The merry glees are still;
The voice of the bird
Shall no more be heard,
Nor the wind on the hill.
    Oh! misery!
Hark! death is calling
While I speak to ye,
The jaw is falling,
The red cheek paling,
The strong limbs failing;
Ice with the warm blood mixing;
The eyeballs fixing.
Nine times goes the passing bell:
Ye merry souls, farewell.
    The old earth
    Had a birth,
    As all men know,
    Long ago.

And the old earth must die.
So let the warm winds range,
And the blue wave beat the shore;
For even and morn
Ye will never see
Thro' eternity.
All things were born.
Ye will come never more,
For all things must die.

LEONINE ELEGIACS

Low-flowing breezes are roaming the broad valley dimm'd in the gloaming:
Thoro' the black-stemm'd pines only the far river shines.
Creeping thro' blossomy rushes and bowers of rose-blowing bushes,
Down by the poplar tall rivulets babble and fall.
Barketh the shepherd-dog cheerly; the grasshopper carolleth clearly;
Deeply the wood-dove coos; shrilly the owlet halloos;
Winds creep; dews fall chilly: in her first sleep earth breathes stilly:
Over the pools in the burn water-gnats murmur and mourn.
Sadly the far kine loweth: the glimmering water out-floweth:
Twin peaks shadow'd with pine slope to the dark hyaline.
Low-throned Hesper is stayed between the two peaks; but the Naiad
Throbbing in mild unrest holds him beneath in her breast.
The ancient poetess singeth, that Hesperus all things bringeth,
Smoothing the wearied mind: bring me my love, Rosalind.
Thou comest morning or even; she cometh not morning or even.
False-eyed Hesper, unkind, where is my sweet Rosalind?

SUPPOSED CONFESSIONS

OF A SECOND-RATE SENSITIVE MIND

O God! my God! have mercy now.
I faint, I fall. Men say that Thou
Didst die for me, for such as *me*,
Patient of ill, and death, and scorn,

SUPPOSED CONFESSIONS

And that my sin was as a thorn
Among the thorns that girt Thy brow,
Wounding Thy soul.—That even now,
In this extremest misery
Of ignorance, I should require
A sign! and if a bolt of fire
Would rive the slumbrous summer noon
While I do pray to Thee alone,
Think my belief would stronger grow:
Is not my human pride brought low?
The boastings of my spirit still?
The joy I had in my freewill
All cold, and dead, and corpse-like grown?
And what is left to me, but Thou
And faith in Thee? Men pass me by;
Christians with happy countenances—
And children all seem full of Thee!
And women smile with saint-like glances
Like Thine own mother's when she bow'd
Above Thee, on that happy morn
When angels spake to men aloud,
And Thou and peace to earth were born,
Goodwill to me as well as all—
I one of them: my brothers they:
Brothers in Christ—a world of peace
And confidence, day after day;
And trust and hope till things should cease,
And then one Heaven receive us all.

How sweet to have a common faith!
To hold a common scorn of death!
And at a burial to hear
The creaking cords which wound and eat
Into my human heart, whene'er
Earth goes to earth, with grief, not fear,
With hopeful grief, were passing sweet!

Thrice happy state again to be
The trustful infant on the knee!
Who lets his rosy fingers play
About his mother's neck, and knows
Nothing beyond his mother's eyes.
They comfort him by night and day;

They light his little life alway;
He hath no thought of coming woes;
He hath no care of life or death;
Scarce outward signs of joy arise,
Because the Spirit of happiness
And perfect rest so inward is;
And loveth so his innocent heart,
Her temple and her place of birth,
Where she would ever wish to dwell,
Life of the fountain there, beneath
Its salient springs, and far apart,
Hating to wander out on earth,
Or breathe into the hollow air,
Whose chillness would make visible
Her subtil, warm, and golden breath,
Which mixing with the infant's blood,
Fulfils him with beatitude.
Oh! sure it is a special care
Of God, to fortify from doubt,
To arm in proof, and guard about
With triple-mailèd trust, and clear
Delight, the infant's dawning year.

Would that my gloomed fancy were
As thine, my mother, when with brows
Propt on thy knees, my hands upheld
In thine, I listen'd to thy vows,
For me outpour'd in holiest prayer—
For me unworthy!—and beheld
Thy mild deep eyes upraised, that knew
The beauty and repose of faith,
And the clear spirit shining thro'.
Oh! wherefore do we grow awry
From roots which strike so deep? why dare
Paths in the desert? Could not I
Bow myself down, where thou hast knelt,
To the earth—until the ice would melt
Here, and I feel as thou hast felt?
What Devil had the heart to scathe
Flowers thou hadst rear'd—to brush the dew
From thine own lily, when thy grave
Was deep, my mother, in the clay?
Myself? Is it thus? Myself? Had I

SUPPOSED CONFESSIONS

So little love for thee? But why
Prevail'd not thy pure prayers? Why pray
To one who heeds not, who can save
But will not? Great in faith, and strong
Against the grief of circumstance
Wert thou, and yet unheard. What if
Thou pleadest still, and seest me drive
Thro' utter dark a full-sail'd skiff,
Unpiloted i' the echoing dance
Of reboant whirlwinds, stooping low
Unto the death, not sunk! I know
At matins and at evensong,
That thou, if thou wert yet alive,
In deep and daily prayers would'st strive
To reconcile me with thy God.
Albeit, my hope is gray, and cold
At heart, thou wouldest murmur still—
"Bring this lamb back into Thy fold,
My Lord, if so it be Thy will."
Would'st tell me I must brook the rod
And chastisement of human pride;
That pride, the sin of devils, stood
Betwixt me and the light of God!
That hitherto I had defied
And had rejected God—that grace
Would drop from his o'er-brimming love,
As manna on my wilderness,
If I would pray—that God would move
And strike the hard, hard rock, and thence,
Sweet in their utmost bitterness,
Would issue tears of penitence
Which would keep green hope's life. Alas!
I think that pride hath now no place
Nor sojourn in me. I am void,
Dark, formless, utterly destroyed.

Why not believe then? Why not yet
Anchor thy frailty there, where man
Hath moor'd and rested? Ask the sea
At midnight, when the crisp slope waves
After a tempest, rib and fret
The broad-imbased beach, why he
Slumbers not like a mountain tarn?

Wherefore his ridges are not curls
And ripples of an island mere?
Wherefore he moaneth thus, nor can
Draw down into his vexed pools
All that blue heaven which hues and paves
The other? I am too forlorn,
Too shaken: my own weakness fools
My judgment, and my spirit whirls,
Moved from beneath with doubt and fear.

"Yet," said I in my morn of youth,
The unsunn'd freshness of my strength,
When I went forth in quest of truth,
"It is man's privilege to doubt,
If so be that from doubt at length,
Truth may stand forth unmoved of change,
An image with profulgent brows,
And perfect limbs, as from the storm
Of running fires and fluid range
Of lawless airs, at last stood out
This excellence and solid form
Of constant beauty. For the Ox
Feeds in the herb, and sleeps, or fills
The horned valleys all about,
And hollows of the fringed hills
In summer heats, with placid lows
Unfearing, till his own blood flows
About his hoof. And in the flocks
The lamb rejoiceth in the year,
And raceth freely with his fere,
And answers to his mother's calls
From the flower'd furrow. In a time,
Of which he wots not, run short pains
Thro' his warm heart; and then, from whence
He knows not, on his light there falls
A shadow; and his native slope,
Where he was wont to leap and climb,
Floats from his sick and filmed eyes,
And something in the darkness draws
His forehead earthward, and he dies.
Shall man live thus, in joy and hope
As a young lamb, who cannot dream,
Living, but that he shall live on?

Shall we not look into the laws
Of life and death, and things that seem,
And things that be, and analyze
Our double nature, and compare
All creeds till we have found the one,
If one there be?" Ay me! I fear
All may not doubt, but everywhere
Some must clasp Idols. Yet, my God,
Whom call I Idol? Let Thy dove
Shadow me over, and my sins
Be unremember'd, and Thy love
Enlighten me. Oh teach me yet
Somewhat before the heavy clod
Weighs on me, and the busy fret
Of that sharp-headed worm begins
In the gross blackness underneath.

O weary life! O weary death!
O spirit and heart made desolate!
O damned vacillating state!

The Kraken

Below the thunders of the upper deep;
Far, far beneath in the abysmal sea,
His ancient, dreamless, uninvaded sleep
The Kraken sleepeth: faintest sunlights flee
About his shadowy sides: above him swell
Huge sponges of millennial growth and height;
And far away into the sickly light,
From many a wondrous grot and secret cell
Unnumber'd and enormous polypi
Winnow with giant arms the slumbering green.

There hath he lain for ages and will lie
Battening upon huge seaworms in his sleep.
Until the latter fire shall heat the deep;
Then once by man and angels to be seen,
In roaring he shall rise and on the surface die.

Song

The winds, as at their hour of birth,
  Leaning upon the ridged sea,
Breathed low around the rolling earth
  With mellow preludes, "We are free."

The streams through many a lilied row
  Down-carolling to the crisped sea,
Low-tinkled with a bell-like flow
  Atween the blossoms, "We are free."

Lilian

I

Airy, fairy Lilian,
  Flitting, fairy Lilian,
When I ask her if she love me,
Clasps her tiny hands above me,
  Laughing all she can;
She'll not tell me if she love me,
  Cruel little Lilian.

II

When my passion seeks
Pleasance in love-sighs,
She, looking thro' and thro' me
Thoroughly to undo me,
  Smiling, never speaks:
So innocent-arch, so cunning-simple,
From beneath her gathered wimple
  Glancing with black-beaded eyes,
Till the lightning laughters dimple
  The baby-roses in her cheeks;
  Then away she flies.

III

Prithee weep, May Lilian!
  Gayety without eclipse
Wearieth me, May Lilian:

Thro' my very heart it thrilleth
  When from crimson-threaded lips
Silver-treble laughter trilleth:
  Prithee weep, May Lilian.

IV

  Praying all I can,
If prayers will not hush thee,
  Airy Lilian,
Like a rose-leaf I will crush thee,
  Fairy Lilian.

Isabel

I

Eyes not down-dropt nor over-bright, but fed
  With the clear-pointed flame of chastity,
  Clear, without heat, undying, tended by
    Pure vestal thoughts in the translucent fane
Of her still spirit; locks not wide-dispread,
    Madonna-wise on either side her head;
    Sweet lips whereon perpetually did reign
  The summer calm of golden charity,
Were fixed shadows of thy fixed mood,
    Revered Isabel, the crown and head,
The stately flower of female fortitude,
    Of perfect wifehood and pure lowlihead.

II

The intuitive decision of a bright
  And thorough-edged intellect to part
    Error from crime; a prudence to withhold;
    The laws of marriage character'd in gold
  Upon the blanched tablets of her heart;
A love still burning upward, giving light
To read those laws; an accent very low
In blandishment, but a most silver flow
    Of subtle-paced counsel in distress,
Right to the heart and brain, tho' undescried,
    Winning its way with extreme gentleness
Thro' all the outworks of suspicious pride;

A courage to endure and to obey;
A hate of gossip parlance, and of sway,
Crown'd Isabel, thro' all her placid life,
The queen of marriage, a most perfect wife.

III

The mellow'd reflex of a winter moon;
A clear stream flowing with a muddy one,
  Till in its onward current it absorbs
    With swifter movement and in purer light
      The vexed eddies of its wayward brother:
    A leaning and upbearing parasite,
      Clothing the stem, which else had fallen quite
  With cluster'd flower-bells and ambrosial orbs
    Of rich fruit-bunches leaning on each other—
      Shadow forth thee:—the world hath not another
(Tho' all her fairest forms are types of thee,
And thou of God in thy great charity)
Of such a finish'd chasten'd purity.

Mariana

    "Mariana in the moated grange."
            Measure for Measure.

With blackest moss the flower-plots
  Were thickly crusted, one and all:
The rusted nails fell from the knots
  That held the pear to the gable-wall.
The broken sheds look'd sad and strange:
  Unlifted was the clinking latch;
  Weeded and worn the ancient thatch
Upon the lonely moated grange.
    She only said, "My life is dreary,
      He cometh not," she said;
    She said, "I am aweary, aweary,
      I would that I were dead!"

Her tears fell with the dews at even;
  Her tears fell ere the dews were dried;
She could not look on the sweet heaven,
  Either at morn or eventide.

MARIANA

After the flitting of the bats,
  When thickest dark did trance the sky,
  She drew her casement-curtain by,
And glanced athwart the glooming flats.
    She only said, "The night is dreary,
      He cometh not," she said;
    She said, "I am aweary, aweary,
      I would that I were dead!"

Upon the middle of the night,
  Waking she heard the night-fowl crow:
The cock sung out an hour ere light:
  From the dark fen the oxen's low
Came to her: without hope of change,
  In sleep she seem'd to walk forlorn,
  Till cold winds woke the gray-eyed morn
About the lonely moated grange.
    She only said, "The day is dreary,
      He cometh not," she said;
    She said, "I am aweary, aweary,
      I would that I were dead!"

About a stone-cast from the wall
  A sluice with blacken'd waters slept,
And o'er it many, round and small,
  The cluster'd marish-mosses crept.
Hard by a poplar shook alway,
  All silver-green with gnarled bark:
  For leagues no other tree did mark
The level waste, the rounding gray.
    She only said, "My life is dreary,
      He cometh not," she said;
    She said, "I am aweary, aweary,
      I would that I were dead!"

And ever when the moon was low,
  And the shrill winds were up and away,
In the white curtain, to and fro,
  She saw the gusty shadow sway.
But when the moon was very low,
  And wild winds bound within their cell,
  The shadow of the poplar fell
Upon her bed, across her brow.

She only said, "The night is dreary,
  He cometh not," she said;
She said, "I am aweary, aweary,
  I would that I were dead!"

All day within the dreamy house,
  The doors upon their hinges creak'd;
The blue fly sung in the pane; the mouse
  Behind the mouldering wainscot shriek'd,
Or from the crevice peer'd about.
  Old faces glimmer'd thro' the doors,
  Old footsteps trod the upper floors,
Old voices called her from without.
  She only said, "My life is dreary,
    He cometh not," she said;
  She said, "I am aweary, aweary,
    I would that I were dead!"

The sparrows chirrup on the roof,
  The slow clock ticking, and the sound
Which to the wooing wind aloof
  The poplar made, did all confound
Her sense; but most she loathed the hour
  When the thick-moated sunbeam lay
  Athwart the chambers, and the day
Was sloping toward his western bower.
  Then, said she, "I am very dreary,
    He will not come," she said;
  She wept, "I am aweary, aweary,
    Oh, God, that I were dead!"

MARIANA IN THE SOUTH

WITH one black shadow at its feet,
  The house thro' all the level shines,
Close-latticed to the brooding heat,
  And silent in its dusty vines:
A faint-blue ridge upon the right,
  An empty river-bed before,
  And shallows on a distant shore,
In glaring sand and inlets bright.

MARIANA IN THE SOUTH

But "Ave Mary," made she moan,
  And "Ave Mary," night and morn,
And "Ah," she sang, "to be all alone,
  To live forgotten, and love forlorn."

She, as her carol sadder grew,
  From brow and bosom slowly down
Thro' rosy taper fingers drew
  Her streaming curls of deepest brown
To left and right, and made appear
  Still-lighted in a secret shrine,
  Her melancholy eyes divine,
The home of woe without a tear.
  And "Ave Mary," was her moan,
    "Madonna, sad is night and morn,"
  And "Ah," she sang, "to be all alone,
    To live forgotten, and love forlorn."

Till all the crimson changed, and past
  Into deep orange o'er the sea,
Low on her knees herself she cast,
  Before Our Lady murmur'd she;
Complaining, "Mother, give me grace
  To help me of my weary load."
And on the liquid mirror glow'd
The clear perfection of her face.
  "Is this the form," she made her moan,
    "That won his praises night and morn?"
  And "Ah," she said, "but I wake alone,
    I sleep forgotten, I wake forlorn."

Nor bird would sing, nor lamb would bleat,
  Nor any cloud would cross the vault,
But day increased from heat to heat,
  On stony drought and steaming salt;
Till now at noon she slept again,
  And seem'd knee-deep in mountain grass,
  And heard her native breezes pass,
And runlets babbling down the glen.
  She breathed in sleep a lower moan,
    And murmuring, as at night and morn,
  She thought, "My spirit is here alone,
    Walks forgotten, and is forlorn."

Dreaming, she knew it was a dream:
  She felt he was and was not there.
She woke: the babble of the stream
  Fell, and, without, the steady glare
Shrank one sick willow sear and small.
  The river-bed was dusty-white;
  And all the furnace of the light
Struck up against the blinding wall.
    She whisper'd, with a stifled moan
      More inward than at night or morn,
    "Sweet Mother, let me not here alone
      Live forgotten, and die forlorn."

And, rising, from her bosom drew
  Old letters, breathing of her worth,
For "Love," they said, "must needs be true,
  To what is loveliest upon earth."
An image seem'd to pass the door,
  To look at her with slight, and say
  "But now thy beauty flows away,
So be alone forevermore."
    "O cruel heart," she changed her tone,
      "And cruel love, whose end is scorn,
    Is this the end to be left alone,
      To live forgotten, and die forlorn?"

But sometimes in the falling day
  An image seem'd to pass the door,
To look into her eyes and say,
  "But thou shalt be alone no more."
And flaming downward over all
  From heat to heat the day decreased,
  And slowly rounded to the east
The one black shadow from the wall.
    "The day to night," she made her moan,
      "The day to night, the night to morn,
    And day and night I am left alone
      To live forgotten, and love forlorn."

At eve a dry cicala sung,
  There came a sound as of the sea;
Backward the lattice-blind she flung,
  And lean'd upon the balcony.

TO ——

There all in spaces rosy-bright
   Large Hesper glitter'd on her tears,
   And deepening thro' the silent spheres
Heaven over Heaven rose the night.
And weeping then she made her moan,
   "The night comes on that knows not morn,
When I shall cease to be all alone,
   To live forgotten, and love forlorn."

To ——

I

CLEAR-HEADED friend, whose joyful scorn,
   Edged with sharp laughter, cuts atwain
      The knots that tangle human creeds,
   The wounding cords that bind and strain
      The heart until it bleeds,
Ray-fringed eyelids of the morn
   Roof not a glance so keen as thine:
   If aught of prophecy be mine,
Thou wilt not live in vain.

II

Low-cowering shall the Sophist sit;
   Falsehood shall bare her plaited brow:
   Fair-fronted Truth shall droop not now
With shrilling shafts of subtle wit.
Nor martyr-flames, nor trenchant swords
   Can do away that ancient lie;
   A gentler death shall Falsehood die,
Shot thro' and thro' with cunning words.

III

Weak Truth a-leaning on her crutch,
   Wan, wasted Truth in her utmost need,
   Thy kingly intellect shall feed,
      Until she be an athlete bold,
And weary with a finger's touch
   Those writhed limbs of lightning speed;
Like that strange angel which of old,

Until the breaking of the light,
Wrestled with wandering Israel,
   Past Yabbok brook the livelong night,
And heaven's mazed signs stood still
In the dim tract of Penuel.

MADELINE

I

THOU are not steep'd in golden languors,
   No tranced summer calm is thine,
   Ever varying Madeline.
   Thro' light and shadow thou dost range,
   Sudden glances, sweet and strange,
Delicious spites and darling angers,
   And airy forms of flitting change.

II

Smiling, frowning, evermore,
Thou art perfect in love-lore.
Revealings deep and clear are thine
Of wealthy smiles: but who may know
Whether smile or frown be fleeter?
Whether smile or frown be sweeter,
   Who may know?
Frowns perfect-sweet along the brow
Light-glooming over eyes divine,
Like little clouds sun-fringed, are thine,
   Ever varying Madeline.

Thy smile and frown are not aloof
   From one another,
   Each to each is dearest brother;
Hues of the silken sheeny woof
   Momently shot into each other.
   All the mystery is thine;
Smiling, frowning, evermore,
Thou art perfect in love-lore,
   Ever varying Madeline.

III

A subtle, sudden flame,
  By veering passion fann'd,
    About thee breaks and dances:
When I would kiss thy hand,
The flush of anger'd shame
    O'erflows thy calmer glances,
And o'er black brows drops down
A sudden-curved frown:
But when I turn away,
Thou, willing me to stay,
  Wooest not, nor vainly wranglest;
    But, looking fixedly the while,
  All my bounding heart entanglest
    In a golden-netted smile;
Then in madness and in bliss,
If my lips should dare to kiss
Thy taper fingers amorously,
Again thou blushest angerly;
And o'er black brows drops down
A sudden-curved frown.

Song: The Owl

I

WHEN cats run home and light is come
  And dew is cold upon the ground,
And the far-off stream is dumb,
  And the whirring sail goes round,
  And the whirring sail goes round;
    Alone and warming his five wits,
    The white owl in the belfry sits.

II

When merry milkmaids click the latch,
  And rarely smells the new-mown hay,
And the cock hath sung beneath the thatch
  Twice or thrice his roundelay,
  Twice or thrice his roundelay;
    Alone and warming his five wits,
    The white owl in the belfry sits.

Second Song

TO THE SAME

I

Thy tuwhits are lull'd, I wot,
　Thy tuwhoos of yesternight,
Which upon the dark afloat,
　So took echo with delight,
　So took echo with delight,
　　That her voice untuneful grown,
　　Wears all day a fainter tone.

II

I would mock thy chant anew;
　But I cannot mimic it;
Not a whit of thy tuwhoo,
　Thee to woo to thy tuwhit,
　Thee to woo to thy tuwhit,
　　With a lengthen'd loud halloo,
　　Tuwhoo, tuwhit, tuwhit, tuwhoo-o-o.

Recollections of the Arabian Nights

When the breeze of a joyful dawn blew free
In the silken sail of infancy,
The tide of time flow'd back with me,
　The forward-flowing tide of time;
And many a sheeny summer-morn,
Adown the Tigris I was borne,
By Bagdat's shrines of fretted gold,
High-walled gardens green and old;
True Mussulman was I and sworn,
For it was in the golden prime
　　Of good Haroun Alraschid.

Anight my shallop, rustling thro'
The low and bloomed foliage, drove
The fragrant, glistening deeps, and clove
The citron-shadows in the blue:

By garden porches on the brim,
The costly doors flung open wide,
Gold glittering thro' lamplight dim,
And broider'd sofas on each side:
  In sooth it was a goodly time,
  For it was in the golden prime
    Of good Haroun Alraschid.

Often, where clear-stemm'd platans guard
The outlet, did I turn away
The boat-head down a broad canal
From the main river sluiced, where all
The sloping of the moon-lit sward
Was damask-work, and deep inlay
Of braided blooms unmown, which crept
Adown to where the water slept.
  A goodly place, a goodly time,
  For it was in the golden prime
    Of good Haroun Alraschid.

A motion from the river won
Ridged the smooth level, bearing on
My shallop thro' the star-strown calm,
Until another night in night
I enter'd, from the clearer light,
Imbower'd vaults of pillar'd palm,
Imprisoning sweets, which, as they clomb
Heavenward, were stay'd beneath the dome
  Of hollow boughs.—A goodly time,
  For it was in the golden prime
    Of good Haroun Alraschid.

Still onward; and the clear canal
Is rounded to as clear a lake.
From the green rivage many a fall
Of diamond rillets musical,
Thro' little crystal arches low
Down from the central fountain's flow
Fall'n silver-chiming, seemed to shake
The sparkling flints beneath the prow.
  A goodly place, a goodly time,
  For it was in the golden prime
    Of good Haroun Alraschid.

Above thro' many a bowery turn
A walk with vary-color'd shells
Wander'd engrain'd. On either side
All round about the fragrant marge
From fluted vase, and brazen urn
In order, eastern flowers large,
Some dropping low their crimson bells
Half-closed, and others studded wide
  With disks and tiars, fed the time
  With odor in the golden prime
    Of good Haroun Alraschid.

Far off, and where the lemon grove
In closest coverture upsprung,
The living airs of middle night
Died round the bulbul as he sung;
Not he: but something which possess'd
The darkness of the world, delight,
Life, anguish, death, immortal love,
Ceasing not, mingled, unrepress'd,
  Apart from place, withholding time,
  But flattering the golden prime
    Of good Haroun Alraschid.

Black the garden-bowers and grots
Slumber'd: the solemn palms were ranged
Above, unwoo'd of summer wind:
A sudden splendor from behind
Flush'd all the leaves with rich gold-green,
And, flowing rapidly between
Their interspaces, counterchanged
The level lake with diamond-plots
  Of dark and bright. A lovely time,
  For it was in the golden prime
    Of good Haroun Alraschid.

Dark-blue the deep sphere overhead,
Distinct with vivid stars inlaid,
Grew darker from that under-flame:
So, leaping lightly from the boat,
With silver anchor left afloat,
In marvel whence that glory came

RECOLLECTIONS OF THE ARABIAN NIGHTS

Upon me, as in sleep I sank
In cool soft turf upon the bank,
   Entranced with that place and time,
   So worthy of the golden prime
     Of good Haroun Alraschid.

Thence thro' the garden I was drawn—
A realm of pleasance, many a mound,
And many a shadow-checker'd lawn
Full of the city's stilly sound,
And deep myrrh-thickets blowing round
The stately cedar, tamarisks,
Thick rosaries of scented thorn,
Tall orient shrubs, and obelisks
   Graven with emblems of the time,
   In honor of the golden prime
     Of good Haroun Alraschid.

With dazed visions unawares
From the long alley's latticed shade
Emerged, I came upon the great
Pavilion of the Caliphat.
Right to the carven cedarn doors,
Flung inward over spangled floors,
Broad-based flights of marble stairs
Ran up with golden balustrade,
   After the fashion of the time,
   And humor of the golden prime
     Of good Haroun Alraschid.

The fourscore windows all alight
As with the quintessence of flame,
A million tapers flaring bright
From twisted silvers look'd to shame
The hollow-vaulted dark, and stream'd
Upon the mooned domes aloof
In inmost Bagdat, till there seem'd
Hundreds of crescents on the roof
   Of night new-risen, that marvellous time
   To celebrate the golden prime
     Of good Haroun Alraschid.

Then stole I up, and trancedly
Gazed on the Persian girl alone,
Serene with argent-lidded eyes
Amorous, and lashes like to rays
Of darkness, and a brow of pearl
Tressed with redolent ebony,
In many a dark delicious curl,
Flowing beneath her rose-hued zone;
  The sweetest lady of the time,
  Well worthy of the golden prime
    Of good Haroun Alraschid.

Six columns, three on either side,
Pure silver, underpropt a rich
Throne of the massive ore, from which
Down-droop'd, in many a floating fold,
Engarlanded and diaper'd
With inwrought flowers, a cloth of gold.
Thereon, his deep eye laughter-stirr'd
With merriment of kingly pride,
  Sole star of all that place and time,
  I saw him—in his golden prime,
    THE GOOD HAROUN ALRASCHID.

ODE TO MEMORY

ADDRESSED TO ——

I

THOU who stealest fire,
From the fountains of the past,
To glorify the present; oh, haste,
  Visit my low desire!
Strengthen me, enlighten me!
I faint in this obscurity,
Thou dewy dawn of memory.

II

Come not as thou camest of late,
Flinging the gloom of yesternight
On the white day; but robed in soften'd light
  Of orient state.

ODE TO MEMORY

Whilom thou camest with the morning mist,
  Even as a maid, whose stately brow
The dew-impearled winds of dawn have kiss'd.
  When, she, as thou,
Stays on her floating locks the lovely freight
Of overflowing blooms, and earliest shoots
Of orient green, giving safe pledge of fruits,
Which in wintertide shall star
The black earth with brilliance rare.

III

Whilom thou camest with the morning mist,
    And with the evening cloud,
Showering thy gleaned wealth into my open breast
(Those peerless flowers which in the rudest wind
    Never grow sear,
When rooted in the garden of the mind,
  Because they are the earliest of the year).
    Nor was the night thy shroud.
In sweet dreams softer than unbroken rest
Thou leddest by the hand thine infant Hope.
The eddying of her garments caught from thee
The light of thy great presence; and the cope
  Of the half-attain'd futurity,
  Tho' deep not fathomless,
Was cloven with the million stars which tremble
O'er the deep mind of dauntless infancy.
Small thought was there of life's distress;
For sure she deem'd no mist of earth could dull
Those spirit-thrilling eyes so keen and beautiful:
Sure she was nigher to heaven's spheres,
Listening the lordly music flowing from
    The illimitable years.
  O strengthen me, enlighten me!
  I faint in this obscurity,
  Thou dewy dawn of memory.

IV

Come forth, I charge thee, arise,
Thou of the many tongues, the myriad eyes!
Thou comest not with showers of flaunting vines
    Unto mine inner eye,
    Divinest Memory!

Thou wert not nursed by the waterfall
Which ever sounds and shines
  A pillar of white light upon the wall
Of purple cliffs, aloof descried:
Come from the woods that belt the gray hill-side,
  The seven elms, the poplars four
  That stand beside my father's door,
And chiefly from the brook that loves
To purl o'er matted cress and ribbed sand,
Or dimple in the dark of rushy coves,
Drawing into his narrow earthen urn,
    In every elbow and turn,
The filter'd tribute of the rough woodland,
    O! hither lead thy feet!
Pour round mine ears the livelong bleat
Of the thick-fleeced sheep from wattled folds,
    Upon the ridged wolds,
When the first matin-song hath waken'd loud
Over the dark dewy earth forlorn,
What time the amber morn
Forth gushes from beneath a low-hung cloud.

v

Large dowries doth the raptured eye
  To the young spirit present
    When first she is wed;
      And like a bride of old
    In triumph led,
      With music and sweet showers
      Of festal flowers,
Unto the dwelling she must sway.
Well hast thou done, great artist Memory,
  In setting round thy first experiment
    With royal frame-work of wrought gold;
Needs must thou dearly love thy first essay,
And foremost in thy various gallery
  Place it, where sweetest sunlight falls
  Upon the storied walls;
    For the discovery
And newness of thine art so pleased thee,
That all which thou hast drawn of fairest
  Or boldest since, but lightly weighs
With thee unto the love thou bearest

The first-born of thy genius. Artist-like,
Ever retiring thou dost gaze
On the prime labor of thine early days:
No matter what the sketch might be;
Whether the high field on the bushless Pike,
Or even a sand-built ridge
Of heaped hills that mound the sea,
Overblown with murmurs harsh,
Or even a lowly cottage whence we see
Stretch'd wide and wild the waste enormous marsh,
Where from the frequent bridge,
Like emblems of infinity,
The trenched waters run from sky to sky;
Or a garden bower'd close
With plaited alleys of the trailing rose,
Long alleys falling down to twilight grots,
Or opening upon level plots
Of crowned lilies, standing near
Purple spiked lavender:
Whither in after life retired
From brawling storms,
From weary wind,
With youthful fancy re-inspired,
    We may hold converse with all forms
Of the many-sided mind,
And those whom passion hath not blinded,
Subtle-thoughted, myriad-minded.

My friend, with you to live alone,
Were how much better than to own
A crown, a sceptre, and a throne!

O strengthen me, enlighten me!
I faint in this obscurity,
Thou dewy dawn of memory.

Song

I

A SPIRIT haunts the year's last hours
Dwelling amid these yellowing bowers:
    To himself he talks;
For at eventide, listening earnestly,
At his work you may hear him sob and sigh
    In the walks;
    Earthward he boweth the heavy stalks
Of the mouldering flowers:
  Heavily hangs the broad sunflower
  Over its grave i' the earth so chilly;
  Heavily hangs the hollyhock,
    Heavily hangs the tiger-lily.

II

The air is damp, and hush'd, and close,
As a sick man's room when he taketh repose
    An hour before death;
My very heart faints and my whole soul grieves
At the moist rich smell of the rotting leaves,
    And the breath
    Of the fading edges of box beneath,
And the year's last rose.
  Heavily hangs the broad sunflower
    Over its grave i' the earth so chilly;
  Heavily hangs the hollyhock,
    Heavily hangs the tiger-lily.

A Character

WITH a half-glance upon the sky
At night he said, "The wanderings
Of this most intricate Universe
Teach me the nothingness of things."
Yet could not all creation pierce
Beyond the bottom of his eye.

He spake of beauty; that the dull
Saw no divinity in grass,
Life in dead stones, or spirit in air;
Then looking as 'twere in a glass,
He smooth'd his chin and sleek'd his hair,
And said the earth was beautiful.

He spake of virtue: not the gods
More purely, when they wish to charm
Pallas and Juno sitting by:
And with a sweeping of the arm,
And a lack-lustre dead-blue eye,
Devolved his rounded periods.

Most delicately hour by hour
He canvass'd human mysteries,
And trod on silk, as if the winds
Blew his own praises in his eyes,
And stood aloof from other minds
In impotence of fancied power.

With lips depress'd as he were meek,
Himself unto himself he sold:
Upon himself himself did feed:
Quiet, dispassionate, and cold,
And other than his form of creed,
With chisell'd features clear and sleek.

The Poet

The poet in a golden clime was born,
 With golden stars above;
Dower'd with the hate of hate, the scorn of scorn,
 The love of love.

He saw thro' life and death, thro' good and ill,
 He saw thro' his own soul,
The marvel of the everlasting will
 An open scroll,

Before him lay: with echoing feet he threaded
    The secretest walks of fame:
The viewless arrows of his thoughts were headed
    And wing'd with flame,

Like Indian reeds blown from his silver tongue,
    And of so fierce a flight,
From Calpe unto Caucasus they sung
    Filling with light

And vagrant melodies the winds which bore
    Them earthward till they lit;
Then, like the arrow-seeds of the field flower,
    The fruitful wit

Cleaving, took root, and springing forth anew
    Where'er they fell, behold,
Like to the mother plant in semblance, grew
    A flower all gold,

And bravely furnish'd all abroad to fling
    Thy winged shafts of truth,
To throng with stately blooms the breathing spring
    Of Hope and Youth.

So many minds did gird their orbs with beams,
    Tho' one did fling the fire.
Heaven flow'd upon the soul in many dreams
    Of high desire.

Thus truth was multiplied on truth, the world
    Like one great garden show'd,
And thro' the wreaths of floating dark upcurl'd,
    Rare sunrise flow'd.

And Freedom rear'd in that august sunrise
    Her beautiful bold brow,
When rites and forms before his burning eyes
    Melted like snow.

There was no blood upon her maiden robes
    Sunn'd by those orient skies;
But round about the circles of the globes
    Of her keen eyes

And in her raiment's hem was traced in flame
    WISDOM, a name to shake
All evil dreams of power—a sacred name.
    And when she spake,

Her words did gather thunder as they ran,
    And as the lightning to the thunder
Which follows it, riving the spirit of man,
    Making earth wonder,

So was their meaning to her words. No sword
    Of wrath her right arm whirl'd,
But one poor poet's scroll, and with *his* word
    She shook the world.

THE POET'S MIND

I

Vex not thou the poet's mind
  With thy shallow wit:
Vex not thou the poet's mind;
  For thou canst not fathom it.
Clear and bright it should be ever,
Flowing like a crystal river;
Bright as light, and clear as wind.

II

Dark-brow'd sophist, come not anear;
  All the place is holy ground;
  Hollow smile and frozen sneer
    Come not here.
  Holy water will I pour
  Into every spicy flower
Of the laurel-shrubs that hedge it around.
The flowers would faint at your cruel cheer.

In your eye there is death,
There is frost in your breath
Which would blight the plants.
   Where you stand you cannot hear
      From the groves within
      The wild-bird's din.
In the heart of the garden the merry bird chants.
It would fall to the ground if you came in.
   In the middle leaps a fountain
      Like sheet lightning,
      Ever brightening
   With a low melodious thunder;
All day and all night it is ever drawn
   From the brain of the purple mountain
   Which stands in the distance yonder:
It springs on a level of bowery lawn,
And the mountain draws it from Heaven above,
And it sings a song of undying love;
And yet, tho' its voice be so clear and full,
You never would hear it; your ears are so dull;
So keep where you are: you are foul with sin;
It would shrink to the earth if you came in.

The Sea-Fairies

Slow sail'd the weary mariners and saw,
Betwixt the green brink and the running foam,
Sweet faces, rounded arms, and bosoms prest
To little harps of gold; and while they mused
Whispering to each other half in fear,
Shrill music reach'd them on the middle sea.

Whither away, whither away, whither away? fly no more.
Whither away from the high green field, and the happy blossoming shore?
Day and night to the billow the fountain calls:
Down shower the gambolling waterfalls
From wandering over the lea:
Out of the live-green heart of the dells
They freshen the silvery-crimson shells,
And thick with white bells the clover-hill swells

THE SEA-FAIRIES

High over the full-toned sea:
O hither, come hither and furl your sails,
Come hither to me and to me:
Hither, come hither and frolic and play;
Here it is only the mew that wails;
We will sing to you all the day:
Mariner, mariner, furl your sails,
For here are the blissful downs and dales,
And merrily, merrily carol the gales,
And the spangle dances in bight and bay,
And the rainbow forms and flies on the land
Over the islands free;
And the rainbow lives in the curve of the sand;
Hither, come hither and see;
And the rainbow hangs on the poising wave,
And sweet is the color of cove and cave,
And sweet shall your welcome be:
O hither, come hither, and be our lords,
For merry brides are we:
We will kiss sweet kisses, and speak sweet words:
O listen, listen, your eyes shall glisten
With pleasure and love and jubilee:
O listen, listen, your eyes shall glisten
When the sharp clear twang of the golden chords
Runs up the ridged sea.
Who can light on as happy a shore
All the world o'er, all the world o'er?
Whither away? listen and stay: mariner, mariner, fly no more.

The Deserted House

I

Life and Thought have gone away
    Side by side,
    Leaving door and windows wide:
Careless tenants they!

II

    All within is dark as night:
    In the windows is no light;
    And no murmur at the door,
    So frequent on its hinge before.

III

Close the door, the shutters close,
    Or thro' the windows we shall see
    The nakedness and vacancy
Of the dark deserted house.

IV

Come away: no more of mirth
    Is here or merry-making sound.
The house was builded of the earth,
    And shall fall again to ground.

V

Come away: for Life and Thought
    Here no longer dwell;
      But in a city glorious—
A great and distant city—have bought
  A mansion incorruptible.
Would they could have staid with us!

THE DYING SWAN

I

THE plain was grassy, wild and bare,
Wide, wild, and open to the air,
Which had built up everywhere
    An under-roof of doleful gray.
With an inner voice the river ran,
Adown it floated a dying swan,
    And loudly did lament.
  It was the middle of the day.
Ever the weary wind went on,
    And took the reed-tops as it went.

II

Some blue peaks in the distance rose,
And white against the cold-white sky,
Shone out their crowning snows.
    One willow over the river wept,
And shook the wave as the wind did sigh;
Above in the wind was the swallow,

THE DYING SWAN

    Chasing itself at its own wild will,
    And far thro' the marish green and still
    The tangled water-courses slept,
Shot over with purple, and green, and yellow.

III

The wild swan's death-hymn took the soul
Of that waste place with joy
Hidden in sorrow: at first to the ear
The warble was low, and full and clear;
And floating about the under-sky,
Prevailing in weakness, the coronach stole
Sometimes afar, and sometimes anear;
But anon her awful jubilant voice,
With a music strange and manifold,
Flow'd forth on a carol free and bold;
As when a mighty people rejoice
With shawms, and with cymbals, and harps of gold,
And the tumult of their acclaim is roll'd
Thro' the open gates of the city afar,
To the shepherd who watcheth the evening star.

And the creeping mosses and clambering weeds,
And the willow-branches hoar and dank,
And the wavy swell of the soughing reeds,
And the wave-worn horns of the echoing bank,
And the silvery marish-flowers that throng
The desolate creeks and pools among,
Were flooded over with eddying song.

A DIRGE

I

    Now is done thy long day's work;
    Fold thy palms across thy breast,
    Fold thine arms, turn to thy rest.
        Let them rave.
    Shadows of the silver birk
    Sweep the green that folds thy grave.
        Let them rave.

II

Thee nor carketh care nor slander;
Nothing but the small cold worm
Fretteth thine enshrouded form.
    Let them rave.
Light and shadow ever wander
O'er the green that folds thy grave.
    Let them rave.

III

Thou wilt not turn upon thy bed;
Chanteth not the brooding bee
Sweeter tones than calumny?
    Let them rave.
Thou wilt never raise thine head
From the green that folds thy grave.
    Let them rave.

IV

Crocodiles wept tears for thee;
The woodbine and eglatere
Drip sweeter dews than traitor's tear.
    Let them rave.
Rain makes music in the tree
O'er the green that folds thy grave.
    Let them rave.

V

Round thee blow, self-pleached deep,
Bramble roses, faint and pale,
And long purples of the dale.
    Let them rave.
These in every shower creep
Thro' the green that folds thy grave.
    Let them rave.

VI

The gold-eyed kingcups fine;
The frail bluebell peereth over
Rare broidry of the purple clover.
    Let them rave.

Kings have no such couch as thine,
As the green that folds thy grave.
     Let them rave.

VII

Wild words wander here and there:
God's great gift of speech abused
Makes thy memory confused:
     But let them rave.
The balm-cricket carols clear
In the green that folds thy grave.
     Let them rave.

LOVE AND DEATH

WHAT time the mighty moon was gathering light
Love paced the thymy plots of Paradise,
And all about him roll'd his lustrous eyes;
When, turning round a cassia, full in view,
Death, walking all alone beneath a yew,
And talking to himself, first met his sight:
"You must begone," said Death, "these walks are mine."
Love wept and spread his sheeny vans for flight;
Yet ere he parted said, "This hour is thine:
Thou are the shadow of life, and as the tree
Stands in the sun and shadows all beneath,
So in the light of great eternity
Life eminent creates the shade of death;
The shadow passeth when the tree shall fall,
But I shall reign forever over all."

THE BALLAD OF ORIANA

My heart is wasted with my woe,
          Oriana.
There is no rest for me below,
          Oriana,
When the long dun wolds are ribb'd with snow,
And loud the Norland whirlwinds blow,
          Oriana,
Alone I wander to and fro,
          Oriana,

Ere the light on dark was growing,
    Oriana,
At midnight the cock was crowing,
    Oriana:
Winds were blowing, waters flowing,
We heard the steeds to battle going,
    Oriana;
Aloud the hollow bugle blowing,
    Oriana.

In the yew-wood black as night,
    Oriana,
Ere I rode into the fight,
    Oriana,
While blissful tears blinded my sight
By star-shine and by moonlight,
    Oriana,
I to thee my troth did plight,
    Oriana.

She stood upon the castle wall,
    Oriana:
She watch'd my crest among them all,
    Oriana:
She saw me fight, she heard me call,
When forth there stept a foeman tall,
    Oriana,
Atween me and the castle wall,
    Oriana.

The bitter arrow went aside,
    Oriana:
The false, false arrow went aside,
    Oriana:
The damned arrow glanced aside,
And pierced thy heart, my love, my bride,
    Oriana!
Thy heart, my life, my love, my bride,
    Oriana!

Oh! narrow, narrow was the space,
    Oriana.
Loud, loud rung out the bugle's brays,
    Oriana.

THE BALLAD OF ORIANA

Oh! deathful stabs were dealt apace,
The battle deepen'd in its place,
        Oriana;
But I was down upon my face,
        Oriana.

They should have stabb'd me where I lay,
        Oriana!
How could I rise and come away,
        Oriana?
How could I look upon the day?
They should have stabb'd me where I lay,
        Oriana—
They should have trod me into clay,
        Oriana.

O breaking heart that will not break,
        Oriana!
O pale, pale face so sweet and meek,
        Oriana!
Thou smilest, but thou dost not speak,
And then the tears run down my cheek,
        Oriana:
What wantest thou? whom dost thou seek,
        Oriana?

I cry aloud: none hear my cries,
        Oriana.
Thou comest atween me and the skies,
        Oriana.
I feel the tears of blood arise
Up from my heart unto my eyes,
        Oriana.
Within thy heart my arrow lies,
        Oriana.

O cursed hand! O cursed blow!
        Oriana!
O happy thou that liest low,
        Oriana!
All night the silence seems to flow

Beside me in my utter woe,
    Oriana.
A weary, weary way I go,
    Oriana.

When Norland winds pipe down the sea,
    Oriana,
I walk, I dare not think of thee,
    Oriana.
Thou liest beneath the greenwood tree,
I dare not die and come to thee,
    Oriana.
I hear the roaring of the sea,
    Oriana.

CIRCUMSTANCE

Two children in two neighbor villages
Playing mad pranks along the heathy-leas;
Two strangers meeting at a festival;
Two lovers whispering by an orchard wall;
Two lives bound fast in one with golden ease;
Two graves grass-green beside a gray church-tower,
Wash'd with still rains and daisy blossomed;
Two children in one hamlet born and bred;
So runs the round of life from hour to hour.

THE MERMAN

I

Who would be
A merman bold,
Sitting alone,
Singing alone
Under the sea,
With a crown of gold,
On a throne?

THE MERMAN

II

I would be a merman bold,
I would sit and sing the whole of the day;
I would fill the sea-halls with a voice of power;
But at night I would roam abroad and play
With the mermaids in and out of the rocks,
Dressing their hair with the white sea-flower;
And holding them back by their flowing locks
I would kiss them often under the sea,
And kiss them again till they kiss'd me
    Laughingly, laughingly;
And then we would wander away, away
To the pale-green sea-groves straight and high,
    Chasing each other merrily.

III

There would be neither moon nor star;
But the wave would make music above us afar—
Low thunder and light in the magic night—
    Neither moon nor star.
We would call aloud in the dreamy dells,
Call to each other and whoop and cry
    All night, merrily, merrily;
They would pelt me with starry spangles and shells,
Laughing and clapping their hands between,
    All night, merrily, merrily:
But I would throw to them back in mine
Turkis and agate and almondine:
Then leaping out upon them unseen
I would kiss them often under the sea,
And kiss them again till they kiss'd me
    Laughingly, laughingly.
Oh! what a happy life were mine
Under the hollow-hung ocean green!
Soft are the moss-beds under the sea;
We would live merrily, merrily.

The Mermaid

I

Who would be
A mermaid fair,
Singing alone,
Combing her hair
Under the sea,
In a golden curl
With a comb of pearl,
On a throne?

II

I would be a mermaid fair;
I would sing to myself the whole of the day;
With a comb of pearl I would comb my hair;
And still as I comb'd I would sing and say,
"Who is it loves me? who loves not me?"
I would comb my hair till my ringlets would fall
      Low adown, low adown,
From under my starry sea-bud crown
      Low adown and around,
And I should look like a fountain of gold
      Springing alone
    With a shrill inner sound,
      Over the throne
    In the midst of the hall;
Till that great sea-snake under the sea
From his coiled sleeps in the central deeps
Would slowly trail himself sevenfold
Round the hall where I sate, and look in at the gate
With his large calm eyes for the love of me.
And all the mermen under the sea
Would feel their immortality
Die in their hearts for the love of me.

III

But at night I would wander away, away,
    I would fling on each side my low-flowing locks,
And lightly vault from the throne and play
    With the mermen in and out of the rocks;

We would run to and fro, and hide and seek,
   On the broad sea-wolds in the crimson shells,
   Whose silvery spikes are nighest the sea.
But if any came near I would call, and shriek,
And adown the steep like a wave I would leap
   From the diamond-ledges that jut from the dells;
For I would not be kiss'd by all who would list,
Of the bold merry mermen under the sea;
They would sue me, and woo me, and flatter me,
In the purple twilights under the sea;
But the king of them all would carry me,
Woo me, and win me, and marry me,
In the branching jaspers under the sea;
Then all the dry pied things that be
In the hueless mosses under the sea
Would curl round my silver feet silently,
All looking up for the love of me.
And if I should carol aloud, from aloft
All things that are forked, and horned, and soft
Would lean out from the hollow sphere of the sea,
All looking down for the love of me.

Adeline

I

Mystery of mysteries,
   Faintly smiling Adeline,
   Scarce of earth nor all divine,
Nor unhappy, nor at rest,
   But beyond expression fair
   With thy floating flaxen hair;
Thy rose-lips and full blue eyes
   Take the heart from out my breast.
   Wherefore those dim looks of thine,
   Shadowy, dreaming Adeline?

II

Whence that aery bloom of thine,
   Like a lily which the sun
Looks thro' in his sad decline,
   And a rose-bush leans upon,

Thou that faintly smilest still,
   As a Naiad in a well,
   Looking at the set of day,
Or a phantom two hours old
   Of a maiden past away,
Ere the placid lips be cold?
Wherefore those faint smiles of thine,
   Spiritual Adeline?

III

What hope or fear or joy is thine?
Who talketh with thee, Adeline?
   For sure thou art not all alone.
      Do beating hearts of salient springs
      Keep measure with thine own?
         Hast thou heard the butterflies
         What they say betwixt their wings?
         Or in stillest evenings
With what voice the violet woos
To his heart the silver dews?
      Or when little airs arise,
      How the merry bluebell rings
         To the mosses underneath?
         Hast thou look'd upon the breath
         Of the lilies at sunrise?
Wherefore that faint smile of thine,
Shadowy, dreamy Adeline?

IV

Some honey-converse feeds thy mind,
   Some spirit of a crimson rose
   In love with thee forgets to close
   His curtains, wasting odorous sighs
All night long on darkness blind.
What aileth thee? whom waitest thou
With thy soften'd, shadow'd brow,
      And those dew-lit eyes of thine,
      Thou faint smiler, Adeline?

V

Lovest thou the doleful wind
      When thou gazest at the skies?
   Doth the low-tongued Orient
      Wander from the side of the morn,

Dripping with Sabæan spice
On thy pillow, lowly bent
With melodious airs lovelorn,
Breathing Light against thy face,
While his locks a-drooping twined
Round thy neck in subtle ring
Make a carcanet of rays,
And ye talk together still,
In the language wherewith Spring
Letters cowslips on the hill?
Hence that look and smile of thine,
Spiritual Adeline.

MARGARET

I

O SWEET pale Margaret,
O rare pale Margaret,
What lit your eyes with tearful power,
Like moonlight on a falling shower?
Who lent you, love, your mortal dower
Of pensive thought and aspect pale,
Your melancholy sweet and frail
As perfume of the cuckoo-flower?
From the westward-winding flood,
From the evening-lighted wood,
From all things outward you have won
A tearful grace, as tho' you stood
Between the rainbow and the sun.
The very smile before you speak,
That dimples your transparent cheek,
Encircles all the heart, and feedeth
The senses with a still delight
Of dainty sorrow without sound,
Like the tender amber round,
Which the moon about her spreadeth,
Moving thro' a fleecy night.

II

You love, remaining peacefully,
To hear the murmur of the strife,
But enter not the toil of life.

Your spirit is the calmed sea,
    Laid by the tumult of the fight.
You are the evening star, alway
    Remaining betwixt dark and bright:
Lull'd echoes of laborious day
    Come to you, gleams of mellow light
    Float by you on the verge of night.

III

What can it matter, Margaret,
    What songs below the waning stars
The lion-heart, Plantagenet,
    Sang looking thro' his prison bars?
      Exquisite Margaret, who can tell
The last wild thought of Chatelet,
    Just ere the falling axe did part
    The burning brain from the true heart,
      Even in her sight he loved so well?

IV

A fairy shield your Genius made
    And gave you on your natal day.
Your sorrow, only sorrow's shade,
    Keeps real sorrow far away.
You move not in such solitudes,
    You are not less divine,
But more human in your moods,
    Than your twin-sister, Adeline.
Your hair is darker, and your eyes
    Touch'd with a somewhat darker hue,
    And less aerially blue,
    But ever-trembling thro' the dew
Of dainty-woful sympathies.

V

    O sweet pale Margaret,
    O rare pale Margaret,
Come down, come down, and hear me speak:
Tie up the ringlets on your cheek:
    The sun is just about to set,
The arching limes are tall and shady,
    And faint, rainy lights are seen,
      Moving in the leavy beech.

Rise from the feast of sorrow, lady,
　　　　Where all day long you sit between
　　　　　Joy and woe, and whisper each.
Or only look across the lawn,
　　Look out below your bower-eaves,
Look down, and let your blue eyes dawn
　　Upon me thro' the jasmine-leaves.

ROSALIND

I

My Rosalind, my Rosalind,
My frolic falcon, with bright eyes,
Whose free delight, from any height of rapid flight,
Stoops at all game that wing the skies,
My Rosalind, my Rosalind,
My bright-eyed, wild-eyed falcon whither,
Careless both of wind and weather,
Whither fly ye, what game spy ye,
Up or down the streaming wind?

II

The quick lark's closest-caroll'd strains,
The shadow rushing up the sea,
The lightning flash atween the rains,
The sunlight driving down the lea,
The leaping stream, the very wind,
That will not stay, upon his way,
To stoop the cowslip to the plains,
Is not so clear and bold and free
As you, my falcon Rosalind.
You care not for another's pains,
Because you are the soul of joy,
Bright metal all without alloy.
Life shoots and glances thro' your veins,
And flashes off a thousand ways,
Thro' lips and eyes in subtle rays.
Your hawk-eyes are keen and bright,
Keen with triumph, watching still
To pierce me thro' with pointed light;
But oftentimes they flash and glitter

Like sunshine on a dancing rill,
And your words are seeming-bitter,
Sharp and few, but seeming-bitter
From excess of swift delight.

III

Come down, come home, my Rosalind,
My gay young hawk, my Rosalind:
Too long you keep the upper skies;
Too long you roam and wheel at will;
But we must hood your random eyes,
That care not whom they kill,
And your cheek, whose brilliant hue
Is so sparkling-fresh to view,
Some red heath-flower in the dew,
Touch'd with sunrise. We must bind
And keep you fast, my Rosalind,
Fast, fast, my wild-eyed Rosalind,
And clip your wings, and make you love:
When we have lured you from above,
And that delight of frolic flight, by day or night,
From North to South,
We'll bind you fast in silken cords
And kiss away the bitter words
From off your rosy mouth.

ELEÄNORE

I

THY dark eyes open'd not,
  Nor first reveal'd themselves to English air,
    For there is nothing here,
Which, from the outward to the inward brought,
Moulded thy baby thought.
Far off from human neighborhood,
  Thou wert born, on a summer morn,
A mile beneath the cedar-wood.
Thy bounteous forehead was not fann'd
  With breezes from our oaken glades,
But thou wert nursed in some delicious land
  Of lavish lights, and floating shades:

ELEÄNORE

And flattering thy childish thought
    The oriental fairy brought,
      At the moment of thy birth,
From old well-heads of haunted rills,
And the hearts of purple hills,
    And shadow'd coves on a sunny shore,
      The choicest wealth of all the earth,
    Jewel or shell, or starry ore,
    To deck thy cradle, Eleänore.

II

Or the yellow-banded bees,
Thro' half-open lattices
Coming in the scented breeze,
    Fed thee, a child, lying alone,
      With whitest honey in fairy gardens cull'd—
    A glorious child, dreaming alone,
    In silk-soft folds, upon yielding down,
With the hum of swarming bees
    Into dreamful slumber lull'd.

III

Who may minister to thee?
Summer herself should minister
    To thee, with fruitage golden-rinded
    On golden salvers, or it may be,
Youngest Autumn, in a bower
Grape-thicken'd from the light, and blinded
    With many a deep-hued bell-like flower
Of fragrant trailers, when the air
    Sleepeth over all the heaven,
    And the crag that fronts the Even,
    All along the shadowing shore,
Crimsons over an inland mere,
      Eleänore!

IV

How many full-sail'd verse express,
    How many measured words adore
      The full-flowing harmony
Of thy swan-like stateliness,
      Eleänore?
      The luxuriant symmetry

Of thy floating gracefulness,
    Eleänore?
  Every turn and glance of thine,
  Every lineament divine,
    Eleänore,
  And the steady sunset glow,
    That stays upon thee? For in thee
    Is nothing sudden, nothing single;
Like two streams of incense free
  From one censer in one shrine,
  Thought and motion mingle,
Mingle ever. Motions flow
To one another, even as tho'
They were modulated so
  To an unheard melody,
Which lives about thee, and a sweep
  Of richest pauses, evermore
Drawn from each other mellow-deep;
  Who may express thee, Eleänore?

V

I stand before thee, Eleänore;
  I see thy beauty gradually unfold,
Daily and hourly, more and more.
I muse, as in a trance, the while
  Slowly, as from a cloud of gold,
Comes out thy deep ambrosial smile.
I muse, as in a trance, whene'er
  The languors of thy love-deep eyes
Float on to me. I would I were
  So tranced, so rapt in ecstasies,
To stand apart, and to adore,
Gazing on thee forevermore,
Serene, imperial Eleänore!

VI

Sometimes, with most intensity
Gazing, I seem to see
Thought folded over thought, smiling asleep,
Slowly awaken'd, grow so full and deep
In thy large eyes, that, overpower'd quite,
I cannot veil, or droop my sight,
But am as nothing in its light:

As tho' a star, in inmost heaven set,
Ev'n while we gaze on it,
Should slowly round his orb, and slowly grow
To a full face, there like a sun remain
Fix'd—then as slowly fade again,
   And draw itself to what it was before;
     So full, so deep, so slow,
     Thought seems to come and go
In thy large eyes, imperial Eleänore.

VII

As thunder-clouds that, hung on high,
    Roof'd the world with doubt and fear,
Floating thro' an evening atmosphere,
Grow golden all about the sky;
In thee all passion becomes passionless,
Touch'd by thy spirit's mellowness,
Losing his fire and active might
    In a silent meditation,
Falling into a still delight,
    And luxury of contemplation:
As waves that up a quiet cove
    Rolling slide, and lying still
       Shadow forth the banks at will:
Or sometimes they swell and move,
   Pressing up against the land,
   With motions of the outer sea:
     And the self-same influence
     Controlleth all the soul and sense
Of Passion gazing upon thee.
His bow-string slacken'd, languid Love,
   Leaning his cheek upon his hand,
   Droops both his wings, regarding thee,
     And so would languish evermore,
     Serene, imperial Eleänore.

VIII

But when I see thee roam, with tresses unconfined,
While the amorous, odorous wind
   Breathes low between the sunset and the moon;
     Or, in a shadowy saloon,
On silken cushions half reclined;
     I watch thy grace; and in its place

My heart a charm'd slumber keeps,
   While I muse upon thy face;
And a languid fire creeps
   Thro' my veins to all my frame,
Dissolvingly and slowly: soon
   From thy rose-red lips MY name
Floweth; and then, as in a swoon,
   With dinning sound my ears are rife,
   My tremulous tongue faltereth,
I lose my color, I lose my breath,
I drink the cup of a costly death,
Brimm'd with delirious draughts of warmest life.
   I die with my delight, before
      I hear what I would hear from thee;
      Yet tell my name again to me,
   I *would* be dying evermore,
   So dying ever, Eleänore.

EARLY SONNETS

I

To ——

As when with downcast eyes we muse and brood,
And ebb into a former life, or seem
To lapse far back in some confused dream
To states of mystical similitude;
If one but speaks or hems or stirs his chair,
Ever the wonder waxeth more and more,
So that we say, "All this hath been before,
All this hath been, I know not when or where."
So, friend, when first I look'd upon your face,
Our thought gave answer each to each, so true—
Opposed mirrors each reflecting each—
That tho' I knew not in what time or place,
Methought that I had often met with you,
And either lived in either's heart and speech.

II

To J. M. K.

My hope and heart is with thee—thou wilt be
A latter Luther, and a soldier-priest
To scare church-harpies from the master's feast;
Our dusted velvets have much need of thee:
Thou art no sabbath-drawler of old saws,
Distill'd from some worm-canker'd homily;
But spurr'd at heart with fieriest energy
To embattail and to wall about thy cause
With iron-worded proof, hating to hark
The humming of the drowsy pulpit-drone
Half God's good sabbath, while the worn-out clerk
Brow-beats his desk below. Thou from a throne
Mounted in heaven wilt shoot into the dark
Arrows of lightnings. I will stand and mark.

III

Mine be the strength of spirit, full and free,
Like some broad river rushing down alone,
With the self-same impulse wherewith he was thrown
From his loud fount upon the echoing lea:—
Which with increasing might doth forward flee
By town, and tower, and hill, and cape, and isle,
And in the middle of the green salt sea
Keeps his blue waters fresh for many a mile.
Mine be the power which ever to its sway
Will win the wise at once, and by degrees
May into uncongenial spirits flow;
Ev'n as the warm gulf-stream of Florida
Floats far away into the Northern seas
The lavish growths of southern Mexico.

IV

Alexander

Warrior of God, whose strong right arm debased
The throne of Persia, when her Satrap bled
At Issus by the Syrian gates, or fled
Beyond the Memmian naphtha-pits, disgraced
Forever—thee (thy pathway sand-erased)
Gliding with equal crowns two serpents led
Joyful to that palm-planted fountain-fed
Ammonian Oasis in the waste.
There in a silent shade of laurel brown
Apart the Chamian Oracle divine
Shelter'd his unapproached mysteries:
High things were spoken there, unhanded down;
Only they saw thee from the secret shrine
Returning with hot cheek and kindled eyes.

V

Buonaparte

He thought to quell the stubborn hearts of oak,
Madman!—to chain with chains, and bind with bands
That island queen who sways the floods and lands,
From Ind to Ind, but in fair daylight woke,
When from her wooden walls,—lit by sure hands,—
With thunders, and with lightnings, and with smoke,—
Peal after peal, the British battle broke,

Lulling the brine against the Coptic sands.
We taught him lowlier moods, when Elsinore
Heard the war moan along the distant sea,
Rocking with shatter'd spars, with sudden fires
Flamed over: at Trafalgar yet once more
We taught him: late he learned humility
Perforce, like those whom Gideon school'd with briers.

VI

Poland

How long, O God, shall men be ridden down,
And trampled under by the last and least
Of men? The heart of Poland hath not ceased
To quiver, tho' her sacred blood doth drown
The fields, and out of every smouldering town
Cries to Thee, lest brute Power be increased,
Till that o'ergrown Barbarian in the East
Transgress his ample bound to some new crown:—
Cries to Thee, "Lord, how long shall these things be?
How long this icy-hearted Muscovite
Oppress the region?" Us, O Just and Good,
Forgive, who smiled when she was torn in three;
Us, who stand now, when we should aid the right—
A matter to be wept with tears of blood!

VII

Caress'd or chidden by the slender hand,
And singing airy trifles this or that,
Light Hope at Beauty's call would perch and stand,
And run thro' every change of sharp and flat;
And Fancy came and at her pillow sat,
When Sleep had bound her in his rosy band,
And chased away the still-recurring gnat,
And woke her with a lay from fairy land.
But now they live with Beauty less and less,
For Hope is other Hope and wanders far,
Nor cares to lisp in love's delicious creeds;
And Fancy watches in the wilderness,
Poor Fancy sadder than a single star,
That sets at twilight in a land of reeds.

VIII

The form, the form alone is eloquent!
A nobler yearning never broke her rest
Than but to dance and sing, be gayly drest,
And win all eyes with all accomplishment:
Yet in the whirling dances as we went,
My fancy made me for a moment blest
To find my heart so near the beauteous breast
That once had power to rob it of content.
A moment came the tenderness of tears,
The phantom of a wish that once could move,
A ghost of passion that no smiles restore—
For ah! the slight coquette, she cannot love,
And if you kiss'd her feet a thousand years,
She still would take the praise, and care no more.

IX

Wan Sculptor, weepest thou to take the cast
Of those dead lineaments that near thee lie?
O sorrowest thou, pale Painter, for the past,
In painting some dead friend from memory?
Weep on: beyond his object Love can last:
His object lives: more cause to weep have I:
My tears, no tears of love, are flowing fast,
No tears of love, but tears that Love can die.
I pledge her not in any cheerful cup,
Nor care to sit beside her where she sits—
Ah pity—hint it not in human tones,
But breathe it into earth and close it up
With secret death forever, in the pits
Which some green Christmas crams with weary bones.

X

If I were loved, as I desire to be,
What is there in the great sphere of the earth,
And range of evil between death and birth,
That I should fear,—if I were loved by thee?
All the inner, all the outer world of pain
Clear Love would pierce and cleave, if thou wert mine,
As I have heard that, somewhere in the main,
Fresh-water springs come up through bitter brine.

'Twere joy, not fear, claspt hand-in-hand with thee,
To wait for death—mute—careless of all ills,
Apart upon a mountain, tho' the surge
Of some new deluge from a thousand hills
Flung leagues of roaring foam into the gorge
Below us, as far on as eye could see.

XI

The Bridesmaid

O BRIDESMAID, ere the happy knot was tied,
Thine eyes so wept that they could hardly see;
Thy sister smiled and said, "No tears for me!
A happy bridesmaid makes a happy bride."
And then, the couple standing side by side,
Love lighted down between them full of glee,
And over his left shoulder laugh'd at thee,
"O happy bridesmaid, make a happy bride."
And all at once a pleasant truth I learn'd,
For while the tender service made thee weep,
I loved thee for the tear thou couldst not hide,
And prest thy hand, and knew the press return'd,
And thought, "My life is sick of single sleep:
O happy bridesmaid, make a happy bride!"

THE LADY OF SHALOTT

PART I

ON either side of the river lie
Long fields of barley and of rye,
That clothe the wold and meet the sky;
And thro' the field the road runs by
    To many-tower'd Camelot;
And up and down the people go,
Gazing where the lilies blow
Round an island there below
    The island of Shalott.

Willows whiten, aspens quiver,
Little breezes dusk and shiver
Thro' the wave that runs forever
By the island in the river
    Flowing down to Camelot.

Four gray walls, and four gray towers,
Overlook a space of flowers,
And the silent isle embowers
    The Lady of Shalott.

By the margin, willow-veil'd,
Slide the heavy barges trail'd.
By slow horses; and unhail'd
The shallop flitteth silken-sail'd
    Skimming down to Camelot:
But who hath seen her wave her hand?
Or at the casement seen her stand?
Or is she known in all the land,
    The Lady of Shalott?

Only reapers, reaping early
In among the bearded barley,
Hear a song that echoes cheerly
From the river winding clearly,
    Down to tower'd Camelot:
And by the moon the reaper weary,
Piling sheaves in uplands airy,
Listening, whispers " 'Tis the fairy
    Lady of Shalott."

PART II

THERE she weaves by night and day
A magic web with colors gay.
She has heard a whisper say,
A curse is on her if she stay
    To look down to Camelot.
She knows not what the curse may be,
And so she weaveth steadily,
And little other care hath she,
    The Lady of Shalott.

And moving thro' a mirror clear
That hangs before her all the year,
Shadows of the world appear.
There she sees the highway near
    Winding down to Camelot:

THE LADY OF SHALOTT

There the river eddy whirls,
And there the surly village-churls,
And the red cloaks of market girls,
    Pass onward from Shalott.

Sometimes a troop of damsels glad,
An abbot on an ambling pad,
Sometimes a curly shepherd-lad,
Or long-hair'd page in crimson clad,
    Goes by to tower'd Camelot;
And sometimes thro' the mirror blue
The knights come riding two and two;
She hath no loyal knight and true,
    The Lady of Shalott.

But in her web she still delights
To weave the mirror's magic sights,
For often thro' the silent nights
A funeral, with plumes and lights
    And music, went to Camelot:
Or when the moon was overhead,
Came two young lovers lately wed;
"I am half sick of shadows," said
    The Lady of Shalott.

PART III

A BOW-SHOT from her bower-eaves,
He rode between the barley-sheaves,
The sun came dazzling thro' the leaves,
And flamed upon the brazen greaves
    Of bold Sir Lancelot.
A red-cross knight forever kneel'd
To a lady in his shield,
That sparkled on the yellow field,
    Beside remote Shalott.

The gemmy bridle glitter'd free,
Like to some branch of stars we see
Hung in the golden Galaxy,
The bridle bells rang merrily
    As he rode down to Camelot:

And from his blazon'd baldric slung
A mighty silver bugle hung,
And as he rode his armor rung,
    Beside remote Shalott.

All in the blue unclouded weather
Thick-jewell'd shone the saddle-leather,
The helmet and the helmet-feather
Burn'd like one burning flame together,
    As he rode down to Camelot.
As often thro' the purple night,
Below the starry clusters bright,
Some bearded meteor, trailing light,
    Moves over still Shalott.

His broad clear brow in sunlight glow'd;
On burnish'd hooves his war-horse trode;
From underneath his helmet flow'd
His coal-black curls as on he rode,
    As he rode down to Camelot.
From the bank and from the river
He flash'd into the crystal mirror,
"Tirra lirra," by the river
    Sang Sir Lancelot.

She left the web, she left the loom,
She made three paces thro' the room,
She saw the water-lily bloom,
She saw the helmet and the plume,
    She look'd down to Camelot.
Out flew the web and floated wide;
The mirror crack'd from side to side;
"The curse is come upon me," cried
    The Lady of Shalott.

PART IV

In the stormy east-wind straining,
The pale yellow woods were waning,
The broad stream in his banks complaining,
Heavily the low sky raining,
    Over tower'd Camelot;

THE LADY OF SHALOTT

Down she came and found a boat
Beneath a willow left afloat,
And round about the prow she wrote
    The Lady of Shalott.

And down the river's dim expanse
Like some bold seer in a trance,
Seeing all his own mischance—
With a glassy countenance
    Did she look to Camelot.
And at the closing of the day
She loosed the chain, and down she lay;
The broad stream bore her far away,
    The Lady of Shalott.

Lying, robed in snowy white,
That loosely flew to left and right—
The leaves upon her falling light—
Thro' the noises of the night
    She floated down to Camelot:
And as the boat-head wound along
The willowy hills and fields among,
They heard her singing her last song,
    The Lady of Shalott.

Heard a carol, mournful, holy,
Chanted loudly, chanted lowly,
Till her blood was frozen slowly,
And her eyes were darken'd wholly,
    Turn'd to tower'd Camelot.
For ere she reach'd upon the tide
The first house by the water-side,
Singing in her song she died,
    The Lady of Shalott.

Under tower and balcony,
By garden-wall and gallery,
A gleaming shape she floated by,
Dead-pale between the houses high,
    Silent into Camelot.
Out upon the wharfs they came,
Knight and burgher, lord and dame,
And round the prow they read her name,
    The Lady of Shalott.

Who is this? and what is here?
And in the lighted palace near
Died the sound of royal cheer;
And they cross'd themselves for fear,
    All the knights at Camelot:
But Lancelot mused a little space;
He said, "She has a lovely face;
God in his mercy lend her grace,
    The Lady of Shalott."

The Two Voices

A STILL small voice spake unto me,
"Thou art so full of misery,
Were it not better not to be?"

Then to the still small voice I said;
"Let me not cast in endless shade
What is so wonderfully made."

To which the voice did urge reply;
"To-day I saw the dragon-fly
Come from the wells where he did lie.

"An inner impulse rent the veil
Of his old husk: from head to tail
Came out clear plates of sapphire mail.

"He dried his wings: like gauze they grew;
Thro' crofts and pastures wet with dew
A living flash of light he flew."

I said, "When first the world began,
Young Nature thro' five cycles ran,
And in the sixth she moulded man.

"She gave him mind, the lordliest
Proportion, and, above the rest,
Dominion in the head and breast."

THE TWO VOICES

Thereto the silent voice replied;
"Self-blinded are you by your pride:
Look up thro' night: the world is wide.

"This truth within thy mind rehearse,
That in a boundless universe
Is boundless better, boundless worse.

"Think you this mould of hopes and fears
Could find no statelier than his peers
In yonder hundred million spheres?"

It spake, moreover, in my mind;
"Tho' thou wert scatter'd to the wind,
Yet is there plenty of the kind."

Then did my response clearer fall:
"No compound of this earthly ball
Is like another, all in all."

To which he answer'd scoffingly;
"Good soul! suppose I grant it thee,
Who'll weep for thy deficiency?

"Or will one beam be less intense,
When thy peculiar difference
Is cancell'd in the world of sense?"

I would have said, "Thou canst not know,"
But my full heart, that work'd below,
Rain'd thro' my sight its overflow.

Again the voice spake unto me:
"Thou art so steep'd in misery,
Surely 'twere better not to be.

"Thine anguish will not let thee sleep,
Nor any train of reason keep:
Thou canst not think, but thou wilt weep."

I said, "The years with change advance:
If I make dark my countenance,
I shut my life from happier chance.

"Some turn this sickness yet might take,
Ev'n yet." But he: "What drug can make
A wither'd palsy cease to shake?"

I wept, "Tho' I should die, I know
That all about the thorn will blow
In tufts of rosy-tinted snow;

"And men, thro' novel spheres of thought
Still moving after truth long sought,
Will learn new things when I am not."

"Yet," said the secret voice, "some time,
Sooner or later, will gray prime
Make thy grass hoar with early rime.

"Not less swift souls that yearn for light,
Rapt after heaven's starry flight,
Would sweep the tracts of day and night.

"Not less the bee would range her cells,
The furzy prickle fire the dells,
The foxglove cluster dappled bells."

I said that "all the years invent;
Each month is various to present
The world with some development.

"Were this not well, to bide mine hour,
Tho' watching from a ruin'd tower
How grows the day of human power?"

"The highest-mounted mind," he said,
"Still sees the sacred morning spread
The silent summit overhead.

"Will thirty seasons render plain
Those lonely lights that still remain,
Just breaking over land and main?

"Or make that morn, from his cold crown
And crystal silence creeping down,
Flood with full daylight glebe and town?

"Forerun thy peers, thy time, and let
Thy feet, millenniums hence, be set
In midst of knowledge, dream'd not yet.

"Thou hast not gain'd a real height,
Nor art thou nearer to the light,
Because the scale is infinite.

"'Twere better not to breathe or speak,
Than cry for strength, remaining weak,
And seem to find, but still to seek.

"Moreover, but to seem to find
Asks what thou lackest, thought resign'd,
A healthy frame, a quiet mind."

I said, "When I am gone away,
'He dared not tarry,' men will say,
Doing dishonor to my clay."

"This is more vile," he made reply,
"To breathe and loathe, to live and sigh,
Than once from dread of pain to die.

"Sick art thou—a divided will
Still heaping on the fear of ill
The fear of men, a coward still.

"Do men love thee? Art thou so bound
To men, that how thy name may sound
Will vex thee lying underground?

"The memory of the wither'd leaf
In endless time is scarce more brief
Than of the garner'd Autumn-sheaf.

"Go, vexed Spirit, sleep in trust;
The right ear, that is fill'd with dust,
Hears little of the false or just."

"Hard task, to pluck resolve," I cried,
"From emptiness and the waste wide
Of that abyss, or scornful pride!

"Nay—rather yet that I could raise
One hope that warm'd me in the days
While still I yearn'd for human praise.

"When, wide in soul and bold of tongue,
Among the tents I paused and sung,
The distant battle flash'd and rung.

"I sung the joyful Pæan clear,
And, sitting, burnish'd without fear
The brand, the buckler, and the spear—

"Waiting to strive a happy strife,
To war with falsehood to the knife,
And not to lose the good of life—

"Some hidden principle to move,
To put together, part and prove,
And mete the bounds of hate and love—

"As far as might be, to carve out
Free space for every human doubt,
That the whole mind might orb about—

"To search through all I felt or saw,
The springs of life, the depths of awe,
And reach the law within the law:

"At least, not rotting like a weed,
But, having sown some generous seed,
Fruitful of further thought and deed,

"To pass when Life her light withdraws,
Not void of righteous self-applause,
Nor in a merely selfish cause—

"In some good cause, not in mine own
To perish, wept for, honor'd, known,
And like a warrior overthrown;

"Whose eyes are dim with glorious tears,
When soil'd with noble dust, he hears
His country's war-song thrill his ears:

"Then dying of a mortal stroke,
What time the foeman's line is broke,
And all the war is rolled in smoke."

"Yea!" said the voice, "thy dream was good,
While thou abodest in the bud.
It was the stirring of the blood.

"If Nature put not forth her power
About the opening of the flower,
Who is it that could live an hour?

"Then comes the check, the change, the fall,
Pain rises up, old pleasures pall.
There is one remedy for all.

"Yet hadst thou, thro' enduring pain,
Link'd month to month with such a chain
Of knitted purport, all were vain.

"Thou hadst not between death and birth
Dissolved the riddle of the earth.
So were thy labor little-worth.

"That men with knowledge merely play'd,
I told thee—hardly nigher made,
Tho' scaling slow from grade to grade;

"Much less this dreamer, deaf and blind,
Named man, may hope some truth to find,
That bears relation to the mind.

"For every worm beneath the moon
Draws different threads, and late and soon
Spins, toiling out his own cocoon.

"Cry, faint not: either Truth is born
Beyond the polar gleam forlorn,
Or in the gateways of the morn.

"Cry, faint not, climb: the summits slope
Beyond the furthest flights of hope,
Wrapt in dense cloud from base to cope.

"Sometimes a little corner shines,
As over rainy mist inclines
A gleaming crag with belts of pines.

"I will go forward, sayest thou,
I shall not fail to find her now.
Look up, the fold is on her brow.

"If straight thy track, or if oblique,
Thou know'st not. Shadows thou dost strike,
Embracing cloud, Ixion-like;

"And owning but a little more
Than beasts, abidest lame and poor,
Calling thyself a little lower

"Than angels. Cease to wail and brawl!
Why inch by inch to darkness crawl?
There is one remedy for all."

"O dull, one-sided voice," said I,
"Wilt thou make every thing a lie,
To flatter me that I may die?

"I know that age to age succeeds,
Blowing a noise of tongues and deeds,
A dust of systems and of creeds.

"I cannot hide that some have striven,
Achieving calm, to whom was given
The joy that mixes man with Heaven:

"Who, rowing hard against the stream,
Saw distant gates of Eden gleam,
And did not dream it was a dream;

"But heard, by secret transport led,
Ev'n in the charnels of the dead,
The murmur of the fountain-head—

"Which did accomplish their desire,
Bore and forebore, and did not tire,
Like Stephen, an unquenched fire.

THE TWO VOICES

"He heeded not reviling tones,
Nor sold his heart to idle moans,
Tho' cursed and scorn'd, and bruised with stones:

"But looking upward, full of grace,
He pray'd, and from a happy place
God's glory smote him on the face."

The sullen answer slid betwixt:
"Not that the grounds of hope were fix'd,
The elements were kindlier mix'd."

I said, "I toil beneath the curse,
But, knowing not the universe,
I fear to slide from bad to worse.

"And that, in seeking to undo,
One riddle, and to find the true,
I knit a hundred others new:

"Or that this anguish fleeting hence,
Unmanacled from bonds of sense,
Be fix'd and froz'n to permanence:

"For I go, weak from suffering here:
Naked I go, and void of cheer:
What is it that I may not fear?"

"Consider well," the voice replied,
"His face, that two hours since hath died;
Wilt thou find passion, pain or pride?

"Will he obey when one commands?
Or answer should one press his hands?
He answers not, nor understands.

"His palms are folded on his breast:
There is no other thing express'd
But long disquiet merged in rest.

"His lips are very mild and meek:
Tho' one should smite him on the cheek,
And on the mouth, he will not speak.

"His little daughter, whose sweet face
He kiss'd, taking his last embrace,
Becomes dishonor to her race—

"His sons grow up that bear his name,
Some grow to honor, some to shame,—
But he is chill to praise or blame.

"He will not hear the north-wind rave,
Nor, moaning, household shelter crave
From winter rains that beat his grave.

"High up the vapors fold and swim:
About him broods the twilight dim:
The place he knew forgetteth him."

"If all be dark, vague voice," I said,
"These things are wrapt in doubt and dread,
Nor canst thou show the dead are dead.

"The sap dries up: the plant declines.
A deeper tale my heart divines.
Know I not Death? the outward signs?

"I found him when my years were few;
A shadow on the graves I knew,
And darkness in the village yew.

"From grave to grave the shadow crept:
In her still place the morning wept:
Touch'd by his feet the daisy slept.

"The simple senses crown'd his head:
'Omega! thou art Lord,' they said,
'We find no motion in the dead.'

"Why, if man rot in dreamless ease,
Should that plain fact, as taught by these,
Not make him sure that he shall cease?

"Who forged that other influence,
That heat of inward evidence,
By which he doubts against the sense?

THE TWO VOICES

"He owns the fatal gift of eyes,
That read his spirit blindly wise,
Not simple as a thing that dies.

"Here sits he shaping wings to fly:
His heart forebodes a mystery:
He names the name Eternity.

"That type of Perfect in his mind
In Nature can he nowhere find.
He sows himself on every wind.

"He seems to hear a Heavenly Friend,
And thro' thick veils to apprehend
A labor working to an end.

"The end and the beginning vex
His reason: many things perplex,
With motions, checks, and counter-checks.

"He knows a baseness in his blood
At such strange war with something good,
He may not do the thing he would.

"Heaven opens inward, chasms yawn,
Vast images in glimmering dawn,
Half shown, are broken and withdrawn.

"Ah! sure within him and without,
Could his dark wisdom find it out,
There must be answer to his doubt.

"But thou canst answer not again.
With thine own weapon art thou slain,
Or thou wilt answer but in vain.

"The doubt would rest, I dare not solve.
In the same circle we revolve.
Assurance only breeds resolve."

As when a billow, blown against,
Falls back, the voice with which I fenced
A little ceased, but recommenced.

"Where wert thou when thy father play'd
In his free field, and pastime made,
A merry boy in sun and shade?

"A merry boy they call'd him then,
He sat upon the knees of men
In days that never come again.

"Before the little ducts began
To feed thy bones with lime, and ran
Their course, till thou wert also man:

"Who took a wife, who rear'd his race,
Whose wrinkles gather'd on his face,
Whose troubles number with his days:

"A life of nothings, nothing-worth,
From that first nothing ere his birth
To that last nothing under earth!"

"These words," I said, "are like the rest;
No certain clearness, but at best
A vague suspicion of the breast:

"But if I grant, thou mightst defend
The thesis which thy words intend—
That to begin implies to end;

"Yet how should I for certain hold
Because my memory is so cold,
That I first was in human mould?

"I cannot make this matter plain,
But I would shoot, howe'er in vain,
A random arrow from the brain.

"It may be that no life is found,
Which only to one engine bound
Falls off, but cycles always round.

"As old mythologies relate,
Some draught of Lethe might await
The slipping thro' from state to state.

"As here we find in trances, men
Forget the dream that happens then,
Until they fall in trance again.

"So might we, if our state were such
As one before, remember much,
For those two likes might meet and touch.

"But if I lapsed from nobler place,
Some legend of a fallen race
Alone might hint of my disgrace;

"Some vague emotion of delight
In gazing up an Alpine height,
Some yearning toward the lamps of night;

"Or, if thro' lower lives I came—
Tho' all experience past became
Consolidate in mind and frame—

"I might forget my weaker lot;
For is not our first year forgot?
The haunts of memory echo not.

"And men, whose reason long was blind,
From cells of madness unconfined,
Oft lose whole years of darker mind.

"Much more, if first I floated free,
As naked essence, must I be
Incompetent of memory:

"For memory dealing but with time,
And he with matter, could she climb
Beyond her own material prime?

"Moreover, something is or seems,
That touches me with mystic gleams,
Like glimpses of forgotten dreams—

"Of something felt, like something here;
Of something done, I know not where;
Such as no language may declare."

The still voice laugh'd. "I talk," said he,
"Not with thy dreams. Suffice it thee
Thy pain is a reality."

"But thou," said I, "hast missed thy mark,
Who sought'st to wreck thy mortal ark,
By making all the horizon dark.

"Why not set forth, if I should do
This rashness, that which might ensue
With this old soul in organs new?

"Whatever crazy sorrow saith,
No life that breathes with human breath
Has ever truly long'd for death.

"'Tis life, whereof our nerves are scant,
Oh life, not death, for which we pant;
More life, and fuller, that I want."

I ceased, and sat as one forlorn.
Then said the voice, in quiet scorn,
"Behold, it is the Sabbath morn."

And I arose, and I released
The casement, and the light increased
With freshness in the dawning east.

Like soften'd airs that blowing steal,
When meres begin to uncongeal,
The sweet church bells began to peal.

On to God's house the people prest:
Passing the place where each must rest,
Each enter'd like a welcome guest.

One walk'd between his wife and child,
With measured footfall firm and mild,
And now and then he gravely smiled.

The prudent partner of his blood
Lean'd on him, faithful, gentle, good,
Wearing the rose of womanhood.

And in their double love secure,
The little maiden walk'd demure,
Pacing with downward eyelids pure.

These three made unity so sweet,
My frozen heart began to beat,
Remembering its ancient heat.

I blest them, and they wander'd on:
I spoke, but answer came there none:
The dull and bitter voice was gone.

A second voice was at mine ear,
A little whisper silver-clear,
A murmur, "Be of better cheer."

As from some blissful neighborhood,
A notice faintly understood,
"I see the end, and know the good."

A little hint to solace woe,
A hint, a whisper breathing low,
"I may not speak of what I know."

Like an Æolian harp that wakes
No certain air, but overtakes
Far thought with music that it makes:

Such seem'd the whisper at my side:
"What is it thou knowest, sweet voice?" I cried.
"A hidden hope," the voice replied:

So heavenly-toned, that in that hour
From out my sullen heart a power
Broke, like the rainbow from the shower,

To feel, altho' no tongue can prove,
That every cloud, that spreads above
And veileth love, itself is love.

And forth into the fields I went,
And Nature's living motion lent
The pulse of hope to discontent.

I wonder'd at the bounteous hours,
The slow result of winter showers:
You scarce could see the grass for flowers.

I wonder'd while I paced along:
The woods were fill'd so full with song,
There seem'd no room for sense of wrong;

And all so variously wrought,
I marvell'd how the mind was brought
To anchor by one gloomy thought;

And wherefore rather I made choice
To commune with that barren voice,
Than him that said, "Rejoice! Rejoice!"

The Miller's Daughter

I SEE the wealthy miller yet,
  His double chin, his portly size,
And who that knew him could forget
  The busy wrinkles round his eyes?
The slow wise smile that, round about
  His dusty forehead dryly curl'd,
Seem'd half-within and half-without,
  And full of dealings with the world?

In yonder chair I see him sit,
  Three fingers round the old silver cup—
I see his gray eyes twinkle yet
  At his own jest—gray eyes lit up
With summer lightnings of a soul
  So full of summer warmth, so glad,
So healthy, sound, and clear and whole,
  His memory scarce can make me sad.

Yet fill my glass: give me one kiss:
  My own sweet Alice, we must die.
There's somewhat in this world amiss
  Shall be unriddled by and by.

THE MILLER'S DAUGHTER

There's somewhat flows to us in life,
  But more is taken quite away.
Pray, Alice, pray, my darling wife,
  That we may die the self-same day.

Have I not found a happy earth?
  I least should breathe a thought of pain.
Would God renew me from my birth
  I'd almost live my life again.
So sweet it seems with thee to walk,
  And once again to woo thee mine—
It seems in after-dinner talk
  Across the walnuts and the wine—

To be the long and listless boy
  Late-left an orphan of the squire,
Where this old mansion mounted high
  Looks down upon the village spire:
For even here, where I and you
  Have lived and loved alone so long,
Each morn my sleep was broken thro'
  By some wild skylark's matin song.

And oft I heard the tender dove
  In firry woodlands making moan;
But ere I saw your eyes, my love,
  I had no motion of my own.
For scarce my life with fancy play'd
  Before I dream'd that pleasant dream—
Still hither thither idly sway'd
  Like those long mosses in the stream.

Or from the bridge I lean'd to hear
  The milldam rushing down with noise,
And see the minnows everywhere
  In crystal eddies glance and poise,
The tall flag-flowers when they sprung
  Below the range of stepping-stones,
Or those three chestnuts near, that hung
  In masses thick with milky cones.

But, Alice, what an hour was that,
  When after roving in the woods
('Twas April then), I came and sat
  Below the chestnuts, when their buds

Were glistening to the breezy blue;
  And on the slope, an absent fool,
I cast me down, nor thought of you,
  But angled in the higher pool.

A love-song I had somewhere read,
  An echo from a measured strain,
Beat time to nothing in my head
  From some odd corner of the brain.
It haunted me, the morning long,
  With weary sameness in the rhymes,
The phantom of a silent song,
  That went and came a thousand times.

Then leapt a trout. In lazy mood
  I watch'd the little circles die;
They past into the level flood,
  And there a vision caught my eye;
The reflex of a beauteous form,
  A glowing arm, a gleaming neck,
As when a sunbeam wavers warm
  Within the dark and dimpled beck.

For you remember, you had set,
  That morning, on the casement-edge
A long green box of mignonette,
  And you were leaning from the ledge:
And when I raised my eyes, above
  They met with two so full and bright—
Such eyes! I swear to you, my love,
  That these have never lost their light.

I loved, and love dispell'd the fear
  That I should die an early death:
For love possess'd the atmosphere,
  And fill'd the breast with purer breath.
My mother thought, What ails the boy?
  For I was alter'd, and began
To move about the house with joy,
  And with the certain step of man.

I loved the brimming wave that swam
  Thro' quiet meadows round the mill,
The sleepy pool above the dam,
  The pool beneath it never still,

THE MILLER'S DAUGHTER

The meal-sacks on the whiten'd floor,
  The dark round of the dripping wheel,
The very air about the door
  Made misty with the floating meal.

And oft in ramblings on the wold,
  When April nights began to blow,
And April's crescent glimmer'd cold,
  I saw the village lights below;
I knew your taper far away,
  And full at heart of trembling hope,
From off the wold I came, and lay
  Upon the freshly-flower'd slope.

The deep brook groan'd beneath the mill;
  And "by that lamp," I thought, "she sits!"
The white chalk-quarry from the hill
  Gleam'd to the flying moon by fits.
"O that I were beside her now!
  O will she answer if I call?
O would she give me vow for vow,
  Sweet Alice, if I told her all?"

Sometimes I saw you sit and spin:
  And, in the pauses of the wind,
Sometimes I heard you sing within;
  Sometimes your shadow cross'd the blind.
At last you rose and moved the light,
  And the long shadow of the chair
Flitted across into the night,
  And all the casement darken'd there.

But when at last I dared to speak,
  The lanes, you know, were white with may,
Your ripe lips moved not, but your cheek
  Flush'd like the coming of the day;
And so it was—half-sly, half-shy,
  You would, and would not, little one!
Although I pleaded tenderly,
  And you and I were all alone.

And slowly was my mother brought
   To yield consent to my desire:
She wish'd me happy, but she thought
   I might have look'd a little higher;
And I was young—too young to wed:
   "Yet must I love her for your sake;
Go fetch your Alice here," she said:
   Her eyelid quiver'd as she spake.

And down I went to fetch my bride:
   But, Alice, you were ill at ease;
This dress and that by turns you tried,
   Too fearful that you should not please.
I loved you better for your fears,
   I knew you could not look but well;
And dews, that would have fall'n in tears,
   I kiss'd away before they fell.

I watch'd the little flutterings,
   The doubt my mother would not see;
She spoke at large of many things,
   And at the last she spoke of me;
And turning look'd upon your face,
   As near this door you sat apart,
And rose, and, with a silent grace
   Approaching, press'd you heart to heart.

Ah, well—but sing the foolish song
   I gave you, Alice, on the day
When, arm in arm, we went along,
   A pensive pair, and you were gay
With bridal flowers—that I may seem,
   As in the nights of old, to lie
Beside the mill-wheel in the stream,
   While those full chestnuts whisper by.

      It is the miller's daughter
         And she is grown so dear, so dear,
     That I would be the jewel
         That trembles in her ear:
     For hid in ringlets day and night,
     I'd touch her neck so warm and white.

And I would be the girdle
  About her dainty dainty waist,
And her heart would beat against me,
  In sorrow and in rest:
And I should know if it beat right,
I'd clasp it round so close and tight.

And I would be the necklace,
  And all day long to fall and rise
Upon her balmy bosom,
  With her laughter or her sighs,
And I would lie so light, so light,
I scarce should be unclasp'd at night.

A trifle, sweet! which true love spells—
  True love interprets—right alone.
His light upon the letter dwells,
  For all the spirit is his own.
So, if I waste words now, in truth
  You must blame Love. His early rage
Had force to make me rhyme in youth,
  And makes me talk too much in age.

And now those vivid hours are gone,
  Like mine own life to me thou art,
Where Past and Present, wound in one,
  Do make a garland for the heart:
So sing that other song I made,
  Half-anger'd with my happy lot,
The day, when in the chestnut-shade
  I found the blue Forget-me-not.

> Love that hath us in the net
> Can he pass, and we forget?
> Many suns arise and set.
> Many a chance the years beget.
> Love the gift is Love the debt.
>   Even so.
>
> Love is hurt with jar and fret.
> Love is made a vague regret.
> Eyes with idle tears are wet.
> Idle habit links us yet.
> What is love? for we forget:
>   Ah, no! no!

Look thro' mine eyes with thine. True wife,
  Round my true heart thine arms intwine
My other dearer life in life,
  Look thro' my very soul with thine!
Untouch'd with any shade of years,
  May those kind eyes forever dwell!
They have not shed a many tears,
  Dear eyes, since first I knew them well.

Yet tears they shed: they had their part
  Of sorrow: for when time was ripe,
The still affection of the heart
  Became an outward breathing type,
That into stillness past again,
  And left a want unknown before;
Although the loss has brought us pain,
  That loss but made us love the more,

With farther lookings on. The kiss,
  The woven arms, seem but to be
Weak symbols of the settled bliss,
  The comfort, I have found in thee:
But that God bless thee, dear—who wrought
  Two spirits to one equal mind—
With blessings beyond hope or thought,
  With blessings which no words can find.

Arise, and let us wander forth,
  To yon old mill across the wolds;
For look, the sunset, south and north,
  Winds all the vale in rosy folds,
And fires your narrow casement glass,
  Touching the sullen pool below:
On the chalk-hill the bearded grass
  Is dry and dewless. Let us go.

FATIMA

O Love, Love, Love! O withering might!
O sun, that from thy noonday height
Shudderest when I strain my sight,
Throbbing thro' all thy heat and light,

FATIMA

Lo, falling from my constant mind,
Lo, parch'd and wither'd, deaf and blind,
I whirl like leaves in roaring wind.

Last night I wasted hateful hours
Below the city's eastern towers:
I thirsted for the brooks, the showers:
I roll'd among the tender flowers:
    I crush'd them on my breast, my mouth;
    I look'd athwart the burning drouth
    Of that long desert to the south.

Last night, when some one spoke his name,
From my swift blood that went and came
A thousand little shafts of flame
Were shiver'd in my narrow frame.
    O Love, O fire! once he drew
    With one long kiss my whole soul thro'
    My lips, as sunlight drinketh dew.

Before he mounts the hill, I know
He cometh quickly: from below
Sweet gales, as from deep gardens, blow
Before him, striking on my brow.
    In my dry brain my spirit soon,
    Down-deepening from swoon to swoon,
    Faints like a dazzled morning moon.

The wind sounds like a silver wire,
And from beyond the noon a fire
Is pour'd upon the hills, and nigher
The skies stoop down in their desire;
    And, isled in sudden seas of light,
    My heart, pierced thro' with fierce **delight**,
    Bursts into blossom in his sight.

My whole soul waiting silently,
All naked in a sultry sky,
Droops blinded with his shining eye:
I *will* possess him or will die.
    I will grow round him in his place,
    Grow, live, die looking on his face,
    Die, dying clasp'd in his embrace.

ŒNONE

THERE lies a vale in Ida, lovelier
Than all the valleys of Ionian hills.
The swimming vapor slopes athwart the glen,
Puts forth an arm, and creeps from pine to pine,
And loiters, slowly drawn. On either hand
The lawns and meadow-ledges midway down
Hang rich in flowers, and far below them roars
The long brook falling thro' the clov'n ravine
In cataract after cataract to the sea.
Behind the valley topmost Gargarus
Stands up and takes the morning: but in front
The gorges, opening wide apart, reveal
Troas and Ilion's column'd citadel,
The crown of Troas.

                    Hither came at noon
Mournful Œnone, wandering forlorn
Of Paris, once her playmate on the hills.
Her cheek had lost the rose, and round her neck
Floated her hair or seem'd to float in rest.
She, leaning on a fragment twined with vine,
Sang to the stillness, till the mountain-shade
Sloped downward to her seat from the upper cliff.

"O mother Ida, many-fountain'd Ida,
Dear mother Ida, hearken ere I die.
For now the noonday quiet holds the hill:
The grasshopper is silent in the grass:
The lizard, with his shadow on the stone,
Rests like a shadow, and the winds are dead.
The purple flower droops: the golden bee
Is lily-cradled: I alone awake.
My eyes are full of tears, my heart of love,
My heart is breaking, and my eyes are dim,
And I am all aweary of my life.

"O mother Ida, many-fountain'd Ida,
Dear mother Ida, hearken ere I die.
Hear me, O Earth, hear me, O Hills, O Caves
That house the cold crown'd snake! O mountain brooks,
I am the daughter of a River God,

Hear me, for I will speak, and build up all
My sorrow with my song, as yonder walls
Rose slowly to a music slowly breathed,
A cloud that gather'd shape: for it may be
That, while I speak of it, a little while
My heart may wander from its deeper woe.

"O mother Ida, many-fountain'd Ida,
Dear mother Ida, hearken ere I die.
I waited underneath the dawning hills,
Aloft the mountain lawn was dewy-dark,
And dewy-dark aloft the mountain pine:
Beautiful Paris, evil-hearted Paris,
Leading a jet-black goat white-horn'd, white-hooved,
Came up from reedy Simois all alone.

"O mother Ida, hearken ere I die.
Far-off the torrent call'd me from the cleft:
Far up the solitary morning smote
The streaks of virgin snow. With down-dropt eyes
I sat alone: white-breasted like a star
Fronting the dawn he moved; a leopard skin
Droop'd from his shoulder, but his sunny hair
Cluster'd about his temples like a God's:
And his cheek brighten'd as the foam-bow brightens
When the wind blows the foam, and all my heart
Went forth to embrace him coming ere he came.

"Dear mother Ida, hearken ere I die.
He smiled, and opening out his milk-white palm
Disclosed a fruit of pure Hesperian gold,
That smelt ambrosially, and while I look'd
And listen'd, the full-flowing river of speech
Came down upon my heart.
      " 'My own Œnone,
Beautiful-brow'd Œnone, my own soul,
Behold this fruit, whose gleaming rind ingrav'n
"For the most fair," would seem to award it thine,
As lovelier than whatever Oread haunt
The knolls of Ida, loveliest in all grace
Of movement, and the charm of married brows.'

"Dear mother Ida, hearken ere I die.
He prest the blossom of his lips to mine,
And added 'This was cast upon the board,
When all the full-faced presence of the Gods
Ranged in the halls of Peleus; whereupon
Rose feud, with question unto whom 'twere due:
But light-foot Iris brought it yester-eve,
Delivering, that to me, by common voice
Elected umpire, Herè comes to-day,
Pallas and Aphroditè, claiming each
This meed of fairest. Thou, within the cave
Behind yon whispering tuft of oldest pine,
Mayst well behold them unbeheld, unheard
Hear all, and see thy Paris judge of Gods.'

"Dear mother Ida, hearken ere I die.
It was the deep midnoon: one silvery cloud
Had lost his way between the piney sides
Of this long glen. Then to the bower they came,
Naked they came to that smooth-swarded bower,
And at their feet the crocus brake like fire,
Violet, amaracus, and asphodel,
Lotos and lilies: and a wind arose,
And overhead the wandering ivy and vine,
This way and that, in many a wild festoon
Ran riot, garlanding the gnarled boughs
With bunch and berry and flower thro' and thro'.

"O mother Ida, hearken ere I die.
On the tree-tops a crested peacock lit,
And o'er him flow'd a golden cloud, and lean'd
Upon him, slowly dropping fragrant dew.
Then first I heard the voice of her, to whom
Coming thro' Heaven, like a light that grows
Larger and clearer, with one mind the Gods
Rise up for reverence. She to Paris made
Proffer of royal power, ample rule
Unquestion'd overflowing revenue
Wherewith to embellish state, 'from many a vale
And river-sunder'd champaign clothed with corn,
Or labor'd mine undrainable of ore.
Honor,' she said, and homage, tax and toll,

From many an inland town and haven large,
Mast-throng'd beneath her shadowing citadel
In glassy bays among her tallest towers.'

"O mother Ida, hearken ere I die.
Still she spake on and still she spake of power,
'Which in all action is the end of all;
Power fitted to the season; wisdom-bred
And throned of wisdom—from all neighbor crowns
Alliance and Allegiance, till thy hand
Fail from the sceptre-staff. Such boon from me,
From me, Heaven's Queen, Paris, to thee king-born,
A shepherd all thy life but yet king-born,
Should come most welcome, seeing men in power
Only, are likest gods, who have attain'd
Rest in a happy place and quiet seats
Above the thunder, with undying bliss
In knowledge of their own supremacy.'

"Dear mother Ida, hearken ere I die.
She ceased, and Paris held the costly fruit
Out at arm's-length, so much the thought of power
Flatter'd his spirit; but Pallas where she stood
Somewhat apart, her clear and bared limbs
O'erthwarted with the brazen-headed spear
Upon her pearly shoulder leaning cold,
The while, above, her full and earnest eye
Over her snow-cold breast and angry cheek
Kept watch, waiting decision, made reply.

" 'Self-reverence, self-knowledge, self-control,
These three alone lead life to sovereign power.
Yet not for power (power of herself
Would come uncall'd for) but to live by law,
Acting the law we live by without fear;
And, because right is right, to follow right
Were wisdom in the scorn of consequence.'

"Dear mother Ida, hearken ere I die.
Again she said: 'I woo thee not with gifts.
Sequel of guerdon could not alter me

To fairer. Judge thou me by what I am,
So shalt thou find me fairest.

        Yet, indeed,
If gazing on divinity disrobed
Thy mortal eyes are frail to judge of fair,
Unbiass'd by self-profit, oh! rest thee sure
That I shall love thee well and cleave to thee,
So that my vigor, wedded to thy blood,
Shall strike within thy pulses, like a God's,
To push thee forward thro' a life of shocks,
Dangers, and deeds, until endurance grow
Sinew'd with action, and the full-grown will,
Circled thro' all experiences, pure law,
Commeasure perfect freedom.'

        "Here she ceas'd,
And Paris ponder'd, and I cried, 'O Paris,
Give it to Pallas!' but he heard me not,
Or hearing would not hear me, woe is me!

"O mother Ida, many-fountain'd Ida,
Dear mother Ida, hearken ere I die.
Idalian Aphroditè beautiful,
Fresh as the foam, new-bathed in Paphian wells,
With rosy slender fingers backward drew
From her warm brows and bosom her deep hair
Ambrosial, golden round her lucid throat
And shoulder: from the violets her light foot
Shone rosy-white, and o'er her rounded form
Between the shadows of the vine-bunches
Floated the glowing sunlights, as she moved.

"Dear mother Ida, hearken ere I die.
She with a subtle smile in her mild eyes,
The herald of her triumph, drawing nigh
Half-whisper'd in his ear, 'I promise thee
The fairest and most loving wife in Greece,'
She spoke and laugh'd: I shut my sight for fear:
But when I look'd, Paris had raised his arm,
And I beheld great Herè's angry eyes,
As she withdrew into the golden cloud,
And I was left alone within the bower;
And from that time to this I am alone,
And I shall be alone until I die.

ŒNONE

"Yet, mother Ida, hearken ere I die.
Fairest—why fairest wife? am I not fair?
My love hath told me so a thousand times.
Methinks I must be fair, for yesterday,
When I past by, a wild and wanton pard,
Eyed like the evening star, with playful tail
Crouch'd fawning in the weed. Most loving is she?
Ah me, my mountain shepherd, that my arms
Were wound about thee, and my hot lips prest
Close, close to thine in that quick-falling dew
Of fruitful kisses, thick as Autumn rains
Flash in the pools of whirling Simois.

"O mother, hear me yet before I die.
They came, they cut away my tallest pines,
My tall dark pines, that plumed the craggy ledge
High over the blue gorge, and all between
The snowy peak and snow-white cataract
Foster'd the callow eaglet—from beneath
Whose thick mysterious boughs in the dark morn
The panther's roar came muffled, while I sat
Low in the valley. Never, never more
Shall lone Œnone see the morning mist
Sweep thro' them; never see them overlaid
With narrow moon-lit slips of silver cloud,
Between the loud stream and the trembling stars.

"O mother, hear me yet before I die.
I wish that somewhere in the ruin'd folds,
Among the fragments tumbled from the glens,
Or the dry thickets, I could meet with her
The Abominable, that uninvited came
Into the fair Peleïan banquet-hall,
And cast the golden fruit upon the board,
And bred this change; that I might speak my mind,
And tell her to her face how much I hate
Her presence, hated both of Gods and men.

"O mother, hear me yet before I die.
Hath he not sworn his love a thousand times,
In this green valley, under this green hill,
Ev'n on this hand, and sitting on this stone?
Seal'd it with kisses? water'd it with tears?

O happy tears, and how unlike to these!
O happy Heaven, how canst thou see my face?
O happy earth, how canst thou bear my weight?
O death, death, death, thou ever-floating cloud,
There are enough unhappy on this earth,
Pass by the happy souls, that love to live:
I pray thee, pass before my light of life,
And shadow all my soul that I may die.
Thou weighest heavy on the heart within,
Weigh heavy on my eyelids: let me die.

"O mother, hear me yet before I die.
I will not die alone, for fiery thoughts
Do shape themselves within me, more and more,
Whereof I catch the issue, as I hear
Dead sounds at night come from the inmost hills,
Like footsteps upon wool. I dimly see
My far-off doubtful purpose, as a mother
Conjectures of the features of her child
Ere it is born: her child!—a shudder comes
Across me: never child be born of me,
Unblest, to vex me with his father's eyes!

"O mother, hear me yet before I die.
Hear me, O earth. I will not die alone,
Lest their shrill happy laughter come to me
Walking the cold and starless road of Death
Uncomforted, leaving my ancient love
With the Greek woman. I will rise and go
Down into Troy, and ere the stars come forth
Talk with the wild Cassandra, for she says
A fire dances before her, and a sound
Rings ever in her ears of armed men.
What this may be I know not, but I know
That, whereso'er I am by night and day,
All earth and air seem only burning fire."

THE SISTERS

WE were two daughters of one race:
She was the fairest in the face:
   The wind is blowing in turret and tree.

THE SISTERS

They were together, and she fell;
Therefore revenge became me well.
   O the Earl was fair to see!

She died: she went to burning flame:
She mix'd her ancient blood with shame.
   The wind is howling in turret and tree.
Whole weeks and months, and early and late,
To win his love I lay in wait:
   O the Earl was fair to see!

I made a feast; I bade him come;
I won his love, I brought him home.
   The wind is roaring in turret and tree.
And after supper, on a bed,
Upon my lap he laid his head:
   O the Earl was fair to see!

I kiss'd his eyelids into rest:
His ruddy cheek upon my breast.
   The wind is raging in turret and tree.
I hated him with the hate of hell.
But I loved his beauty passing well.
   O the Earl was fair to see!

I rose up in the silent night:
I made my dagger sharp and bright.
   The wind is raving in turret and tree.
As half-asleep his breath he drew,
Three times I stabb'd him thro' and thro'.
   O the Earl was fair to see!

I curl'd and comb'd his comely head,
He look'd so grand when he was dead.
   The wind is blowing in turret and tree.
I wrapt his body in the sheet,
And laid him at his mother's feet.
   O the Earl was fair to see!

To ——

WITH THE FOLLOWING POEM

I SEND you here a sort of allegory,
 (For you will understand it) of a soul,
A sinful soul possess'd of many gifts,
A spacious garden full of flowering weeds,
A glorious Devil, large in heart and brain,
That did love Beauty only, (Beauty seen
In all varieties of mould and mind)
And Knowledge for its beauty; or if Good,
Good only for its beauty, seeing not
That Beauty, Good, and Knowledge, are three sisters
That dote upon each other, friends to man,
Living together under the same roof,
And never can be sunder'd without tears.
And he that shuts Love out, in turn shall be
Shut out from Love, and on her threshold lie
Howling in outer darkness. Not for this
Was common clay ta'en from the common earth
Moulded by God, and temper'd with the tears
Of angels to the perfect shape of man.

The Palace of Art

I BUILT my soul a lordly pleasure-house,
 Wherein at ease for aye to dwell.
I said, "O soul, make merry and carouse,
 Dear soul, for all is well."

A huge crag-platform, smooth as burnish'd brass
 I chose. The ranged ramparts bright
From level meadow-bases of deep grass
 Suddenly scaled the light.

Thereon I built it firm. Of ledge or shelf
 The rock rose clear, or winding stair.
My soul would live alone unto herself
 In her high palace there.

And "while the world runs round and round," I said,
  "Reign thou apart, a quiet king,
Still as, while Saturn whirls, his steadfast shade
    Sleeps on his luminous ring."

To which my soul made answer readily:
  "Trust me, in bliss I shall abide
In this great mansion that is built for me,
    So royal-rich and wide."

    *   *   *   *   *

Four courts I made, East, West and South and North,
  In each a squared lawn, wherefrom
The golden gorge of dragons spouted forth
    A flood of fountain-foam.

And round the cool green courts there ran a row
  Of cloisters, branch'd like mighty woods,
Echoing all night to that sonorous flow
    Of spouted fountain-floods.

And round the roofs a gilded gallery
  That lent broad verge to distant lands,
Far as the wild swan wings, to where the sky
    Dipt down to sea and sands.

From those four jets four currents in one swell
  Across the mountain stream'd below
In misty folds, that floating as they fell
    Lit up a torrent-bow.

And high on every peak a statue seem'd
  To hang on tiptoe, tossing up
A cloud of incense of all odor steam'd
    From out a golden cup.

So that she thought, "And who shall gaze upon
  My palace with unblinded eyes,
While this great bow will waver in the sun,
    And that sweet incense rise?"

For that sweet incense rose and never fail'd,
   And, while day sank or mounted higher,
The light aerial gallery, golden-rail'd,
   Burnt like a fringe of fire.

Likewise the deep-set windows, stain'd and traced,
   Would seem slow-flaming crimson fires
From shadow'd grots of arches interlaced,
   And tipt with frost-like spires.

* * * * *

Full of long-sounding corridors it was,
   That over-vaulted grateful gloom,
Thro' which the livelong day my soul did pass,
   Well-pleased, from room to room.

Full of great rooms and small the palace stood,
   All various, each a perfect whole
From living Nature, fit for every mood
   And change of my still soul.

For some were hung with arras green and blue,
   Showing a gaudy summer-morn,
Where with puff'd cheek the belted hunter blew
   His wreathed bugle-horn.

One seem'd all dark and red—a tract of sand,
   And some one pacing there alone,
Who paced forever in a glimmering land,
   Lit with a low large moon.

One show'd an iron coast and angry waves.
   You seem'd to hear them climb and fall
And roar rock-thwarted under bellowing caves,
   Beneath the windy wall.

And one, a full-fed river winding slow
   By herds upon an endless plain,
The ragged rims of thunder brooding low,
   With shadow-streaks of rain.

THE PALACE OF ART

And one, the reapers at their sultry toil.
    In front they bound the sheaves. Behind
Were realms of upland, prodigal in oil,
    And hoary to the wind.

And one a foreground black with stones and slags,
    Beyond, a line of heights, and higher
All barr'd with long white cloud the scornful crags,
    And highest, snow and fire.

And one, an English home—gray twilight pour'd
    On dewy pastures, dewy trees,
Softer than sleep—all things in order stored,
    A haunt of ancient Peace.

Nor these alone, but every landscape fair,
    As fit for every mood of mind,
Or gay, or grave, or sweet, or stern, was there
    Not less than truth design'd.

    *   *   *   *   *

Or the maid-mother by a crucifix,
    In tracts of pasture sunny-warm.
Beneath branch-work of costly sardonyx
    Sat smiling, babe in arm.

Or in a clear-wall'd city on the sea,
    Near gilded organ-pipes, her hair
Wound with white roses, slept St. Cecily;
    An angel look'd at her.

Or thronging all one porch of Paradise
    A group of Houris bow'd to see
The dying Islamite, with hands and eyes
    That said, We wait for thee.

Or mythic Uther's deeply-wounded son
    In some fair space of sloping greens
Lay, dozing in the vale of Avalon,
    And watch'd by weeping queens.

Or hollowing one hand against his ear,
    To list a foot-fall, ere he saw
The wood-nymph, stay'd the Ausonian king to hear
    Of wisdom and of law.

Or over hills with peaky tops engrail'd,
    And many a tract of palm and rice,
The throne of Indian Cama slowly sail'd
    A summer fann'd with spice.

Or sweet Europa's mantle blew unclasp'd,
    From off her shoulder backward borne:
From one hand droop'd a crocus: one hand grasp'd
    The mild bull's golden horn.

Or else flush'd Ganymede, his rosy thigh
    Half-buried in the Eagle's down
Sole as a flying star shot thro' the sky
    Above the pillar'd town.

Nor these alone: but every legend fair
    Which the supreme Caucasian mind
Carved out of Nature for itself, was there,
    Not less than life, design'd.

*   *   *   *   *

Then in the towers I placed great bells that swung,
    Moved of themselves, with silver sound;
And with choice paintings of wise men I hung
    The royal dais round.

For there was Milton like a seraph strong,
    Beside him Shakespeare bland and mild;
And there the world-worn Dante grasp'd his song,
    And somewhat grimly smiled.

And there the Ionian father of the rest;
    A million wrinkles carved his skin;
A hundred winters snow'd upon his breast,
    From cheek and throat and chin.

Above, the fair hall-ceiling stately-set
  Many an arch high up did lift,
And angels rising and descending met
  With interchange of gift.

Below was all mosaic choicely plann'd
  With cycles of the human tale
Of this wide world, the times of every land
  So wrought, they will not fail.

The people here, a beast of burden slow,
  Toil'd onward, prick'd with goads and stings;
Here play'd, a tiger, rolling to and fro
  The heads and crowns of kings;

Here rose, an athlete, strong to break or bind
  All force in bonds that might endure,
And here once more like some sick man declined,
  And trusted any cure.

But over these she trod: and those great bells
  Began to chime. She took her throne:
She sat betwixt the shining Oriels,
  To sing her songs alone.

And thro' the topmost Oriels' colored flame
  Two godlike faces gazed below;
Plato the wise, and large-brow'd Verulam,
  The first of those who know.

And all those names, that in their motion were
  Full-welling fountain-heads of change,
Betwixt the slender shafts were blazon'd fair
  In diverse raiment strange:

Thro' which the lights, rose, amber, emerald, blue,
  Flush'd in her temples, and her eyes.
And from her lips, as morn from Memnon, drew
  Rivers of melodies.

No nightingale delighteth to prolong
  Her low preamble all alone,
More than my soul to hear her echo'd song
  Throb thro' the ribbed stone;

Singing and murmuring in her feastful mirth,
    Joying to feel herself alive,
Lord over Nature, Lord of the visible earth,
    Lord of the senses five;

Communing with herself: "All these are mine,
    And let the world have peace or wars,
'Tis one to me." She—when young night divine
    Crown'd dying day with stars,

Making sweet close of his delicious toils—
    Lit light in wreaths and anadems,
And pure quintessences of precious oils
    In hollow'd moons of gems,

To mimic heaven; and clapt her hands and cried,
    "I marvel if my still delight
In this great house so royal-rich, and wide,
    Be flatter'd to the height.

"O all things fair to sate my various eyes!
    O shapes and hues that please me well!
O silent faces of the Great and Wise,
    My Gods, with whom I dwell!

"O God-like isolation which art mine,
    I can but count thee perfect gain,
What time I watch the darkening droves of swine
    That range on yonder plain.

"In filthy sloughs they roll a prurient skin,
    They graze and wallow, breed and sleep;
And oft some brainless devil enters in,
    And drives them to the deep."

Then of the moral instinct would she prate
    And of the rising from the dead,
As hers by right of full-accomplish'd Fate;
    And at the last she said:

THE PALACE OF ART

"I take possession of man's mind and deed.
　　I care not what the sects may brawl,
I sit as God holding no form of creed,
　　　　But contemplating all."

　　　　＊　＊　＊　＊　＊

Full oft the riddle of the painful earth
　　Flash'd thro' her as she sat alone,
Yet not the less held she her solemn mirth,
　　　　And intellectual throne.

And so she throve and prosper'd: so three years
　　She prosper'd: on the fourth she fell,
Like Herod, when the shout was in his ears,
　　　　Struck thro' with pangs of hell.

Lest she should fail and perish utterly,
　　God, before whom ever lie bare
The abysmal deeps of Personality,
　　　　Plagued her with sore despair.

When she would think, where'er she turn'd her sight
　　The airy hand confusion wrought,
Wrote, "Mene, mene," and divided quite
　　　　The kingdom of her thought.

Deep dread and loathing of her solitude
　　Fell on her, from which mood was born
Scorn of herself; again, from out that mood
　　　　Laughter at her self-scorn.

"What! is not this my place of strength," she said,
　　"My spacious mansion built for me,
Whereof the strong foundation-stones were laid
　　　　Since my first memory?"

But in dark corners of her palace stood
　　Uncertain shapes; and unawares
On white-eyed phantasms weeping tears of blood,
　　　　And horrible nightmares,

And hollow shades enclosing hearts of flame,
    And, with dim fretted foreheads all,
On corpses three-months-old at noon she came,
    That stood against the wall.

A spot of dull stagnation, without light
    Or power of movement, seem'd my soul,
'Mid onward-sloping motions infinite
    Making for one sure goal.

A still salt pool, lock'd in with bars of sand,
    Left on the shore; that hears all night
The plunging seas draw backward from the land
    Their moon-led waters white.

A star that with the choral starry dance
    Join'd not, but stood, and standing saw
The hollow orb of moving Circumstance
    Roll'd round by one fix'd law.

Back on herself her serpent pride had curl'd.
    "No voice," she shriek'd in that lone hall,
"No voice breaks thro' the stillness of this world:
    One deep, deep silence all!"

She, mouldering with the dull earth's mouldering sod,
    Inwrapt tenfold in slothful shame,
Lay there exiled from eternal God,
    Lost to her place and name;

And death and life she hated equally,
    And nothing saw, for her despair,
But dreadful time, dreadful eternity,
    No comfort anywhere;

Remaining utterly confused with fears,
    And ever worse with growing time,
And ever unrelieved by dismal tears,
    And all alone in crime:

Shut up as in a crumbling tomb, girt round
    With blackness as a solid wall,
Far off she seem'd to hear the dully sound
    Of human footsteps fall.

As in strange lands a traveller walking slow,
  In doubt and great perplexity,
A little before moon-rise hears the low
  Moan of an unknown sea;

And knows not if it be thunder, or a sound
  Of rocks thrown down, or one deep cry
Of great wild beasts; then thinketh, "I have found
  A new land, but I die."

She howl'd aloud, "I am on fire within.
  There comes no murmur of reply.
What is it that will take away my sin,
  And save me lest I die?"

So when four years were wholly finished,
  She threw her royal robes away.
"Make me a cottage in the vale," she said,
  "Where I may mourn and pray.

"Yet pull not down my palace towers, that are
  So lightly beautifully built:
Perchance I may return with others there
When I have purged my guilt."

LADY CLARA VERE DE VERE

LADY Clara Vere de Vere,
  Of me you shall not win renown:
You thought to break a country heart
  For pastime, ere you went to town.
At me you smiled, but unbeguiled
  I saw the snare, and I retired:
The daughter of a hundred Earls,
  You are not one to be desired.

Lady Clara Vere de Vere,
  I know you proud to bear your name,
Your pride is yet no mate for mine,
  Too proud to care from whence I came.

Nor would I break for your sweet sake
  A heart that dotes on truer charms.
A simple maiden in her flower
  Is worth a hundred coats-of-arms.

Lady Clara Vere de Vere,
  Some meeker pupil you must find,
For were you queen of all that is,
  I could not stoop to such a mind.
You sought to prove how I could love;
  And my disdain is my reply.
The lion on your old stone gates
  Is not more cold to you than I.

Lady Clara Vere de Vere,
  You put strange memories in my head.
Not thrice your branching limes have blown
  Since I beheld young Laurence dead.
Oh your sweet eyes, your low replies:
  A great enchantress you may be;
But there was that across his throat
  Which you had hardly cared to see.

Lady Clara Vere de Vere,
  When thus he met his mother's view,
She had the passions of her kind,
  She spake some certain truths of you.
Indeed I heard one bitter word
  That scarce is fit for you to hear;
Her manners had not that repose
  Which stamps the caste of Vere de Vere.

Lady Clara Vere de Vere,
  There stands a spectre in your hall:
The guilt of blood is at your door:
  You changed a wholesome heart to gall.
You held your course without remorse,
  To make him trust his modest worth,
And, last, you fix'd a vacant stare,
  And slew him with your noble birth.

Trust me, Clara Vere de Vere,
  From yon blue heavens above us bent
The gardener Adam and his wife
  Smile at the claims of long descent.
Howe'er it be, it seems to me,
  'Tis only noble to be good.
Kind hearts are more than coronets,
  And simple faith than Norman blood.

I know you, Clara Vere de Vere,
  You pine among your halls and towers:
The languid light of your proud eyes
  Is wearied of the rolling hours.
In glowing health, with boundless wealth,
  But sickening of a vague disease,
You know so ill to deal with time,
  You needs must play such pranks as these.

Clara, Clara Vere de Vere,
  If time be heavy on your hands,
Are there no beggars at your gate,
  Nor any poor about your lands?
Oh! teach the orphan-boy to read,
  Or teach the orphan-girl to sew,
Pray Heaven for a human heart,
  And let the foolish yeoman go.

The May Queen

You must wake and call me early, call me early, mother dear;
To-morrow 'ill be the happiest time of all the glad New-year;
Of all the glad New-year, mother, the maddest merriest day;
For I'm to be Queen o' the May, mother, I'm to be Queen o' the May.

There's many a black black eye, they say, but none so bright as mine;
There's Margaret and Mary, there's Kate and Caroline:
But none so fair as little Alice in all the land they say,
So I'm to be Queen o' the May, mother, I'm to be Queen o' the May.

I sleep so sound all night, mother, that I shall never wake,
If you do not call me loud when the day begins to break:
But I must gather knots of flowers, and buds and garlands gay,
For I'm to be Queen o' the May, mother, I'm to be Queen o' the May.

As I came up the valley whom think ye should I see,
But Robin leaning on the bridge beneath the hazel-tree?
He thought of that sharp look, mother, I gave him yesterday,
But I'm to be Queen o' the May, mother, I'm to be Queen o' the May.

He thought I was a ghost, mother, for I was all in white,
And I ran by him without speaking, like a flash of light.
They call me cruel-hearted, but I care not what they say,
For I'm to be Queen o' the May, mother, I'm to be Queen o' the May.

They say he's dying all for love, but that can never be:
They say his heart is breaking, mother—what is that to me?
There's many a bolder lad 'ill woo me any summer day,
And I'm to be Queen o' the May, mother, I'm to be Queen o' the May.

Little Effie shall go with me to-morrow to the green,
And you'll be there, too, mother, to see me made the Queen;
For the shepherd lads on every side 'ill come from far away,
And I'm to be Queen o' the May, mother, I'm to be Queen o' the May.

The honeysuckle round the porch has wov'n its wavy bowers,
And by the meadow-trenches blow the faint sweet cuckoo-flowers;
And the wild marsh-marigold shines like fire in swamps and hollows gray,
And I'm to be Queen o' the May, mother, I'm to be Queen o' the May.

The night-winds come and go, mother, upon the meadow-grass,
And the happy stars above them seem to brighten as they pass;
There will not be a drop of rain the whole of the livelong day,
And I'm to be Queen o' the May, mother, I'm to be Queen o' the May.

All the valley, mother, 'ill be fresh and green and still,
And the cowslip and the crowfoot are over all the hill,
And the rivulet in the flowery dale 'ill merrily glance and play,
For I'm to be Queen o' the May, mother, I'm to be Queen o' the May.

So you must wake and call me early, call me early, mother dear,
To-morrow 'ill be the happiest time of all the glad New-year:
To-morrow 'ill be of all the year the maddest merriest day,
For I'm to be Queen o' the May, mother, I'm to be Queen o' the May.

New-Year's Eve

IF you're waking call me early, call me early, mother dear,
For I would see the sun rise upon the glad New-year.
It is the last New-year that I shall ever see,
Then you may lay me low i' the mould and think no more of me.

To-night I saw the sun set: he set and left behind
The good old year, the dear old time, and all my peace of mind;
And the New-year's coming up, mother, but I shall never see
The blossom on the blackthorn, the leaf upon the tree.

Last May we made a crown of flowers: we had a merry day;
Beneath the hawthorn on the green they made me Queen of May;
And we danced about the may-pole and in the hazel copse,
Till Charles's Wain came out above the tall white chimney-tops.

There's not a flower on all the hills: the frost is on the pane:
I only wish to live till the snowdrops come again:
I wish the snow would melt and the sun come out on high:
I long to see a flower so before the day I die.

The building rook 'ill caw from the windy tall elm-tree,
And the tufted plover pipe along the fallow lea,
And the swallow 'ill come back again with summer o'er the wave,
But I shall lie alone, mother, within the mouldering grave.

Upon the chancel-casement, and upon that grave of mine,
In the early morning the summer sun 'ill shine,
Before the red cock crows from the farm upon the hill,
When you are warm-asleep, mother, and all the world is still.

When the flowers come again, mother, beneath the waning light
You'll never see me more in the long gray fields at night;
When from the dry dark wold the summer airs blow cool
On the oat-grass and the sword-grass, and the bulrush in the pool.

You'll bury me, my mother, just beneath the hawthorn shade,
And you'll come sometimes and see me where I am lowly laid.
I shall not forget you, mother, I shall hear you when you pass,
With your feet above my head in the long and pleasant grass.

I have been wild and wayward, but you'll forgive me now;
You'll kiss me, my own mother, and forgive me ere I go;
Nay, nay, you must not weep, nor let your grief be wild,
You should not fret for me, mother, you have another child.

If I can I'll come again, mother, from out my resting-place;
Tho' you'll not see me, mother, I shall look upon your face;
Tho' I cannot speak a word, I shall hearken what you say,
And be often, often with you when you think I'm far away.

Good-night, good-night, when I have said good-night forevermore,
And you see me carried out from the threshold of the door;
Don't let Effie come to see me till my grave be growing green:
She'll be a better child to you than ever I have been.

She'll find my garden-tools upon the granary floor:
Let her take 'em: they are hers: I shall never garden more:
But tell her, when I'm gone, to train the rosebush that I set
About the parlor-window and the box of mignonette.

Good-night, sweet mother: call me before the day is born.
All night I lie awake, but I fall asleep at morn;
But I would see the sun rise upon the glad New-year,
So, if you're waking, call me, call me early, mother dear.

THE MAY QUEEN

Conclusion

I THOUGHT to pass away before, and yet alive I am;
And in the fields all round I hear the bleating of the lamb.
How sadly, I remember, rose the morning of the year!
To die before the snowdrop came, and now the violet's here.

O sweet is the new violet, that comes beneath the skies,
And sweeter is the young lamb's voice to me that cannot rise,
And sweet is all the land about, and all the flowers that blow,
And sweeter far is death than life to me that long to go.

It seem'd so hard at first, mother, to leave the blessed sun,
And now it seems as hard to stay, and yet His will be done!
But still I think it can't be long before I find release;
And that good man, the clergyman, has told me words of peace.

O blessings on his kindly voice and on his silver hair!
And blessings on his whole life long, until he meet me there!
O blessings on his kindly heart and on his silver head!
A thousand times I blest him, as he knelt beside my bed.

He taught me all the mercy, for he show'd me all the sin.
Now, tho' my lamp was lighted late, there's One will let me in:
Nor would I now be well, mother, again if that could be,
For my desire is but to pass to Him that died for me.

I did not hear the dog howl, mother, or the death-watch beat,
There came a sweeter token when the night and morning meet:
But sit beside my bed, mother, and put your hand in mine,
And Effie on the other side, and I will tell the sign.

All in the wild March-morning I heard the angels call;
It was when the moon was setting, and the dark was over all;
The trees began to whisper, and the wind began to roll,
And in the wild March-morning I heard them call my soul.

For lying broad awake I thought of you and Effie dear;
I saw you sitting in the house, and I no longer here;
With all my strength I pray'd for both, and so I felt resign'd,
And up the valley came a swell of music on the wind.

I thought that it was fancy, and I listen'd in my bed,
And then did something speak to me—I know not what was said;
For great delight and shuddering took hold of all my mind,
And up the valley came again the music on the wind.

But you were sleeping; and I said, "It's not for them: it's mine."
And if it come three times, I thought, I take it for a sign.
And once again it came, and close beside the window-bars,
Then seem'd to go right up to Heaven and die among the stars.

So now I think my time is near. I trust it is. I know
The blessed music went that way my soul will have to go.
And for myself, indeed, I care not if I go to-day.
But, Effie, you must comfort *her* when I am past away.

And say to Robin a kind word, and tell him not to fret;
There's many a worthier than I, would make him happy yet.
If I had lived—I cannot tell—I might have been his wife;
But all these things have ceased to be, with my desire of life.

O look! the sun begins to rise, the heavens are in a glow;
He shines upon a hundred fields, and all of them I know.
And there I move no longer now, and there his light may shine—
Wild flowers in the valley for other hands than mine.

O sweet and strange it seems to me, that ere this day is done
The voice, that now is speaking, may be beyond the sun—
Forever and forever with those just souls and true—
And what is life, that we should moan? why make we such ado?

Forever and forever, all in a blessed home—
And there to wait a little while till you and Effie come—
To lie within the light of God, as I lie upon your breast—
And the wicked cease from troubling, and the weary are at rest.

The Lotos-Eaters

"Courage!" he said, and pointed toward the land,
"This mounting wave will roll us shoreward soon."
In the afternoon they came unto a land
In which it seemed always afternoon.
All round the coast the languid air did swoon,
Breathing like one that hath a weary dream.
Full-faced above the valley stood the moon;
And like a downward smoke, the slender stream
Along the cliff to fall and pause and fall did seem.

A land of streams! some, like a downward smoke,
Slow-dropping veils of thinnest lawn, did go;
And some thro' wavering lights and shadows broke,
Rolling a slumbrous sheet of foam below.
They saw the gleaming river seaward flow
From the inner land: far off, three mountain-tops,
Three silent pinnacles of aged snow,
Stood sunset-flush'd; and, dew'd with showery drops,
Up-clomb the shadowy pine above the woven copse.

The charmed sunset linger'd low adown
In the red West: thro' mountain clefts the dale
Was seen far inland, and the yellow down
Border'd with palm, and many a winding vale
And meadow, set with slender galingale;
A land where all things always seem'd the same!
And round about the keel with faces pale,
Dark faces pale against that rosy flame,
The mild-eyed melancholy Lotos-eaters came.

Branches they bore of that enchanted stem,
Laden with flower and fruit, whereof they gave
To each, but whoso did receive of them,
And taste, to him the gushing of the wave
Far far away did seem to mourn and rave
On alien shores; and if his fellow spake,
His voice was thin, as voices from the grave;
And deep-asleep he seem'd, yet all awake,
And music in his ears his beating heart did make.

They sat them down upon the yellow sand,
Between the sun and moon upon the shore;
And sweet it was to dream of Fatherland,
Of child and wife, and slave; but evermore
Most weary seem'd the sea, weary the oar,
Weary the wandering fields of barren foam.
Then some one said, "We will return no more;"
And all at once they sang, "Our island home
Is far beyond the wave; we will no longer roam."

Choric Song

I

There is sweet music here that softer falls
Than petals from blown roses on the grass,
Or night-dews on still waters between walls
Of shadowy granite, in a gleaming pass;
Music that gentlier on the spirit lies,
Than tir'd eyelids upon tir'd eyes;
Music that brings sweet sleep down from the blissful skies.
Here are cool mosses deep,
And thro' the moss the ivies creep,
And in the stream the long-leaved flowers weep,
And from the craggy ledge the poppy hangs in sleep.

II

Why are we weigh'd upon with heaviness,
And utterly consumed with sharp distress,
While all things else have rest from weariness?
All things have rest: why should we toil alone,
We only toil, who are the first of things,
And make perpetual moan,
Still from one sorrow to another thrown:
Nor ever fold our wings,
And cease from wanderings,
Nor steep our brows in slumber's holy balm;
Nor hearken what the inner spirit sings,
"There is no joy but calm!"
Why should we only toil, the roof and crown of things?

III

Lo! in the middle of the wood,
The folded leaf is woo'd from out the bud
With winds upon the branch, and there
Grows green and broad, and takes no care,
Sun-steep'd at noon, and in the moon
Nightly dew-fed; and turning yellow
Falls, and floats adown the air.
Lo! sweeten'd with the summer light,
The full-juiced apple, waxing over-mellow,
Drops in a silent autumn night.
All its allotted length of days,
The flower ripens in its place,
Ripens and fades, and falls, and hath no toil,
Fast-rooted in the fruitful soil.

IV

Hateful is the dark-blue sky,
Vaulted o'er the dark-blue sea.
Death is the end of life; ah, why
Should life all labor be?
Let us alone. Time driveth onward fast,
And in a little while our lips are dumb.
Let us alone. What is it that will last?
All things are taken from us, and become
Portions and parcels of the dreadful Past.
Let us alone. What pleasure can we have
To war with evil? Is there any peace
In ever climbing up the climbing wave?
All things have rest, and ripen toward the grave
In silence; ripen, fall and cease:
Give us long rest or death, dark death, or dreamful ease.

V

How sweet it were, hearing the downward stream,
With half-shut eyes ever to seem
Falling asleep in a half-dream!
To dream and dream, like yonder amber light,
Which will not leave the myrrh-bush on the height;

To hear each other's whisper'd speech;
Eating the Lotos day by day,
To watch the crisping ripples on the beach,
And tender curving lines of creamy spray;
To lend our hearts and spirit wholly
To the influence of mild-minded melancholy;
To muse and brood and live again in memory,
With those old faces of our infancy
Heap'd over with a mound of grass,
Two handfuls of white dust, shut in an urn of brass!

VI

Dear is the memory of our wedded lives,
And dear the last embraces of our wives
And their warm tears: but all hath suffer'd change:
For surely now our household hearths are cold:
Our sons inherit us: our looks are strange:
And we should come like ghosts to trouble joy.
Or else the island princes over-bold
Have eat our substance, and the minstrel sings,
Before them of the ten years' war in Troy,
And our great deeds, as half-forgotten things.
Is there confusion in the little isle?
Let what is broken so remain.
The Gods are hard to reconcile:
'Tis hard to settle order once again.
There *is* confusion worse than death,
Trouble on trouble, pain on pain,
Long labor unto aged breath,
Sore task to hearts worn out by many wars
And eyes grown dim with gazing on the pilot-stars.

VII

But, propt on beds of amaranth and moly,
How sweet (while warm airs lull us, blowing lowly)
With half-dropt eyelid still,
Beneath a heaven dark and holy,
To watch the long bright river drawing slowly
His waters from the purple hill—
To hear the dewy echoes calling

From cave to cave thro' the thick-twined vine—
To watch the emerald-color'd water falling
Thro' many a wov'n acanthus-wreath divine!
Only to hear and see the far-off sparkling brine,
Only to hear were sweet, stretch'd out beneath the pine.

VIII

The Lotos blooms below the barren peak:
The Lotos blows by every-winding creek:
All day the wind breathes low with mellower tone:
Thro' every hollow cave and alley lone
Round and round the spicy downs the yellow Lotos-dust is blown.
We have had enough of action, and of motion we,
Roll'd to starboard, roll'd to larboard, when the surge was seething free,
Where the wallowing monster spouted his foam-fountains in the sea.
Let us swear an oath, and keep it with an equal mind,
In the hollow Lotos-land to live and lie reclined
On the hills like Gods together, careless of mankind.
For they lie beside their nectar, and the bolts are hurl'd
Far below them in the valleys, and the clouds are lightly curl'd
Round their golden houses, girdled with the gleaming world:
Where they smile in secret, looking over wasted lands,
Blight and famine, plague and earthquake, roaring deeps and fiery sands,
Clanging fights, and flaming towns, and sinking ships, and praying hands.
But they smile, they find a music centred in a doleful song
Steaming up, a lamentation and an ancient tale of wrong,
Like a tale of little meaning tho' the words are strong;
Chanted from an ill-used race of men that cleave the soil,
Sow the seed, and reap the harvest with enduring toil,
Storing yearly little dues of wheat, and wine and oil;
Till they perish and they suffer—some, 'tis whisper'd—down in hell
Suffer endless anguish, others in Elysian valleys dwell,
Resting weary limbs at last on beds of asphodel.
Surely, surely, slumber is more sweet than toil, the shore
Than labor in the deep mid-ocean, wind and wave and oar;
Oh rest ye, brother mariners, we will not wander more.

A Dream of Fair Women

I READ, before my eyelids dropt their shade,
   "*The Legend of Good Women*," long ago
Sung by the morning-star of song, who made
   His music heard below;

Dan Chaucer, the first warbler, whose sweet breath
   Preluded those melodious bursts that fill
The spacious times of great Elizabeth
   With sounds that echo still.

And, for a while, the knowledge of his art
   Held me above the subject, as strong gales
Hold swollen clouds from raining, tho' my heart,
   Brimful of those wild tales,

Charged both mine eyes with tears. In every land
   I saw, wherever light illumineth,
Beauty and anguish walking hand in hand
   The downward slope to death.

Those far-renowned brides of ancient song
   Peopled the hollow dark, like burning stars,
And I heard sounds of insult, shame, and wrong,
   And trumpets blown for wars;

And clattering flints batter'd with clanging hoofs;
   And I saw crowds in column'd sanctuaries;
And forms that pass'd at windows and on roofs
   Of marble palaces;

Corpses across the threshold; heroes tall
   Dislodging pinnacle and parapet
Upon the tortoise creeping to the wall;
   Lances in ambush set;

And high shrine-doors burst thro' with heated blasts
   That run before the fluttering tongues of fire;
White surf wind-scatter'd over sails and masts,
   And ever climbing higher

A DREAM OF FAIR WOMEN

Squadrons and squares of men in brazen plates,
    Scaffolds, still sheets of water, divers woes,
Ranges of glimmering vaults with iron grates,
    And hush'd seraglios.

So shape chased shape as swift as, when to land
    Bluster the winds and tides the self-same way,
Crisp foam-flakes scud along the level sand,
    Torn from the fringe of spray.

I started once, or seem'd to start in pain,
    Resolved on noble things, and strove to speak,
As when a great thought strikes along the brain,
    And flushes all the cheek.

And once my arm was lifted to hew down
    A cavalier from off his saddle-bow,
That bore a lady from a leaguer'd town;
    And then, I know not how,

All those sharp fancies, by down-lapsing thought
    Stream'd onward, lost their edges, and did creep
Roll'd on each other, rounded, smooth'd, and brought
    Into the gulfs of sleep.

At last methought that I had wander'd far
    In an old wood: fresh-wash'd in coolest dew
The maiden splendors of the morning star
    Shook in the steadfast blue.

Enormous elm-tree-boles did stoop and lean
    Upon the dusky brushwood underneath
Their broad curved branches, fledged with clearest green,
    New from its silken sheath.

The dim red morn had died, her journey done,
    And with dead lips smiled at the twilight plain,
Half-fall'n across the threshold of the sun,
    Never to rise again.

There was no motion in the dumb dead air,
    Not any song of bird or sound of rill;
Gross darkness of the inner sepulchre
    Is not so deadly still

As that wide forest. Growths of jasmine turn'd
  Their humid arms festooning tree to tree,
And at the root thro' lush green grasses burn'd
  The red anemone.

I knew the flowers, I knew the leaves, I knew
  The tearful glimmer of the languid dawn
On those long, rank, dark wood-walks drench'd in dew,
  Leading from lawn to lawn.

The smell of violets, hidden in the green,
  Pour'd back into my empty soul and frame
The times when I remember to have been
  Joyful and free from blame.

And from within me a clear undertone
  Thrill'd thro' mine ears in that unblissful clime,
"Pass freely thro': the wood is all thine own,
  Until the end of time."

At length I saw a lady within call,
  Stiller than chisell'd marble, standing there;
A daughter of the gods, divinely tall,
  And most divinely fair.

Her loveliness with shame and with surprise
  Froze my swift speech: she turning on my face
The star-like sorrows of immortal eyes,
  Spoke slowly in her place.

"I had great beauty: ask thou not my name:
  No one can be more wise than destiny.
Many drew swords and died. Where'er I came
  I brought calamity."

"No marvel, sovereign lady: in fair field
  Myself for such a face had boldly died,"
I answer'd free; and turning I appeal'd
  To one that stood beside.

But she, with sick and scornful looks averse,
  To her full height her stately stature draws;
"My youth," she said "was blasted with a curse:
  This woman was the cause.

A DREAM OF FAIR WOMEN

"I was cut off from hope in that sad place,
   Which men call'd Aulis in those iron years:
My father held his hand upon his face;
   I, blinded with my tears,

"Still strove to speak: my voice was thick with sighs
   As in a dream. Dimly I could descry
The stern black-bearded kings with wolfish eyes,
   Waiting to see me die.

"The high masts flicker'd as they lay afloat;
   The crowds, the temples, waver'd, and the shore;
The bright death quiver'd at the victim's throat;
   Touch'd; and I knew no more."

Whereto the other with a downward brow:
   "I would the white cold heavy-plunging foam,
Whirl'd by the wind, had roll'd me deep below,
   Then when I left my home."

Her slow full words sank thro' the silence drear,
   As thunder-drops fall on a sleeping sea:
Sudden I heard a voice that cried, "Come here,
   That I may look on thee."

I turning saw, throned on a flowery rise,
   One sitting on a crimson scarf unroll'd;
A queen, with swarthy cheeks and bold black eyes,
   Brow-bound with burning gold.

She, flashing forth a haughty smile, began:
   "I govern'd men by change, and so I sway'd
All moods. 'Tis long since I have seen a man.
   Once, like the moon, I made

"The ever-shifting currents of the blood
   According to my humor ebb and flow.
I have no men to govern in this wood:
   That makes my only woe.

"Nay—yet it chafes me that I could not bend
   One will; nor tame and tutor with mine eye
That dull cold-blooded Cæsar. Prythee, friend,
   Where is Mark Antony?

"The man, my lover, with whom I rode sublime
  On Fortune's neck: we sat as God by God:
The Nilus would have risen before his time
  And flooded at our nod.

"We drank the Libyan Sun to sleep, and lit
  Lamps which out-burn'd Canopus. O my life
In Egypt! O the dalliance and the wit,
  The flattery and the strife,

"And the wild kiss, when fresh from war's alarms,
  My Hercules, my Roman Antony,
My mailed Bacchus leapt into my arms,
  Contented there to die!

"And there he died: and when I heard my name
  Sigh'd forth with life I would not brook my fear
Of the other: with a worm I balk'd his fame.
  What else was left? look here!"

(With that she tore her robe apart, and half
  The polish'd argent of her breast to sight
Laid bare. Thereto she pointed with a laugh,
  Showing the aspick's bite.)

"I died a Queen. The Roman soldier found
  Me lying dead, my crown about my brows,
A name forever!—lying robed and crown'd,
  Worthy a Roman spouse."

Her warbling voice, a lyre of widest range
  Struck by all passion, did fall down and glance
From tone to tone, and glided thro' all change
  Of liveliest utterance.

When she made pause I knew not for delight:
  Because with sudden motion from the ground
She rais'd her piercing orbs, and fill'd with light
  The interval of sound.

Still with their fires Love tipt his keenest darts;
  As once they drew into two burning rings
All beams of Love, melting the mighty hearts
  Of captains and of kings.

Slowly my sense undazzled. Then I heard
    A noise of some one coming thro' the lawn,
And singing clearer than the crested bird
    That claps his wings at dawn.

"The torrent brooks of hallow'd Israel
    From craggy hollows pouring, late and soon,
Sound all night long, in falling thro' the dell,
    Far-heard beneath the moon.

"The balmy moon of blessed Israel
    Floods all the deep-blue gloom with beams divine:
All night the splinter'd crags that wall the dell
    With spires of silver shine."

As one that museth where broad sunshine laves
    The lawn by some cathedral, thro' the door
Hearing the holy organ rolling waves
    Of sound on roof and floor

Within, and anthem sung, is charm'd and tied
    To where he stands,—so stood I, when that flow
Of music left the lips of her that died
    To save her father's vow;

The daughter of the warrior Gileadite;
    A maiden pure; as when she went along
From Mizpeh's tower'd gate with welcome light,
    With timbrel and with song.

My words leapt forth: "Heaven heads the count of crimes
    With that wild oath." She render'd answer high:
"Not so, nor once alone; a thousand times
    I would be born and die.

"Single I grew, like some green plant, whose root
    Creeps to the garden water-pipes beneath
Feeding the flower; but ere my flower to fruit
    Changed, I was ripe for death.

"My God, my land, my father—these did move
    Me from my bliss of life, that Nature gave,
Lower'd softly with a threefold cord of love
    Down to a silent grave.

"And I went mourning, 'No fair Hebrew boy
　　Shall smile away my maiden blame among
The Hebrew mothers'—emptied of all joy,
　　Leaving the dance and song,

"Leaving the olive-gardens far below,
　　Leaving the promise of my bridal bower,
The valleys of grape-loaded vines that glow
　　Beneath the battled tower.

"The light white cloud swam over us. Anon
　　We heard the lion roaring from his den;
We saw the large white stars rise one by one,
　　Or, from the darken'd glen,

"Saw God divide the night with flying flame,
　　And thunder on the everlasting hills.
I heard Him, for He spake, and grief became
　　A solemn scorn of ills.

"When the next moon was roll'd into the sky,
　　Strength came to me that equall'd my desire.
How beautiful a thing it was to die
　　For God and for my sire!

"It comforts me in this one thought to dwell,
　　That I subdued me to my father's will;
Because the kiss he gave me, ere I fell,
　　Sweetens the spirit still.

"Moreover it is written that my race
　　Hew'd Ammon, hip and thigh, from Aroer
On Arnon unto Minneth." Here her face
　　Glow'd as I look'd at her.

She lock'd her lips: she left me where I stood:
　　"Glory to God," she sang, and past afar,
Thridding the sombre boskage of the wood,
　　Toward the morning-star.

Losing her carol I stood pensively,
　　As one that from a casement leans his head,
When midnight bells cease ringing suddenly,
　　And the old year is dead.

A DREAM OF FAIR WOMEN

"Alas! alas!" a low voice, full of care,
  Murmur'd beside me: "Turn and look on me:
I am that Rosamond, whom men call fair,
  If what I was I be.

"Would I had been some maiden coarse and poor!
  O me, that I should ever see the light!
Those dragon eyes of anger'd Eleanor
  Do hunt me, day and night."

She ceased in tears, fallen from hope and trust:
  To whom the Egyptian: "O, you tamely died!
You should have clung to Fulvia's waist, and thrust
  The dagger thro' her side."

With that sharp sound the white dawn's creeping beams,
  Stol'n to my brain, dissolved the mystery
Of folded sleep. The captain of my dreams
  Ruled in the eastern sky.

Morn broaden'd on the borders of the dark,
  Ere I saw her, who clasp'd in her last trance
Her murder'd father's head, or Joan of Arc,
  A light of ancient France;

Or her who knew that Love can vanquish Death,
  Who kneeling, with one arm about her king,
Drew forth the poison with her balmy breath,
  Sweet as new buds in Spring.

No memory labors longer from the deep
  Gold-mines of thought to lift the hidden ore
That glimpses, moving up, than I from sleep
  To gather and tell o'er

Each little sound and sight. With what dull pain
  Compass'd, how eagerly I sought to strike
Into that wondrous track of dreams again!
    But no two dreams are like.

As when a soul laments, which hath been blest,
  Desiring what is mingled with past years,
In yearnings that can never be exprest
  By signs or groans or tears;

Because all words, tho' cull'd with choicest art,
    Failing to give the bitter of the sweet,
Wither beneath the palate, and the heart
    Faints, faded by its heat.

THE BLACKBIRD

O BLACKBIRD! sing me something well:
    While all the neighbors shoot thee round,
    I keep smooth plats of fruitful ground,
Where thou may'st warble, eat and dwell.

The espaliers and the standards all
    Are thine; the range of lawn and park:
    The unnetted black-hearts ripen dark,
All thine, against the garden wall.

Yet, tho' I spared thee all the spring,
    Thy sole delight is, sitting still,
    With that gold dagger of thy bill
To fret the summer jenneting.

A golden bill! the silver tongue,
    Cold February loved, is dry:
    Plenty corrupts the melody
That made thee famous once, when young:

And in the sultry garden-squares,
    Now thy flute notes are changed to coarse,
    I hear thee not at all, or hoarse
As when a hawker hawks his wares.

Take warning! he that will not sing
    While yon sun prospers in the blue,
    Shall sing for want, ere leaves are new,
Caught in the frozen palms of Spring.

The Death of the Old Year

Full knee-deep lies the winter snow,
   And the winter winds are wearily sighing:
Toll ye the church-bell sad and slow,
And tread softly and speak low,
For the old year lies a-dying.
      Old year, you must not die;
      You came to us so readily,
      You lived with us so steadily,
      Old year, you shall not die.

He lieth still: he doth not move:
He will not see the dawn of day.
He hath no other life above.
He gave me a friend, and a true true-love,
And the New-year will take 'em away.
      Old year, you must not go;
      So long as you have been with us
      Such joy as you have seen with us,
      Old year, you shall not go.

He froth'd his bumpers to the brim;
A jollier year we shall not see.
But tho' his eyes are waxing dim,
And tho' his foes speak ill of him,
He was a friend to me.
      Old year, you shall not die;
      We did so laugh and cry with you,
      I've half a mind to die with you,
      Old year, if you must die.

He was full of joke and jest,
But all his merry quips are o'er.
To see him die, across the waste
His son and heir doth ride post-haste,
But he'll be dead before.
      Every one for his own.
      The night is starry and cold, my friend,
      And the New-year blithe and bold, my friend,
      Comes up to take his own.

How hard he breathes! over the snow
I heard just now the crowing cock.
The shadows flicker to and fro:
The cricket chirps: the light burns low:
'Tis nearly twelve o'clock.
  Shake hands, before you die.
  Old year, we'll dearly rue for you:
  What is it we can do for you?
  Speak out before you die.

His face is growing sharp and thin.
Alack! our friend is gone.
Close up his eyes: tie up his chin:
Step from the corpse, and let him in
That standeth there alone,
  And waiteth at the door.
  There's a new foot on the floor, my friend,
  And a new face at the door, my friend,
  A new face at the door.

To J. S.

THE wind, that beats the mountain, blows
  More softly round the open wold,
And gently comes the world to those
  That are cast in gentle mould.

And me this knowledge bolder made,
  Or else I had not dared to flow
In these words toward you, and invade
  Even with a verse your holy woe.

'Tis strange that those we lean on most,
  Those in whose laps our limbs are nursed,
Fall into shadow, soonest lost:
  Those we love first are taken first.

God gives us love. Something to love
  He lends us; but, when love is grown
To ripeness, that on which it throve
  Falls off, and love is left alone.

TO J. S.

This is the curse of time. Alas!
    In grief I am not all unlearn'd;
Once thro' mine own doors Death did pass;
    One went, who never hath return'd.

He will not smile—not speak to me
    Once more. Two years his chair is seen
Empty before us. That was he
    Without whose life I had not been.

Your loss is rarer; for this star
    Rose with you thro' a little arc
Of heaven, nor having wander'd far
    Shot on the sudden into dark.

I knew your brother: his mute dust
    I honor and his living worth:
A man more pure and bold and just
    Was never born into the earth.

I have not look'd upon you nigh,
    Since that dear soul hath fall'n asleep.
Great Nature is more wise than I:
    I will not tell you not to weep.

And tho' mine own eyes fill with dew,
    Drawn from the spirit thro' the brain,
I will not even preach to you,
    "Weep, weeping dulls the inward pain."

Let Grief be her own mistress still.
    She loveth her own anguish deep
More than much pleasure. Let her will
    Be done—to weep or not to weep.

I will not say, "God's ordinance
    Of Death is blown in every wind";
For that is not a common chance
    That takes away a noble mind.

His memory long will live alone
    In all our hearts, as mournful light
That broods above the fallen sun,
    And dwells in heaven half the night.

Vain solace! Memory standing near
    Cast down her eyes, and in her throat
Her voice seem'd distant, and a tear
    Dropt on the letters as I wrote.

I wrote I know not what. In truth,
    How *should* I soothe you anyway,
Who miss the brother of your youth?
    Yet something I did wish to say:

For he too was a friend to me:
    Both are my friends, and my true breast
Bleedeth for both; yet it may be
    That only silence suiteth best.

Words weaker than your grief would make
    Grief more. 'Twere better I should cease
Although myself could almost take
    The place of him that sleeps in peace.

Sleep sweetly, tender heart, in peace:
    Sleep, holy spirit, blessed soul,
While the stars burn, the moons increase,
    And the great ages onward roll.

Sleep till the end, true soul and sweet.
    Nothing comes to thee new or strange.
Sleep full of rest from head to feet;
    Lie still, dry dust, secure of change.

On a Mourner

I

NATURE, so far as in her lies,
    Imitates God, and turns her face
To every land beneath the skies,
    Counts nothing that she meets with base,
    But lives and loves in every place;

ON A MOURNER

II

Fills out the homely quickset-screens,
  And makes the purple lilac ripe,
Steps from her airy hill, and greens
  The swamp, where hums the dropping snipe,
  With moss and braided marish-pipe;

III

And on thy heart a finger lays,
  Saying, "Beat quicker, for the time
Is pleasant, and the woods and ways
  Are pleasant, and the beech and lime
  Put forth and feel a gladder clime."

IV

And murmurs of a deep voice,
  Going before to some far shrine,
Teach that sick heart the stronger choice,
  Till all thy life one way incline
  With one wide Will that closes thine.

V

And when the zoning eve has died
  Where yon dark valleys wind forlorn,
Come Hope and Memory, spouse and bride,
  From out the borders of the morn,
  With that fair child betwixt them born.

VI

And when no mortal motion jars
  The blackness round the tombing sod,
Thro' silence and the trembling stars
  Comes Faith from tracts no feet have trod,
  And Virtue, like a household god

VII

Promising empire; such as those
  Once heard at dead of night to greet
Troy's wandering prince, so that he rose
  With sacrifice, while all the fleet
  Had rest by stony hills of Crete.

England and America in 1782

O THOU, that sendest out the man
    To rule by land and sea,
Strong mother of a Lion-line,
Be proud of those strong sons of thine
    Who wrench'd their rights from thee!

What wonder, if in noble heart
    Those men thine arms withstood,
Retaught the lesson thou hadst taught,
And in thy spirit with thee fought—
    Who sprang from English blood!

But Thou rejoice with liberal joy,
    Lift up thy rocky face.
And shatter, when the storms are black,
In many a streaming torrent back,
    The seas that shock thy base!

Whatever harmonies of law
    The growing world assume,
Thy work is thine—The single note
From that deep chord which Hampden smote
    Will vibrate to the doom.

The Goose

I KNEW an old wife lean and poor,
    Her rags scarce held together;
There strode a stranger to the door,
    And it was windy weather.

He held a goose upon his arm,
    He utter'd rhyme and reason,
"Here, take the goose, and keep you warm,
    It is a stormy season."

She caught the white goose by the leg,
    A goose—'twas no great matter.
The goose let fall a golden egg
    With cackle and with clatter.

THE GOOSE

She dropt the goose, and caught the pelf,
    And ran to tell her neighbors;
And bless'd herself, and cursed herself,
    And rested from her labors.

And feeding high, and living soft,
    Grew plump and able-bodied;
Until the grave churchwarden doff'd,
    The parson smirk'd and nodded.

So sitting, served by man and maid,
    She felt her heart grow prouder:
But ah! the more the white goose laid
    It clack'd and cackled louder.

It clutter'd here, it chuckled there;
    It stirr'd the old wife's mettle:
She shifted in her elbow-chair,
    And hurl'd the pan and kettle.

"A quinsy choke thy cursed note!"
    Then wax'd her anger stronger.
"Go, take the goose, and wring her throat,
    I will not bear it longer."

Then yelp'd the cur, and yawl'd the cat;
    Ran Gaffer, stumbled Gammer.
The goose flew this way and flew that,
    And fill'd the house with clamor.

As head and heels upon the floor
    They flounder'd all together,
There strode a stranger to the door,
    And it was windy weather:

He took the goose upon his arm,
    He utter'd words of scorning;
"So keep you cold, or keep you warm,
    It is a stormy morning."

The wild wind rang from park and plain,
    And round the attics rumbled,
Till all the tables danced again,
    And half the chimneys tumbled.

The glass blew in, the fire blew out,
  The blast was hard and harder.
Her cap blew off, her gown blew up,
  And a whirlwind clear'd the larder:

And while on all sides breaking loose
  Her household fled the danger,
Quoth she, "The Devil take the goose,
  And God forget the stranger!"

Morte D'Arthur

So all day long the noise of battle roll'd
Among the mountains by the winter sea;
Until King Arthur's table, man by man,
Had fallen in Lyonness about their Lord,
King Arthur: then, because his wound was deep,
The bold Sir Bedivere uplifted him,
Sir Bedivere, the last of all his knights,
And bore him to a chapel nigh the field,
A broken chancel with a broken cross,
That stood on a dark strait of barren land.
On one side lay the Ocean, and on one
Lay a great water, and the moon was full.
  Then spake King Arthur to Sir Bedivere:
"The sequel of to-day unsolders all
The goodliest fellowship of famous knights
Whereof this world holds record. Such a sleep
They sleep—the men I loved. I think that we
Shall nevermore, at any future time,
Delight our souls with talk of knightly deeds,
Walking about the gardens and the halls
Of Camelot, as in the days that were.
I perish by this people which I made,—
Tho' Merlin sware that I should come again
To rule once more—but let what will be, be,
I am so deeply smitten thro' the helm
That without help I cannot last till morn.
Thou therefore take my brand Excalibur,
Which was my pride: for thou rememberest how
In those old days, one summer noon, an arm
Rose up from out the bosom of the lake,

Clothed in white samite, mystic, wonderful,
Holding the sword—and how I row'd across
And took it, and have worn it like a king:
And, wheresoever I am sung or told
In aftertime, this also shall be known:
But now delay not: take Excalibur,
And fling him far into the middle mere:
Watch what thou seëst, and lightly bring me word."

  To him replied the bold Sir Bedivere:
"It is not meet, Sir King, to leave thee thus,
Aidless, alone, and smitten thro' the helm.
A little thing may harm a wounded man.
Yet I thy hest will all perform at full,
Watch what I see, and lightly bring thee word."

  So saying, from the ruin'd shrine he stept
And in the moon athwart the place of tombs,
Where lay the mighty bones of ancient men,
Old knights, and over them the sea-wind sang
Shrill, chill, with flakes of foam. He, stepping down
By zig-zag paths, and juts of pointed rock,
Came on the shining levels of the lake.

  There drew he forth the brand Excalibur,
And o'er him, drawing it, the winter moon,
Brightening the skirts of a long cloud, ran forth
And sparkled keen with frost against the hilt:
For all the haft twinkled with diamond sparks,
Myriads of topaz-lights, and jacinth-work
Of subtlest jewelry. He gazed so long
That both his eyes were dazzled, as he stood,
This way and that dividing the swift mind,
In act to throw: but at the last it seem'd
Better to leave Excalibur conceal'd
There in the many-knotted water-flags,
That whistled stiff and dry about the marge.
So strode he back slow to the wounded King.

  Then spake King Arthur to Sir Bedivere:
"Hast thou perform'd my mission which I gave?
What is it thou hast seen? or what hast heard?"

  And answer made the bold Sir Bedivere:
"I heard the ripple washing in the reeds,
And the wild water lapping on the crag."

  To whom replied King Arthur, faint and pale:
"Thou hast betray'd thy nature and thy name,

Not rendering true answer, as beseem'd
Thy fealty, nor like a noble knight:
For surer sign had follow'd, either hand,
Or voice, or else a motion of the mere.
This is a shameful thing for men to lie.
Yet now, I charge thee, quickly go again
As thou art lief and dear, and do the thing
I bade thee, watch, and lightly bring me word."

   Then went Sir Bedivere the second time
Across the ridge, and paced beside the mere,
Counting the dewy pebbles, fix'd in thought;
But when he saw the wonder of the hilt,
How curiously and strangely chased, he smote
His palms together, and he cried aloud,

   "And if indeed I cast the brand away,
Surely a precious thing, one worthy note,
Should thus be lost for ever from the earth,
Which might have pleased the eyes of many men.
What good should follow this, if this were done?
What harm, undone? deep harm to disobey,
Seeing obedience is the bond of rule.
Were it well to obey them, if a king demand
An act unprofitable, against himself?
The King is sick, and knows not what he does.
What record, or what relic of my lord
Should be to aftertime, but empty breath
And rumors of a doubt? but were this kept,
Stored in some treasure-house of mighty kings,
Some one might show it at a joust of arms,
Saying, 'King Arthur's sword, Excalibur,
Wrought by the lonely maiden of the Lake.
Nine years she wrought it, sitting in the deeps
Upon the hidden bases of the hills.'
So might some old man speak in the aftertime
To all the people, winning reverence.
But now much honor and much fame were lost."

   So spake he, clouded with his own conceit,
And hid Excalibur the second time,
And so strode back slow to the wounded King.

   Then spoke King Arthur, breathing heavily:
"What is it thou hast seen? or what hast heard?"

   And answer made the bold Sir Bedivere:
"I heard the water lapping on the crag,

And the long ripple washing in the reeds."
    To whom replied King Arthur, much in wrath:
"Ah, miserable and unkind, untrue,
Unknightly, traitor-hearted! Woe is me!
Authority forgets a dying king,
Laid widow'd of the power in his eye
That bow'd the will. I see thee what thou art,
For thou, the latest-left of all my knights,
In whom should meet the offices of all,
Thou wouldst betray me for the precious hilt;
Either from lust of gold, or like a girl
Valuing the giddy pleasure of the eyes.
Yet, for a man may fail in duty twice,
And the third time may prosper, get thee hence:
But, if thou spare to fling Excalibur,
I will arise and slay thee with my hands."
    Then quickly rose Sir Bedivere, and ran,
And, leaping down the ridges lightly, plunged
Among the bulrush-beds, and clutch'd the sword,
And strongly wheel'd and threw it. The great brand
Made lightnings in the splendor of the moon,
And flashing round and round, and whirl'd in an arch,
Shot like a streamer of the northern morn,
Seen where the moving isles of winter shock
By night, with noises of the northern sea.
So flash'd and fell the brand Excalibur:
But ere he dipt the surface, rose an arm
Clothed in white samite, mystic, wonderful,
And caught him by the hilt, and brandish'd him
Three times, and drew him under in the mere.
And lightly went the other to the King.
    Then spoke King Arthur, drawing thicker breath:
"Now see I by thine eyes that this is done.
Speak out: what is it thou hast heard, or seen?"
    And answer made the bold Sir Bedivere:
"Sir King, I closed mine eyelids, lest the gems
Should blind my purpose, for I never saw,
Nor shall see, here or elsewhere, till I die,
Not tho' I live three lives of mortal men,
So great a miracle as yonder hilt,
Then with both hands I flung him, wheeling him;
But when I look'd again, behold an arm,
Clothed in white samite, mystic, wonderful,

That caught him by the hilt, and brandish'd him
Three times, and drew him under in the mere."
    And answer made King Arthur, breathing hard:
"My end draws nigh; 'tis time that I were gone.
Make broad thy shoulders to receive my weight,
And bear me to the margin; yet I fear
My wound hath taken cold, and I shall die."
    So saying, from the pavement he half rose,
Slowly, with pain, reclining on his arm,
And looking wistfully with wide blue eyes
As in a picture. Him Sir Bedivere
Remorsefully regarded thro' his tears,
And would have spoken, but he found not words,
Then took with care, and kneeling on one knee,
O'er both his shoulders drew the languid hands,
And rising bore him thro' the place of tombs.
    But, as he walk'd King Arthur panted hard,
Like one that feels a nightmare on his bed
When all the house is mute. So sigh'd the King,
Muttering and murmuring at his ear, "Quick, quick!
I fear it is too late, and I shall die."
But the other swiftly strode from ridge to ridge,
Clothed with his breath, and looking, as he walk'd,
Larger than human on the frozen hills.
He heard the deep behind him, and a cry
Before. His own thought drove him, like a goad.
Dry clash'd his harness in the icy caves
And barren chasms, and all to left and right
The bare black cliff clang'd round him, as he based
His feet on juts of slippery crag that rang
Sharp-smitten with the dint of armed heels—
And on a sudden, lo! the level lake,
And the long glories of the winter moon.
    Then saw they how there hove a dusky barge,
Dark as a funeral scarf from stem to stern,
Beneath them; and descending they were ware
That all the decks were dense with stately forms
Black-stoled, black-hooded, like a dream—by these
Three Queens with crowns of gold—and from them rose
A cry that shiver'd to the tingling stars,
And, as it were one voice an agony
Of lamentation, like a wind, that shrills
All night in a waste land, where no one comes,

Or hath come, since the making of the world.
    Then murmur'd Arthur, "Place me in the barge,"
And to the barge they came. There those three Queens
Put forth their hands, and took the King, and wept.
But she, that rose the tallest of them all
And fairest, laid his head upon her lap,
And loosed the shatter'd casque, and chafed his hands,
And call'd him by his name, complaining loud,
And dropping bitter tears against his brow
Striped with dark blood: for all his face was white
And colorless, and like the wither'd moon
Smote by the fresh beam of the springing east;
And all his greaves and cuisses dash'd with drops
Of onset; and the light and lustrous curls—
That made his forehead like a rising sun
High from the daïs-throne—were parch'd with dust;
Or, clotted into points and hanging loose,
Mix'd with the knightly growth that fringed his lips.
So like a shatter'd column lay the King;
Not like that Arthur who, with lance in rest,
From spur to plume a star of tournament,
Shot thro' the lists at Camelot, and charged
Before the eyes of ladies and of kings.
    Then loudly cried the bold Sir Bedivere,
"Ah! my Lord Arthur, whither shall I go?
Where shall I hide my forehead and my eyes?
For now I see the true old times are dead,
When every morning brought a noble chance,
And every chance brought out a noble knight.
Such times have been not since the light that led
The holy Elders with the gift of myrrh.
But now the whole ROUND TABLE is dissolved
Which was an image of the mighty world;
And I, the last, go forth companionless,
And the days darken round me, and the years,
Among new men, strange faces, other minds."
    And slowly answered Arthur from the barge:
"The old order changeth, yielding place to new,
And God fulfils Himself in many ways,
Lest one good custom should corrupt the world.
Comfort thyself: what comfort is in me?
I have lived my life, and that which I have done
May He within Himself make pure! but thou,

If thou shouldst never see my face again,
Pray for my soul. More things are wrought by prayer
Than this world dreams of. Wherefore, let thy voice
Rise like a fountain for me night and day.
For what are men better than sheep or goats
That nourish a blind life within the brain,
If, knowing God, they lift not hands of prayer
Both for themselves and those who call them friend?
For so the whole round earth is every way
Bound by gold chains about the feet of God.
But now farewell. I am going a long way
With these thou seëst—if indeed I go—
(For all my mind is clouded with a doubt)
To the island-valley of Avilion;
Where falls not hail, or rain, or any snow,
Nor ever wind blows loudly; but it lies
Deep-meadow'd, happy, fair with orchard-lawns
And bowery hollows crown'd with summer sea,
Where I will heal me of my grievous wound."

So said he, and the barge with oar and sail
Moved from the brink, like some full-breasted swan
That, fluting a wild carol ere her death,
Ruffles her pure cold plume, and takes the flood
With swarthy webs. Long stood Sir Bedivere
Revolving many memories, till the hull
Look'd one black dot against the verge of dawn,
And on the mere the wailing died away.

HERE ended Hall, and our last light, that long
Had wink'd and threaten'd darkness, flared and fell:
At which the Parson, sent to sleep with sound,
And waked with silence, grunted "Good!" but we
Sat rapt: it was the tone with which he read—
Perhaps some modern touches here and there
Redeem'd it from the charge of nothingness—
Or else we loved the man, and prized his work;
I know not: but we sitting, as I said,
The cock crew loud; as at that time of year
The lusty bird takes every hour for dawn:
Then Francis, muttering, like a man ill-used,
"There now—that's nothing!" drew a little back,
And drove his heel into the smoulder'd log,
That sent a blast of sparkles up the flue:

And so to bed; where yet in sleep I seem'd
To sail with Arthur under looming shores,
Point after point; till on to dawn, when dreams
Begin to feel the truth and stir of day,
To me, methought, who waited with a crowd,
There came a bark that, blowing forward, bore
King Arthur, like a modern gentleman
Of stateliest port; and all the people cried,
"Arthur is come again: he cannot die."
Then those that stood upon the hills behind
Repeated—"Come again, and thrice as fair;"
And, further inland, voices echoed—"Come
With all good things, and war shall be no more."
At this a hundred bells began to peal,
That with the sound I woke, and heard indeed
The clear church-bells ring in the Christmas-morn.

Dora

With farmer Allan at the farm abode
William and Dora. William was his son,
And she his niece. He often look'd at them,
And often thought, "I'll make them man and wife."
Now Dora felt her uncle's will in all,
And yearn'd towards William; but the youth, because
He had been always with her in the house,
Thought not of Dora.
   Then there came a day
When Allan call'd his son, and said, "My son:
I married late, but I would wish to see
My grandchild on my knees before I die:
And I have set my heart upon a match.
Now therefore look to Dora; she is well
To look to; thrifty too beyond her age.
She is my brother's daughter: he and I
Had once hard words, and parted, and he died
In foreign lands; but for his sake I bred
His daughter Dora: take her for your wife;
For I have wish'd this marriage, night and day,
For many years." But William answer'd short;
"I cannot marry Dora; by my life,
I will not marry Dora." Then the old man

Was wroth, and doubled up his hands, and said:
"You will not, boy! you dare to answer thus!
But in my time a father's word was law,
And so it shall be now for me. Look to it;
Consider, William: take a month to think,
And let me have an answer to my wish;
Or, by the Lord that made me, you shall pack
And never more darken my doors again."
But William answer'd madly; bit his lips,
And broke away. The more he look'd at her
The less he liked her; and his ways were harsh;
But Dora bore them meekly. Then before
The month was out he left his father's house,
And hired himself to work within the fields;
And half in love, half spite, he woo'd and wed
A laborer's daughter, Mary Morrison.

Then, when the bells were ringing, Allan call'd
His niece and said: "My girl, I love you well;
But if you speak with him that was my son,
Or change a word with her he calls his wife,
My home is none of yours. My will is law."
And Dora promised, being meek. She thought,
"It cannot be: my uncle's mind will change!"

And days went on, and there was born a boy
To William; then distresses came on him;
And day by day he pass'd his father's gate,
Heart-broken, and his father help'd him not.
But Dora stored what little she could save,
And sent it them by stealth, nor did they know
Who sent it; till at last a fever seized
On William, and in harvest time he died.

Then Dora went to Mary. Mary sat
And look'd with tears upon her boy, and thought
Hard things of Dora. Dora came and said:
"I have obey'd my uncle until now,
And I have sinn'd, for it was all thro' me
This evil came on William at the first.
But, Mary, for the sake of him that's gone,
And for your sake, the woman that he chose,
And for this orphan, I am come to you:
You know there has not been for these five years
So full a harvest: let me take the boy,
And I will set him in my uncle's eye

Among the wheat; that when his heart is glad
Of the full harvest, he may see the boy,
And bless him for the sake of him that's gone."
    And Dora took the child, and went her way
Across the wheat, and sat upon a mound
That was unsown, where many poppies grew.
Far off the farmer came into the field
And spied her not; for none of all his men
Dare tell him Dora waited with the child;
And Dora would have risen and gone to him,
But her heart fail'd her; and the reapers reap'd,
And the sun fell, and all the land was dark.
    But when the morrow came, she rose and took
The child once more, and sat upon the mound;
And made a little wreath of all the flowers
That grew about, and tied it round his hat
To make him pleasing in her uncle's eye.
Then when the farmer pass'd into the field
He spied her, and he left his men at work,
And came and said: "Where were you yesterday?
Whose child is that? What are you doing here?"
So Dora cast her eyes upon the ground,
And answer'd softly, "This is William's child!"
"And did I not," said Allan, "did I not
Forbid you, Dora?" Dora said again:
"Do with me as you will, but take the child,
And bless him for the sake of him that's gone!"
And Allan said, "I see it is a trick
Got up betwixt you and the woman there.
I must be taught my duty, and by you!
You knew my word was law, and yet you dared
To slight it. Well—for I will take the boy;
But go you hence, and never see me more."
    So saying, he took the boy that cried aloud
And struggled hard. The wreath of flowers fell
At Dora's feet. She bow'd upon her hands,
And the boy's cry came to her from the field,
More and more distant. She bow'd down her head,
Remembering the day when first she came,
And all the things that had been. She bow'd down
And wept in secret; and the reapers reap'd,
And the sun fell, and all the land was dark.
    Then Dora went to Mary's house, and stood

Upon the threshold. Mary saw the boy
Was not with Dora. She broke out in praise
To God, that help'd her in her widowhood.
And Dora said, "My uncle took the boy;
But, Mary, let me live and work with you:
He says that he will never see me more."
Then answer'd Mary, "This shall never be,
That thou shouldst take my trouble on thyself:
And, now I think, he shall not have the boy,
For he will teach him hardness, and to slight
His mother; therefore thou and I will go,
And I will have my boy, and bring him home;
And I will beg of him to take thee back:
But if he will not take thee back again,
Then thou and I will live within one house,
And work for William's child, until he grows
Of age to help us."
    So the women kiss'd
Each other, and set out, and reach'd the farm.
The door was off the latch: they peep'd, and saw
The boy set up betwixt his grandsire's knees,
Who thrust him in the hollows of his arm,
And clapt him on the hands and on the cheeks,
Like one that loved him: and the lad stretch'd out
And babbled for the golden seal, that hung
From Allan's watch, and sparkled by the fire.
Then they came in: but when the boy beheld
His mother, he cried out to come to her:
And Allan set him down, and Mary said:

"O Father!—if you let me call you so—
I never came a-begging for myself,
Or William, or this child; but now I come
For Dora: take her back; she loves you well.
O Sir, when William died, he died at peace
With all men; for I ask'd him, and he said,
He could not ever rue his marrying me—
I had been a patient wife: but, Sir, he said
That he was wrong to cross his father thus:
'God bless him!' he said, 'and may he never know
The troubles I have gone thro'!' Then he turn'd
His face and pass'd—unhappy that I am!
But now, Sir, let me have my boy, for you
Will make him hard, and he will learn to slight

His father's memory; and take Dora back,
And let all this be as it was before."
　　So Mary said, and Dora hid her face
By Mary. There was silence in the room;
And all at once the old man burst in sobs:—
　　"I have been to blame—to blame. I have killed my son.
I have kill'd him—but I loved him—my dear son.
May God forgive me!—I have been to blame.
Kiss me, my children."
　　　　　　　　　Then they clung about
The old man's neck, and kiss'd him many times.
And all the man was broken with remorse;
And all his love came back a hundredfold;
And for three hours he sobb'd o'er William's child
Thinking of William.
　　　　　　　So those four abode
Within one house together; and as years
Went forward, Mary took another mate;
But Dora lived unmarried till her death.

AUDLEY COURT

"THE Bull, the Fleece are cramm'd, and not a room
For love or money. Let us picnic there
At Audley Court."
　　　　　　　I spoke, while Audley feast
Humm'd like a hive all round the narrow quay,
To Francis, with a basket on his arm,
To Francis just alighted from the boat,
And breathing of the sea. "With all my heart,"
Said Francis. Then we shoulder'd thro' the swarm,
And rounded by the stillness of the beach
To where the bay runs up its latest horn.
　　We left the dying ebb that faintly lipp'd
The flat red granite; so by many a sweep
Of meadow smooth from aftermath we reach'd
The griffin-guarded gates, and pass'd thro' all
The pillar'd dusk of sounding sycamores,
And cross'd the garden to the gardener's lodge,
With all its casements bedded, and its walls
And chimneys muffled in the leafy vine.
　　There, on a slope of orchard, Francis laid

A damask napkin wrought with horse and hound,
Brought out a dusky loaf that smelt of home,
And, half-cut-down, a pasty costly-made,
Where quail and pigeon, lark and leveret lay,
Like fossils of the rock, with golden yolks
Imbedded and injellied; last, with these,
A flask of cider from his father's vats,
Prime, which I knew; and so we sat and eat
And talk'd old matters over; who was dead,
Who married, who was like to be, and how
The races went, and who would rent the hall:
Then touch'd upon the game, how scarce it was
This season; glancing thence, discuss'd the farm,
The four-field system, and the price of grain;
And struck upon the corn-laws, where we split,
And came again together on the king
With heated faces; till he laugh'd aloud;
And, while the blackbird on the pippin hung
To hear him, clapt his hand in mine and sang—

"Oh! who would fight and march and countermarch,
Be shot for sixpence in a battle-field,
And shovell'd up into some bloody trench
Where no one knows? but let me live my life.

"Oh! who would cast and balance at a desk,
Perch'd like a crow upon a three-legg'd stool,
Till all his juice is dried, and all his joints
Are full of chalk? but let me live my life.

"Who'd serve the state? for if I carved my name
Upon the cliffs that guard my native land,
I might as well have traced it in the sands;
The sea wastes all: but let me live my life.

"Oh! who would love? I woo'd a woman once,
But she was sharper than an eastern wind,
And all my heart turn'd from her, as a thorn
Turns from the sea; but let me live my life."

He sang his song, and I replied with mine:
I found it in a volume, all of songs,
Knock'd down to me, when old Sir Robert's pride,
His books—the more the pity, so I said—
Came to the hammer here in March—and this—
I set the words, and added names I knew.

"Sleep, Ellen Aubrey, sleep, and dream of me:
Sleep, Ellen, folded in thy sister's arm,

And sleeping, haply dream her arm is mine.
"Sleep, Ellen, folded in Emilia's arm;
Emilia, fairer than all else but thou,
For thou art fairer than all else that is.
"Sleep, breathing health and peace upon her breast:
Sleep, breathing love and trust against her lip:
I go to-night: I come to-morrow morn.
"I go, but I return: I would I were
The pilot of the darkness and the dream.
Sleep, Ellen Aubrey, love, and dream of me."
So sang we each to either, Francis Hale,
The farmer's son, who lived across the bay,
My friend; and I, that having wherewithal,
And in the fallow leisure of my life
A rolling stone of here and everywhere,
Did what I would; but ere the night we rose
And saunter'd home beneath a moon, that, just
In crescent, dimly rain'd about the leaf
Twilights of airy silver, till we reach'd
The limit of the hills; and as we sank
From rock to rock upon the glooming quay,
The town was hush'd beneath us: lower down
The bay was oily calm; the harbor buoy,
Sole star of phosphorescence in the calm,
With one green sparkle ever and anon
Dipt by itself, and we were glad at heart.

WALKING TO THE MAIL

John. I'M glad I walk'd. How fresh the meadows look
Above the river, and, but a month ago,
The whole hill-side was redder than a fox.
Is yon plantation where this byway joins
The turnpike?
James.   Yes.
John. And when does this come by?
James. The mail? At one o'clock.
John.   What is it now?
James. A quarter to.
John.   Whose house is that I see?
No, not the County Member's with the vane:
Up higher with the yew-tree by it, and half

A score of gables.
   James. That? Sir Edward Head's:
But he's abroad: the place is to be sold.
   John. Oh, his. He was not broken.
   James.   No, sir, he,
Vex'd with a morbid devil in his blood
That veil'd the world with jaundice, hid his face
From all men, and commercing with himself,
He lost the sense that handles daily life—
That keeps us all in order more or less—
And sick of home went overseas for change.
   John. And whither?
   James. Nay, who knows? he's here and there.
But let him go; his devil goes with him,
As well as with his tenant, Jocky Dawes.
   John. What's that?
   James. You saw the man—on Monday, was it?—
There by the humpback'd willow; half stands up
And bristles; half has fall'n and made a bridge;
And there he caught the younker tickling trout—
Caught *in flagrante*—what's the Latin word?—
Delicto: but his house, for so they say,
Was haunted with a jolly ghost, that shook
The curtains, whined in lobbies, tapt at doors,
And rummaged like a rat: no servant stay'd:
The farmer vext packs up his beds and chairs,
And all his household stuff; and with his boy
Betwixt his knees, his wife upon the tilt,
Sets out, and meets a friend who hails him, "What!
You're flitting!" "Yes, we're flitting," says the ghost
(For they had pack'd the thing among the beds,)
"Oh well," says he, "you flitting with us too—
Jack, turn the horses' heads and home again."
   John. He left *his* wife behind; for so I heard.
   James. He left her, yes. I met my lady once:
A woman like a butt, and harsh as crabs.
   John. Oh yet but I remember, ten years back—
'Tis now at least ten years—and then she was—
You could not light upon a sweeter thing:
A body slight and round, and like a pear
In growing, modest eyes, a hand, a foot
Lessening in perfect cadence, and a skin
As clean and white as privet when it flowers.

WALKING TO THE MAIL

James. Ay, ay, the blossom fades, and they that loved
At first like dove and dove were cat and dog.
She was the daughter of a cottager,
Out of her sphere. What betwixt shame and pride,
New things and old, himself and her, she sour'd
To what she is: a nature never kind!
Like men, like manners: like breeds like, they say:
Kind nature is the best: those manners next
That fit us like a nature second-hand;
Which are indeed the manners of the great.

John. But I had heard it was this bill that past,
And fear of change at home, that drove him hence.

James. That was the last drop in the cup of gall.
I once was near him, when his bailiff brought
A Chartist pike. You should have seen him wince
As from a venomous thing: he thought himself
A mark for all, and shudder'd, lest a cry
Should break his sleep by night, and his nice eyes
Should see the raw mechanic's bloody thumbs
Sweat on his blazon'd chairs, but, sir, you know
That these two parties still divide the world—
Of those that want, and those that have: and still
The same old sore breaks out from age to age
With much the same result. Now I myself,
A Tory to the quick, was as a boy
Destructive, when I had not what I would.
I was at school—a college in the South:
There lived a flayflint near; we stole his fruit,
His hens, his eggs; but there was law for *us;*
We paid in person. He had a sow, sir. She,
With meditative grunts of much content,
Lay great with pig, wallowing in sun and mud.
By night we dragg'd her to the college tower
From her warm bed, and up the corkscrew stair
With hand and rope we haled the groaning sow,
And on the leads we kept her till she pigg'd.
Large range of prospect had the mother sow,
And but for daily loss of one she loved
As one by one we took them—but for this—
As never sow was higher in this world—
Might have been happy: but what lot is pure?
We took them all, till she was left alone
Upon her tower, the Niobe of swine,

And so return'd unfarrow'd to her sty.
John. They found you out?
James.   Not they.
John.   Well—after all—
What know we of the secret of a man?
His nerves were wrong. What ails us, who are sound,
That we should mimic this raw fool the world,
Which charts us all in its coarse blacks or whites,
As ruthless as a baby with a worm,
As cruel as a schoolboy ere he grows
To Pity—more from ignorance than will.

But put your best foot forward, or I fear
That we shall miss the mail: and here it comes
With five at top: as quaint a four-in-hand
As you shall see—three pyebalds and a roan.

EDWIN MORRIS;

OR, THE LAKE

O ME, my pleasant rambles by the lake,
My sweet, wild, fresh three quarters of a year,
My one Oasis in the dust and drouth
Of city life! I was a sketcher then:
See here, my doing: curves of mountain, bridge,
Boat, island, ruins of a castle, built
When men knew how to build, upon a rock
With turrets lichen-gilded like a rock:
And here, new-comers in an ancient hold,
New-comers from the Mersey, millionaires,
Here lived the Hills—a Tudor-chimnied bulk
Of mellow brickwork on an isle of bowers.

O me, my pleasant rambles by the lake
With Edwin Morris and with Edward Bull
The curate; he was fatter than his cure.

But Edwin Morris, he that knew the names,
Long learned names of agaric, moss and fern,
Who forged a thousand theories of the rocks,
Who taught me how to skate, to row, to swim,
Who read me rhymes elaborately good,
His own—I call'd him Crichton, for he seem'd
All-perfect, finish'd to the finger nail.

EDWIN MORRIS

And once I ask'd him of his early life,
And his first passion; and he answer'd me;
And well his words became him: was he not
A full-cell'd honeycomb of eloquence
Stored from all flowers? Poet-like he spoke.

"My love for Nature is as old as I;
But thirty moons, one honeymoon to that,
And three rich sennights more, my love for her.
My love for Nature and my love for her,
Of different ages, like twin-sisters grew,
Twin-sisters differently beautiful.
To some full music rose and sank the sun,
And some full music seem'd to move and change
With all the varied changes of the dark,
And either twilight and the day between;
For daily hope fulfill'd, to rise again
Revolving toward fulfilment, made it sweet
To walk, to sit, to sleep, to wake, to breathe."

Or this or something like to this he spoke.
Then said the fat-faced curate Edward Bull,
"I take it, God made the woman for the man,
And for the good and increase of the world.
A pretty face is well, and this is well,
To have a dame indoors, that trims us up,
And keeps us tight; but these unreal ways
Seem but the theme of writers, and indeed
Worn threadbare. Man is made of solid stuff.
I say, God made the woman for the man,
And for the good and increase of the world."

"Parson," said I, "you pitch the pipe too low:
But I have sudden touches, and can run
My faith beyond my practice into his:
Tho' if, in dancing after Letty Hill,
I do not hear the bells upon my cap,
I scarce have other music: yet say on.
What should one give to light on such a dream?"
I ask'd him half-sardonically.

"Give?
Give all thou art," he answer'd, and a light
Of laughter dimpled in his swarthy cheek;

"I would have hid her needle in my heart,
To save her little finger from a scratch
No deeper than the skin: my ears could hear
Her lightest breath; her least remark was worth
The experience of the wise. I went and came;
Her voice fled always thro' the summer land;
I spoke her name alone. Thrice-happy days!
The flower of each, those moments when we met,
The crown of all, we met to part no more."

Were not his words delicious, I a beast
To take them as I did? but something jarr'd;
Whether he spoke too largely; that there seem'd
A touch of something false, some self-conceit,
Or over-smoothness: howsoe'er it was,
He scarcely hit my humor, and I said:

"Friend Edwin, do not think yourself alone
Of all men happy. Shall not Love to me,
As in the Latin song I learnt at school,
Sneeze out a full God-bless-you right and left?
But you can talk: yours is a kindly vein:
I have, I think,—Heaven knows—as much within;
Have, or should have, but for a thought or two,
That like a purple beech among the greens
Looks out of place: 'tis from no want in her:
It is my shyness, or my self-distrust,
Or something of a wayward modern mind
Dissecting passion. Time will set me right."

So spoke I knowing not the things that were.
Then said the fat-faced curate, Edward Bull:
"God made the woman for the use of man,
And for the good and increase of the world."
And I and Edwin laughed; and now we paused
About the windings of the marge to hear
The soft wind blowing over meadowy holms
And alders, garden-isles; and now we left
The clerk behind us, I and he, and ran
By ripply shallows of the lisping lake,
Delighted with the freshness and the sound.

But, when the bracken rusted on their crags,
My suit had wither'd, nipt to death by him
That was a God, and is a lawyer's clerk,
The rentroll Cupid of our rainy isles.
'Tis true, we met; one hour I had, no more:
She sent a note, the seal an *Elle vous suit,*
The close, "Your Letty, only yours"; and this
Thrice underscored. The friendly mist of morn
Clung to the lake. I boated over, ran
My craft aground, and heard with beating heart
The Sweet-Gale rustle round the shelving keel;
And out I stept, and up I crept: she moved,
Like Proserpine in Enna, gathering flowers:
Then low and sweet I whistled thrice; and she,
She turn'd, we closed, we kiss'd, swore faith, I breathed
In some new planet: a silent cousin stole
Upon us and departed: "Leave," she cried,
"O leave me!" "Never, dearest, never: here
I brave the worst:" and while we stood like fools
Embracing, all at once a score of pugs
And poodles yell'd within, and out they came
Trustees and Aunts and Uncles.

  "What, with him!
Go" (shrill'd the cotton-spinning chorus); "him!"
I choked. Again they shriek'd the burthen—"Him!"
Again with hands of wild rejection "Go!—
Girl, get you in!" She went—and in one month
They wedded her to sixty thousand pounds,
To lands in Kent and messuages in York,
And slight Sir Robert with his watery smile
And educated whisker. But for me,
They set an ancient creditor to work:
It seems I broke a close with force and arms:
There came a mystic token from the king
To greet the sheriff, needless courtesy!
I read, and fled by night, and flying turn'd:
Her taper glimmer'd in the lake below:
I turn'd once more, close-button'd to the storm;
So left the place, left Edwin, nor have seen
Him since, nor heard of her, nor cared to hear.

 Nor cared to hear? perhaps: yet long ago
I have pardon'd little Letty; not indeed,

It may be, for her own dear sake but this,
She seems a part of those fresh days to me;
For in the dust and drouth of London life
She moves among my visions of the lake,
While the prime swallow dips his wing, or then
While the gold-lily blows, and overhead
The light cloud smoulders on the summer crag.

St. Simeon Stylites

ALTHO' I be the basest of mankind,
From scalp to sole one slough and crust of sin,
Unfit for earth, unfit for heaven, scarce meet
For troops of devils, mad with blasphemy,
I will not cease to grasp the hope I hold
O saintdom, and to clamor, mourn and sob,
Battering the gates of heaven with storms of prayer,
Have mercy, Lord, and take away my sin.
 Let this avail, just, dreadful, mighty God,
This not be all in vain, that thrice ten years,
Thrice multiplied by superhuman pangs,
In hungers and in thirsts, fevers and cold,
In coughs, aches, stitches, ulcerous throes and cramps,
A sign betwixt the meadow and the cloud,
Patient on this tall pillar I have borne
Rain, wind, frost, heat, hail, damp, and sleet, and snow;
And I had hoped that ere this period closed
Thou wouldst have caught me up into thy rest,
Denying not these weather-beaten limbs
The meed of saints, the white robe and the palm.
 O take the meaning, Lord: I do not breathe,
Not whisper, any murmur of complaint.
Pain heap'd ten-hundred-fold to this, were still
Less burthen, by ten-hundred-fold, to bear,
Than were those lead-like tons of sin, that crush'd
My spirit flat before thee.
                O Lord, Lord,
Thou knowest I bore this better at the first,
For I was strong and hale of body then;
And tho' my teeth, which now are dropt away,
Would chatter with the cold, and all my beard
Was tagg'd with icy fringes in the moon,

ST. SIMEON STYLITES

I drown'd the whoopings of the owl with sound
Of pious hymns and psalms, and sometimes saw
An angel stand and watch me, as I sang.
Now am I feeble grown; my end draws nigh;
I hope my end draws nigh: half deaf I am,
So that I scarce can hear the people hum
About the column's base, and almost blind,
And scarce can recognize the fields I know;
And both my thighs are rotted with the dew;
Yet cease I not to clamor and to cry,
While my stiff spine can hold my weary head,
Till all my limbs drop piecemeal from the stone,
Have mercy, mercy: take away my sin.

  O Jesus, if thou wilt not save my soul,
Who may be saved? who is it may be saved?
Who may be made a saint, if I fail here?
Show me the man hath suffer'd more than I.
For did not all thy martyrs die one death?
For either they were stoned, or crucified,
Or burn'd in fire, or boil'd in oil, or sawn
In twain beneath the ribs; but I die here
To-day, and whole years long, a life of death
Bear witness, if I could have found a way
 (And heedfully I sifted all my thought)
More slowly-painful to subdue this home
Of sin, my flesh, which I despise and hate,
I had not stinted practice, O my God.

  For not alone this pillar-punishment,
Not this alone I bore: but while I lived
In the white convent down the valley there,
For many weeks about my loins I wore
The robe that haled the buckets from the well,
Twisted as tight as I could knot the noose;
And spake not of it to a single soul,
Until the ulcer, eating thro' my skin,
Betray'd my secret penance, so that all
My brethren marvell'd greatly. More than this
I bore, whereof, O God, thou knowest all.

  Three winters, that my soul might grow to thee,
I lived up there on yonder mountain side.
My right leg chain'd into the crag, I lay
Pent in a roofless close of ragged stones;
Inswathed sometimes in wandering mist, and twice

Black'd with thy branding thunder, and sometimes
Sucking the damps for drink, and eating not,
Except the spare chance-gift of those that came
To touch my body and be heal'd, and live:
And they say then that I work'd miracles,
Whereof my fame is loud amongst mankind,
Cured lameness, palsies, cancers. Thou, O God,
Knowest alone whether this was or no.
Have mercy, mercy! cover all my sin.

   Then, that I might be more alone with thee,
Three years I lived upon a pillar, high
Six cubits, and three years on one of twelve;
And twice three years I crouch'd on one that rose
Twenty by measure; last of all, I grew
Twice ten long weary weary years to this,
That numbers forty cubits from the soil.

   I think that I have borne as much as this—
Or else I dream—and for so long a time,
If I may measure time by yon slow light,
And this high dial, which my sorrow crowns—
So much—even so.
                And yet I know not well,
For that the evil ones come here, and say,
"Fall down, O Simeon: that hast suffer'd long
For ages and for ages!" then they prate
Of penances I cannot have gone thro',
Perplexing me with lies; and oft I fall,
Maybe for months, in such blind lethargies
That Heaven, and Earth, and Time are choked.
                               But yet
Bethink thee, Lord, while thou and all the saints
Enjoy themselves in heaven, and men on earth
House in the shade of comfortable roofs,
Sit with their wives by fires, eat wholesome food,
And wear warm clothes, and even beasts have stalls,
I, 'tween the spring and downfall of the light,
Bow down one thousand and two hundred times,
To Christ, the Virgin Mother, and the saints;
Or in the night, after a little sleep,
I wake: the chill stars sparkle; I am wet
With drenching dews, or stiff with crackling frost.
I wear an undress'd goatskin on my back;
A grazing iron collar grinds my neck;

And in my weak, lean arms I lift the cross,
And strive and wrestle with thee till I die:
O mercy, mercy! wash away my sin.

    O Lord, thou knowest what a man I am;
A sinful man, conceived and born in sin:
'Tis their own doing; this is none of mine;
Lay it not to me. Am I to blame for this,
That here comes those that worship me? Ha! ha!
They think that I am somewhat. What am I?
The silly people take me for a saint,
And bring me offerings of fruit and flowers:
And I, in truth (thou wilt bear witness here)
Have all in all endured as much, and more
Than many just and holy men, whose names
Are register'd and calendar'd for saints.

    Good people, you do ill to kneel to me.
What is it I can have done to merit this?
I am a sinner viler than you all.
It may be I have wrought some miracles,
And cured some halt and maim'd; but what of that?
It may be, no one, even among the saints,
May match his pains with mine; but what of that?
Yet do not rise; for you may look on me,
And in your looking you may kneel to God.
Speak! is there any of you halt or maim'd?
I think you know I have some power with Heaven
From my long penance: let him speak his wish.

    Yes, I can heal him. Power goes forth from me.
They say that they are heal'd. Ah, hark! they shout
"St. Simeon Stylites." Why, if so,
God reaps a harvest in me. O my soul,
God reaps a harvest in thee. If this be,
Can I work miracles and not be saved?
This is not told of any. They were saints.
It cannot be but that I shall be saved;
Yea, crown'd a saint. They shout, "Behold a saint!"
And lower voices saint me from above.
Courage, St. Simeon! This dull chrysalis
Cracks into shining wings, and hope ere death
Spreads more and more and more, that God hath now
Sponged and made blank of crimeful record all
My mortal archives.
                O my sons, my sons,

I, Simeon of the pillar, by surname
Stylites, among men; I, Simeon,
The watcher on the column till the end;
I, Simeon, whose brain the sunshine bakes;
I, whose bald brows in silent hours become
Unnaturally hoar with rime, do now
From my high nest of penance here proclaim
That Pontius and Iscariot by my side
Show'd like fair seraphs. On the coals I lay,
A vessel full of sin: all hell beneath
Made me boil over. Devils pluck'd my sleeve,
Abaddon and Asmodeus caught at me.
I smote them with the cross; they swarm'd again.
In bed like monstrous apes they crush'd my chest:
They flapp'd my light out as I read: I saw
Their faces grow between me and my book;
With colt-like whinny and with hoggish whine
They burst my prayer. Yet this way was left,
And by this way I 'scaped them. Mortify
Your flesh, like me, with scourges and with thorns;
Smite, shrink not, spare not. If it may be, fast
Whole Lents, and pray. I hardly, with slow steps,
With slow, faint steps, and much exceeding pain,
Have scrambled past those pits of fire, that still
Sing in mine ears. But yield not me the praise:
God only through his bounty hath thought fit,
Among the powers and princes of this world,
To make me an example to mankind,
Which few can reach to. Yet I do not say
But that a time may come—yea, even now,
Now, now, his footsteps smite the threshold stairs
Of life—I say, that time is at the doors
When you may worship me without reproach;
For I will leave my relics in your land,
And you may carve a shrine about my dust,
And burn a fragrant lamp before my bones,
When I am gather'd to the glorious saints.

While I spake then, a sting of shrewdest pain
Ran shrivelling thro' me, and a cloudlike change,
In passing, with a grosser film made thick
These heavy, horny eyes. The end! the end!
Surely the end! What's here? a shape, a shade,
A flash of light. Is that the angel there

That holds a crown? Come, blessed brother, come.
I know thy glittering face. I waited long;
My brows are ready. What! deny it now?
Nay, draw, draw, draw nigh. So I clutch it. Christ!
'Tis gone: 'tis here again; the crown! the crown!
So now 'tis fitted on and grows to me,
And from it melt the dews of Paradise,
Sweet! sweet! spikenard, and balm, and frankincense.
Ah! let me not be fool'd, sweet saints: I trust
That I am whole, and clean, and meet for Heaven.

  Speak, if there be a priest, a man of God,
Among you there, and let him presently
Approach, and lean a ladder on the shaft,
And climbing up into my airy home,
Deliver me the blessed sacrament;
For by the warning of the Holy Ghost,
I prophesy that I shall die to-night,
A quarter before twelve.
                  But thou, O Lord,
Aid all this foolish people; let them take
Example, pattern: lead them to thy light.

THE TALKING OAK

    ONCE more the gate behind me falls;
        Once more before my face
    I see the moulder'd Abbey-walls,
        That stand within the chace.

    Beyond the lodge the city lies,
        Beneath its drift of smoke;
    And ah! with what delighted eyes
        I turn to yonder oak.

    For when my passion first began,
        Ere that, which in me burn'd,
    The love, that makes me thrice a man,
        Could hope itself return'd;

    To yonder oak within the field
        I spoke without restraint,
    And with a larger faith appeal'd
        Than Papist unto Saint.

For oft I talk'd with him apart,
   And told him of my choice,
Until he plagiarized a heart,
   And answer'd with a voice.

Tho' what he whisper'd under Heaven
   None else could understand;
I found him garrulously given,
   A babbler in the land.

But since I heard him make reply
   Is many a weary hour;
'Twere well to question him, and try
   If yet he keeps the power.

Hail, hidden to the knees in fern,
   Broad Oak of Sumner-chace,
Whose topmost branches can discern
   The roofs of Sumner-place!

Say thou, whereon I carved her name,
   If ever maid or spouse,
As fair as my Olivia, came
   To rest beneath thy boughs.—

"O Walter, I have shelter'd here
   Whatever maiden grace
The good old Summers, year by year
   Made ripe in Sumner-chace:

"Old Summers, when the monk was fat,
   And, issuing shorn and sleek,
Would twist his girdle tight, and pat
   The girls upon the cheek,

"Ere yet, in scorn of Peter's-pence,
   And number'd bead, and shrift,
Bluff Harry broke into the spence
   And turn'd the cowl's adrift:

"And I have seen some score of those
   Fresh faces, that would thrive
When his man-minded offset rose
   To chase the deer at five;

THE TALKING OAK

"And all that from the town would stroll,
  Till that wild wind made work
In which the gloomy brewer's soul
  Went by me, like a stork:

"The slight she-slips of loyal blood,
  And others, passing praise,
Strait-laced, but all-too-full in bud
  For puritanic stays:

"And I have shadow'd many a group
  Of beauties, that were born
In teacup-times of hood and hoop,
  Or while the patch was worn;

"And, leg and arm with love-knots gay,
  About me leap'd and laugh'd
The modish Cupid of the day,
  And shrill'd his tinsel shaft.

"I swear (and else may insects prick
  Each leaf into a gall)
This girl, for whom your heart is sick,
  Is three times worth them all;

"For those and theirs, by Nature's law,
  Have faded long ago;
But in these latter springs I saw
  Your own Olivia blow,

"From when she gamboll'd on the greens
  A baby-germ, to when
The maiden blossoms of her teens
  Could number five from ten.

"I swear, by leaf, and wind, and rain,
  (And hear me with thine ears,)
That, tho' I circle in the grain
  Five hundred rings of years—

"Yet, since I first could cast a shade,
  Did never creature pass
So slightly, musically made,
  So light upon the grass:

"For as to fairies, that will flit
  To make the greensward fresh,
I hold them exquisitely knit,
  But far too spare of flesh."

Oh, hide thy knotted knees in fern,
  And overlook the chace;
And from thy topmost branch discern
  The roofs of Sumner-place.

But thou, whereon I carved her name,
  That oft has heard my vows,
Declare when last Olivia came
  To sport beneath thy boughs.

"O yesterday, you know, the fair
  Was holden at the town;
Her father left his good arm-chair,
  And rode his hunter down.

"And with him Albert came on his.
  I look'd at him with joy
As cowslip unto oxlip is,
  So seems she to the boy.

"An hour had past—and, sitting straight
  Within the low-wheel'd chaise,
Her mother trundled to the gate
  Behind the dappled grays.

"But as for her, she stay'd at home,
  And on the roof she went,
And down the way you use to come,
  She look'd with discontent.

"She left the novel half-uncut
  Upon the rosewood shelf;
She left the new piano shut:
  She could not please herself.

"Then ran she, gamesome as the colt,
  And livelier than a lark
She sent her voice thro' all the holt
  Before her, and the park.

THE TALKING OAK

"A light wind chased her on the wing,
   And in the chase grew wild,
As close as might be would he cling
   About the darling child:

"But light as any wind that blows
   So fleetly did she stir,
The flower, she touch'd on, dipt and rose,
   And turn'd to look at her.

"And here she came, and round me play'd,
   And sang to me the whole
Of those three stanzas that you made
   About my 'giant bole;'

"And in a fit of frolic mirth
   She strove to span my waist;
Alas, I was so broad of girth,
   I could not be embraced.

"I wish'd myself the fair young beech
   That here beside me stands,
That round me, clasping each in each,
   She might have lock'd her hands.

"Yet seem'd the pressure thrice as sweet
   As woodbine's fragile hold,
Or when I feel about my feet
   The berried briony fold."

O muffle round thy knees with fern,
   And shadow Sumner-chace!
Long may thy topmost branch discern
   The roofs of Sumner-place!

But tell me, did she read the name
   I carved with many vows
When last with throbbing heart I came
   To rest beneath thy boughs?

"O yes, she wander'd round and round
   These knotted knees of mine,
And found, and kiss'd the name she found,
   And sweetly murmur'd thine.

"A teardrop trembled from its source,
  And down my surface crept.
My sense of touch is something coarse,
  But I believe she wept.

"Then flush'd her cheek with rosy light,
  She glanced across the plain;
But not a creature was in sight:
  She kiss'd me once again.

"Her kisses were so close and kind,
  That, trust me on my word,
Hard wood I am, and wrinkled rind,
  But yet my sap was stirr'd:

"And even into my inmost ring
  A pleasure I discern'd,
Like those blind motions of the Spring,
  That show the year is turn'd.

"Thrice-happy he that may caress
  The ringlet's waving balm—
The cushions of whose touch may press
  The maiden's tender palm.

"I, rooted here among the groves,
  But languidly adjust
My vapid vegetable loves
  With anthers and with dust:

"For ah! my friend, the days were brief
  Whereof the poets talk,
When that, which breathes within the leaf,
  Could slip its bark and walk.

"But could I, as in times foregone,
  From spray, and branch, and stem,
Have suck'd and gather'd into one
  The life that spreads in them,

"She had not found me so remiss;
  But lightly issuing thro',
I would have paid her kiss for kiss,
  With usury thereto."

THE TALKING OAK

O flourish high, with leafy towers,
   And overlook the lea,
Pursue thy loves among the bowers
   But leave thou mine to me.

O flourish, hidden deep in fern,
   Old oak, I love thee well;
A thousand thanks for what I learn
   And what remains to tell.

"'Tis little more: the day was warm;
   At last, tired out with play,
She sank her head upon her arm
   And at my feet she lay.

"Her eyelids dropp'd their silken eaves.
   I breathed upon her eyes
Thro' all the summer of my leaves
   A welcome mix'd with sighs.

"I took the swarming sound of life—
   The music from the town—
The murmurs of the drum and fife
   And lull'd them in my own.

"Sometimes I let a sunbeam slip,
   To light her shaded eye;
A second flutter'd round her lip
   Like a golden butterfly;

"A third would glimmer on her neck
   To make the necklace shine;
Another slid, a sunny fleck,
   From head to ankle fine,

"Then close and dark my arms I spread,
   And shadow'd all her rest—
Dropt dews upon her golden head,
   An acorn in her breast.

"But in a pet she started up,
   And pluck'd it out, and drew
My little oakling from the cup,
   And flung him in the dew.

"And yet it was a graceful gift—
  I felt a pang within
As when I see the woodman lift
  His axe to slay my kin.

"I shook him down because he was
  The finest on the tree.
He lies beside thee on the grass.
  O kiss him once for me.

"O kiss him twice and thrice for me,
  That have no lips to kiss,
For never yet was oak on lea
  Shall grow so fair as this."

Step deeper yet in herb and fern,
  Look further thro' the chace,
Spread upward till thy boughs discern
  The front of Sumner-place.

This fruit of thine by Love is blest,
  That but a moment lay
Where fairer fruit of Love may rest
  Some happy future day.

I kiss it twice, I kiss it thrice,
  The warmth it thence shall win
To riper life may magnetize
  The baby-oak within.

But thou, while kingdoms overset,
  Or lapse from hand to hand,
Thy leaf shall never fail, nor yet
  Thine acorn in the land.

May never saw dismember thee,
  Nor wielded axe disjoint,
That art the fairest-spoken tree
  From here to Lizard-point.

O rock upon thy towery-top
  All throats that gurgle sweet!
All starry culmination drop
  Balm-dews to bathe thy feet!

THE TALKING OAK

All grass of silky feather grow—
  And while he sinks or swells
The full south-breeze around thee blow
  The sound of minister bells.

The fat earth feed thy branchy root,
  That under deeply strikes!
The northern morning o'er thee shoot,
  High up, in silver spikes!

Nor ever lightning char thy grain,
  But, rolling as in sleep,
Low thunders bring the mellow rain,
  That makes thee broad and deep!

And hear me swear a solemn oath,
  That only by thy side
Will I to Olive plight my troth,
  And gain her for my bride.

And when my marriage morn may fall,
  She, Dryad-like, shall wear
Alternate leaf and acorn-ball
  In wreath about her hair.

And I will work in prose and rhyme,
  And praise thee more in both
Than bard has honor'd beech or lime,
  Or that Thessalian growth,

In which the swarthy ringdove sat,
  And mystic sentence spoke;
And more than England honors that,
  Thy famous brother-oak,

Wherein the younger Charles abode
  Till all the paths were dim,
And far below the Roundhead rode,
  And humm'd a surly hymn.

LOVE AND DUTY

Of love that never found his earthly close,
What sequel? Streaming eyes and breaking hearts?
Or all the same as if he had not been?
   Not so. Shall Error in the round of time
Still father Truth? O shall the braggart shout
For some blind glimpse of freedom work itself
Thro' madness, hated by the wise, to law
System and empire? Sin itself be found
The cloudy porch oft opening on the Sun?
And only he, this wonder, dead, become
Mere highway dust? or year by year alone
Sit brooding in the ruins of a life,
Nightmare of youth, the spectre of himself?
   If this were thus, if this, indeed, were all,
Better the narrow brain, the stony heart,
The staring eye glazed o'er with sapless days,
The long mechanic pacings to and fro,
The set gray life, and apathetic end.
But am I not the nobler thro' thy love?
O three times less unworthy! likewise thou
Art more thro' Love, and greater than thy years
The Sun will run his orbit, and the Moon
Her circle. Wait, and Love himself will bring
The drooping flower of knowledge changed to fruit
Of wisdom. Wait: my faith is large in Time,
And that which shapes it to some perfect end.
   Will some one say, Then why not ill for good?
Why took ye not your pastime? To that man
My work shall answer, since I knew the right
And did it; for a man is not as God,
But then most Godlike being most a man.
   —So let me think 'tis well for thee and me—
Ill-fated that I am, what lot is mine
Whose foresight preaches peace, my heart so slow
To feel it! For how hard it seem'd to me,
When eyes, love-languid thro' half tears would dwell
One earnest, earnest moment upon mine,
Then not to dare to see! when thy low voice,
Faltering, would break its syllables, to keep

My own full-tuned,—hold passion in a leash,
And not leap forth and fall about thy neck,
And on thy bosom (deep desired relief!)
Rain out the heavy mist of tears, that weigh'd
Upon my brain, my senses and my soul!

For Love himself took part against himself
To warn us off, and Duty loved of Love—
O this world's curse,—beloved but hated—came
Like Death betwixt thy dear embrace and mine,
And crying, "Who is this? behold thy bride,"
She push'd me from thee.
                      If the sense is hard
To alien ears, I did not speak to these—
No, not to thee, but to thyself in me:
Hard is my doom and thine: thou knowest it all.

Could Love part thus? was it not well to speak,
To have spoken once? It could not but be well.
The slow sweet hours that bring us all things good,
The slow sad hours that bring us all things ill,
And all good things from evil, brought the night
In which we sat together and alone,
And to the want, that hollow'd all the heart,
Gave utterance by the yearning of an eye,
That burn'd upon its object thro' such tears
As flow but once a life.
                      The trance gave way
To those caresses, when a hundred times
In that last kiss, which never was the last,
Farewell, like endless welcome, lived and died.
Then follow'd counsel, comfort, and the words
That make a man feel strong in speaking truth;
Till now the dark was worn, and overhead
The lights of sunset and of sunrise mix'd
In that brief night; the summer night that paused
Among her stars to hear us; stars that hung
Love-charm'd to listen: all the wheels of Time
Spun round in station, but the end had come.

O then like those, who clench their nerves to rush
Upon their dissolution, we two rose,
There—closing like an individual life—
In one blind cry of passion and of pain,
Like bitter accusation ev'n to death,

Caught up the whole of love and utter'd it,
And bade adieu for ever.

                            Live—yet live—
Shall sharpest pathos blight us, knowing all
Life needs for life is possible to will—
Live happy; tend thy flowers; be tended by
My blessing! Should my Shadow cross thy thoughts
Too sadly for their peace, remand it thou
For calmer hours to Memory's darkest hold,
If not to be forgotten—not at once—
Not all forgotten. Should it cross thy dreams,
O might it come like one that looks content,
With quiet eyes unfaithful to the truth,
And point thee forward to a distant light,
Or seem to lift a burthen from thy heart
And leave thee freër, till thou wake refresh'd
Then when the first low matin-chirp hath grown
Full quire, and morning driv'n her plow of pearl
Far furrowing into light the mounded rack,
Beyond the fair green field and eastern sea.

THE GOLDEN YEAR

WELL, you shall have that song which Leonard wrote:
It was last summer on a tour in Wales:
Old James was with me: we that day had been
Up Snowdon; and I wish'd for Leonard there,
And found him in Llanberis: then we crost
Between the lakes, and clamber'd half way up
The counter side; and that same song of his
He told me; for I banter'd him, and swore
They said he lived shut up within himself,
A tongue-tied Poet in the feverous days,
That, setting the *how much* before the *how,*
Cry, like the daughters of the horse-leech, "Give,
Cram us with all," but count not me the herd!

  To which "They call me what they will," he said:
"But I was born too late: the fair new forms,
That float about the threshold of an age,
Like truths of Science waiting to be caught—
Catch me who can, and make the catcher crown'd—
Are taken by the forelock. Let it be.

THE GOLDEN YEAR

But if you care indeed to listen, hear
These measured words, my work of yestermorn.
  "We sleep and wake and sleep, but all things move;
The Sun flies forward to his brother Sun;
The dark Earth follows wheel'd in her ellipse;
And human things returning on themselves
Move onward, leading up the golden year.
  "Ah, tho' the times, when some new thought can bud,
Are but as poets' seasons when they flower,
Yet seas, that daily gain upon the shore,
Have ebb and flow conditioning their march,
And slow and sure comes up the golden year.
  "When wealth no more shall rest in mounded heaps,
But smit with freër light shall slowly melt
In many streams to fatten lower lands,
And light shall spread, and man be liker man
Thro' all the season of the golden year.
  "Shall eagles not be eagles? wrens be wrens?
If all the world were falcons, what of that?
The wonder of the eagle were the less,
But he not less the eagle. Happy days
Roll onward, leading up the golden year.
  "Fly, happy happy sails, and bear the Press;
Fly happy with the mission of the Cross;
Knit land to land, and blowing havenward
With silks, and fruits, and spices, clear of toll,
Enrich the markets of the golden year.
  "But we grow old. Ah! when shall all men's good
Be each man's rule, and universal Peace
Lie like a shaft of light across the land,
And like a lane of beams athwart the sea,
Thro' all the circle of the golden year?"
  Thus far he flow'd, and ended; whereupon
"Ah, folly!" in mimic cadence answer'd James—
"Ah, folly! for it lies so far away,
Not in our time, nor in our children's time,
'Tis like the second world to us that live;
'Twere all as one to fix our hopes on Heaven
As on this vision of the golden year."
  With that he struck his staff against the rocks
And broke it,—James,—you know him,—old, but full
Of force and choler, and firm upon his feet,
And like an oaken stock in winter woods,

O'erflourish'd with the hoary clematis:
Then added, all in heat:
                              "What stuff is this!
Old writers push'd the happy season back,—
The more fools they,—we forward: dreamers both:
You most, that in an age, when every hour
Must sweat her sixty minutes to the death,
Live on, God love us, as if the seedsman, rapt
Upon the teeming harvest, should not plunge
His hand into the bag: but well I know
That unto him who works, and feels he works,
This same grand year is ever at the doors."

  He spoke; and, high above, I heard them blast
The steep slate-quarry, and the great echo flap
And buffet round the hills, from bluff to bluff.

ULYSSES

It little profits that an idle king,
By this still hearth, among these barren crags,
Match'd with an aged wife, I mete and dole
Unequal laws unto a savage race,
That hoard, and sleep, and feed, and know not me.
I cannot rest from travel: I will drink
Life to the lees: all times I have enjoy'd
Greatly, have suffer'd greatly, both with those
That loved me, and alone; on shore, and when
Thro' scudding drifts the rainy Hyades
Vext the dim sea: I am become a name;
For always roaming with a hungry heart
Much have I seen and known; cities of men
And manners, climates, councils, governments,
Myself not least, but honor'd of them all;
And drunk delight of battle with my peers,
Far on the ringing plains of windy Troy.
I am a part of all that I have met;
Yet all experience is an arch wherethro'
Gleams that untravell'd world, whose margin fades
For ever and for ever when I move.
How dull it is to pause, to make an end,
To rust unburnish'd, not to shine in use!
As tho' to breathe were life. Life piled on life

Were all too little, and of one to me
Little remains: but every hour is saved
From that eternal silence, something more,
A bringer of new things; and vile it were
For some three suns to store and hoard myself,
And this gray spirit yearning in desire
To follow knowledge like a sinking star,
Beyond the utmost bound of human thought.

    This is my son, mine own Telemachus,
To whom I leave the sceptre and the isle—
Well-loved of me, discerning to fulfil
This labor, by slow prudence to make mild
A rugged people, and thro' soft degrees
Subdue them to the useful and the good.
Most blameless is he, centred in the sphere
Of common duties, decent not to fail
In offices of tenderness, and pay
Meet adoration to my household gods,
When I am gone. He works his work, I mine.

    There lies the port; the vessel puffs her sail:
There gloom the dark broad seas. My mariners,
Souls that have toil'd, and wrought, and thought with me—
That ever with a frolic welcome took
The thunder and the sunshine, and opposed
Free hearts, free foreheads—you and I are old;
Old age hath yet his honor and his toil;
Death closes all: but something ere the end,
Some work of noble note, may yet be done,
Not unbecoming men that strove with Gods.
The lights begin to twinkle from the rocks:
The long day wanes: the slow moon climbs: the deep
Moans round with many voices. Come, my friends,
'Tis not too late to seek a newer world.
Push off, and sitting well in order smite
The sounding furrows; for my purpose holds
To sail beyond the sunset, and the baths
Of all the western stars, until I die.
It may be that the gulfs will wash us down:
It may be we shall touch the Happy Isles,
And see the great Achilles, whom we knew.
Tho' much is taken, much abides; and tho'
We are not now that strength which in old days
Moved earth and heaven; that which we are, we are;

One equal temper of heroic hearts,
Made weak by time and fate, but strong in will
To strive, to seek, to find, and not to yield.

TITHONUS

The woods decay, the woods decay and fall,
The vapors weep their burthen to the ground,
Man comes and tills the field and lies beneath,
And after many a summer dies the swan.
Me only cruel immortality
Consumes: I wither slowly in thine arms,
Here at the quiet limit of the world,
A white-hair'd shadow roaming like a dream
The ever-silent spaces of the East,
Far-folded mists, and gleaming halls of morn.

Alas! for this gray shadow, once a man—
So glorious in his beauty and thy choice,
Who madest him thy chosen, that he seem'd
To his great heart none other than a God!
I ask'd thee, "Give me immortality."
Then didst thou grant mine asking with a smile,
Like wealthy men who care not how they give.
But thy strong Hours indignant work'd their wills,
And beat me down and marr'd and wasted me,
And tho' they could not end me, left me maim'd
To dwell in presence of immortal youth,
Immortal age beside immortal youth,
And all I was, in ashes. Can thy love,
Thy beauty, make amends, tho' even now,
Close over us, the silver star, thy guide,
Shines in those tremulous eyes that fill with tears
To hear me? Let me go: take back thy gift:
Why should a man desire in any way
To vary from the kindly race of men,
Or pass beyond the goal of ordinance
Where all should pause, as is most meet for all?

A soft air fans the cloud apart; there comes
A glimpse of that dark world where I was born.
Once more the old mysterious glimmer steals

TITHONUS

From thy pure brows, and from thy shoulders pure,
And bosom beating with a heart renew'd.
Thy cheek begins to redden thro' the gloom,
Thy sweet eyes brighten slowly close to mine,
Ere yet they blind the stars, and the wild team
Which love thee, yearning for thy yoke, arise,
And shake the darkness from their loosen'd manes,
And beat the twilight into flakes of fire.

   Lo! ever thus thou growest beautiful
In silence, then before thine answer given
Departest, and thy tears are on my cheek.

   Why wilt thou ever scare me with thy tears,
And make me tremble lest a saying learnt,
In days far-off, on that dark earth, be true?
"The Gods themselves cannot recall their gifts."

   Ay me! ay me! with what another heart
In days far-off, and with what other eyes
I used to watch—if I be he that watch'd—
The lucid outline forming round thee; saw
The dim curls kindle into sunny rings;
Changed with thy mystic change, and felt my blood
Glow with the glow that slowly crimson'd all
Thy presence and thy portals, while I lay,
Mouth, forehead, eyelids, growing dewy-warm
With kisses balmier than half-opening buds
Of April, and could hear the lips that kiss'd
Whispering I knew not what of wild and sweet,
Like that strange song I heard Apollo sing,
While Ilion like a mist rose into towers.

   Yet hold me not for ever in thine East:
How can my nature longer mix with thine?
Coldly thy rosy shadows bathe me, cold
Are all thy lights, and cold my wrinkled feet
Upon thy glimmering thresholds, when the steam
Floats up from those dim fields about the homes
Of happy men that have the power to die,
And grassy barrows of the happier dead.
Release me, and restore me to the ground;
Thou seëst all things, thou wilt see my grave:

Thou wilt renew thy beauty morn by morn;
I earth in earth forget these empty courts,
And thee returning on thy silver wheels.

LOCKSLEY HALL

COMRADES, leave me here a little, while as yet 'tis early morn:
Leave me here, and when you want me, sound upon the bugle-horn.

'Tis the place, and all around it, as of old, the curlews call,
Dreary gleams about the moorland flying over Locksley Hall;

Locksley Hall, that in the distance overlooks the sandy tracts,
And the hollow ocean-ridges roaring into cataracts.

Many a night from yonder ivied casement, ere I went to rest,
Did I look on great Orion sloping slowly to the West.

Many a night I saw the Pleiads, rising thro' the mellow shade,
Glitter like a swarm of fire-flies tangled in a silver braid.

Here about the beach I wander'd, nourishing a youth sublime
With the fairy tales of science, and the long result of Time;

When the centuries behind me like a fruitful land reposed;
When I clung to all the present for the promise that it closed:

When I dipt into the future far as human eye could see;
Saw the Vision of the world, and all the wonder that would be.—

In the Spring a fuller crimson comes upon the robin's breast;
In the Spring the wanton lapwing gets himself another crest;

In the Spring a livelier iris changes on the burnish'd dove;
In the Spring a young man's fancy lightly turns to thoughts of love.

Then her cheek was pale and thinner than should be for one so young,
And her eyes on all my motions with a mute observance hung.

And I said, "My cousin Amy, speak, and speak the truth to me,
Trust me, cousin, all the current of my being sets to thee."

On her pallid cheek and forehead came a color and a light,
As I have seen the rosy red flushing in the northern night.

And she turn'd—her bosom shaken with a sudden storm of sighs—
All the spirit deeply dawning in the dark of hazel eyes—

Saying, "I have hid my feelings, fearing they should do me wrong";
Saying, "Dost thou love me, cousin?" weeping, "I have loved thee long."

Love took up the glass of Time, and turn'd it in his glowing hands;
Every moment, lightly shaken, ran itself in golden sands.

Love took up the harp of Life, and smote on all the chords with might;
Smote the chord of Self, that, trembling, pass'd in music out of sight.

Many a morning on the moorland did we hear the copses ring,
And her whisper throng'd my pulses with the fulness of the Spring.

Many an evening by the waters did we watch the stately ships,
And our spirits rush'd together at the touching of the lips.

O my cousin, shallow-hearted! O my Amy, mine no more!
O the dreary, dreary moorland! O the barren, barren shore!

Falser than all fancy fathoms, falser than all songs have sung,
Puppet to a father's threat, and servile to a shrewish tongue!

Is it well to wish thee happy?—having known me—to decline
On a range of lower feelings and a narrower heart than mine!

Yet it shall be: thou shalt lower to his level day by day,
What is fine within thee growing coarse to sympathize with clay.

As the husband is, the wife is: thou art mated with a clown,
And the grossness of his nature will have weight to drag thee down.

He will hold thee, when his passion shall have spent its novel force,
Something better than his dog, a little dearer than his horse.

What is this? his eyes are heavy: think not they are glazed with wine.
Go to him: it is thy duty: kiss him: take his hand in thine.

It may be my lord is weary, that his brain is overwrought:
Soothe him with thy finer fancies, touch him with thy lighter thought.

He will answer to the purpose, easy things to understand—
Better thou wert dead before me, tho' I slew thee with my hand!

Better thou and I were lying, hidden from the heart's disgrace,
Roll'd in one another's arms, and silent in a last embrace.

Cursed be the social wants that sin against the strength of youth!
Cursed be the social lies that warp us from the living truth!

Cursed be the sickly forms that err from honest Nature's rule!
Cursed be the gold that gilds the straiten'd forehead of the fool!

Well—'tis well that I should bluster!—Hadst thou less unworthy proved—
Would to God—for I had loved thee more than ever wife was loved.

Am I mad, that I should cherish that which bears but bitter fruit?
I will pluck it from my bosom, tho' my heart be at the root.

Never, tho' my mortal summers to such length of years should come
As the many-winter'd crow that leads the clanging rookery home.

LOCKSLEY HALL

Where is comfort? in division of the records of the mind?
Can I part her from herself, and love her, as I knew her, kind?

I remember one that perish'd: sweetly did she speak and move:
Such a one do I remember, whom to look at was to love.

Can I think of her as dead, and love her for the love she bore?
No—she never loved me truly: love is love for evermore.

Comfort? comfort scorn'd of devils! this is truth the poet sings,
That a sorrow's crown of sorrow is remembering happier things.

Drug thy memories, lest thou learn it, lest thy heart be put to proof,
In the dead unhappy night, and when the rain is on the roof.

Like a dog, he hunts in dreams, and thou art staring at the wall,
Where the dying night-lamp flickers, and the shadows rise and fall.

Then a hand shall pass before thee, pointing to his drunken sleep,
To thy widow'd marriage-pillows, to the tears that thou wilt weep.

Thou shalt hear the "Never, never," whisper'd by the phantom years,
And a song from out the distance in the ringing of thine ears;

And an eye shall vex thee, looking ancient kindness on thy pain.
Turn thee, turn thee on thy pillow: get thee to thy rest again.

Nay, but Nature brings thee solace; for a tender voice will cry.
'Tis a purer life than thine; a lip to drain thy trouble dry.

Baby lips will laugh me down: my latest rival brings thee rest.
Baby fingers, waxen touches, press me from the mother's breast.

O, the child too clothes the father with a dearness not his due.
Half is thine and half is his: it will be worthy of the two.

O, I see thee old and formal, fitted to thy petty part,
With a little hoard of maxims preaching down a daughter's heart.

"They were dangerous guides the feelings—she herself was not exempt—
Truly, she herself had suffer'd"—Perish in thy self-contempt!

Overlive it—lower yet—be happy! wherefore should I care?
I myself must mix with action, lest I wither by despair.

What is that which I should turn to, lighting upon days like these?
Every door is barr'd with gold, and opens but to golden keys.

Every gate is throng'd with suitors, all the markets overflow.
I have but an angry fancy: what is that which I should do?

I had been content to perish, falling on the foeman's ground,
When the ranks are roll'd in vapor, and the winds are laid with sound

But the jingling of the guinea helps the hurt that Honor feels,
And the nations do but murmur, snarling at each other's heels.

Can I but relive in sadness? I will turn that earlier page.
Hide me from thy deep emotion, O thou wondrous Mother-Age!

Make me feel the wild pulsation that I felt before the strife,
When I heard my days before me, and the tumult of my life;

Yearning for the large excitement that the coming years would yield,
Eager-hearted as a boy when first he leaves his father's field,

And at night along the dusky highway near and nearer drawn,
Sees in heaven the light of London flaring like a dreary dawn;

And his spirit leaps within him to be gone before him then,
Underneath the light he looks at, in among the throngs of men:

Men, my brothers, men the workers, ever reaping something new:
That which they have done but earnest of the things that they shall do:

For I dipt into the future, far as human eye could see,
Saw the Vision of the world, and all the wonder that would be;

Saw the heavens fill with commerce, argosies of magic sails,
Pilots of the purple twilight, dropping down with costly bales;

Heard the heavens fill with shouting, and there rain'd a ghastly dew
From the nations' airy navies grappling in the central blue;

Far along the world-wide whisper of the south-wind rushing warm,
With the standards of the peoples plunging thro' the thunderstorm;

Till the war-drum throbb'd no longer, and the battle-flags were furl'd
In the Parliament of man, the Federation of the world.

There the common sense of most shall hold a fretful realm in awe,
And the kindly earth shall slumber, lapt in universal law.

So I triumph'd ere my passion sweeping thro' me left me dry,
Left me with the palsied heart, and left me with the jaundiced eye;

Eye, to which all order festers, all things here are out of joint:
Science moves, but slowly slowly, creeping on from point to point:

Slowly comes a hungry people, as a lion creeping nigher,
Glares at one that nods and winks behind a slowly-dying fire.

Yet I doubt not thro' the ages one increasing purpose runs,
And the thoughts of men are widen'd with the process of the suns.

What is that to him that reaps not harvest of his youthful joys,
Tho' the deep heart of existence beat for ever like a boy's?

Knowledge comes, but wisdom lingers, and I linger on the shore,
And the individual withers, and the world is more and more.

Knowledge comes, but wisdom lingers, and he bears a laden breast,
Full of sad experience, moving toward the stillness of his rest.

Hark, my merry comrades call me, sounding on the bugle-horn,
They to whom my foolish passion were a target for their scorn:

Shall it not be scorn to me to harp on such a moulder'd string?
I am shamed thro' all my nature to have loved so slight a thing.

Weakness to be wroth with weakness! woman's pleasure, woman's pain—
Nature made them blinder motions bounded in a shallower brain:

Woman is the lesser man, and all thy passions, match'd with mine,
Are as moonlight unto sunlight, and as water unto wine—

Here at least, where nature sickens, nothing. Ah, for some retreat
Deep in yonder shining Orient, where my life began to beat;

Where in wild Mahratta-battle fell my father evil-starr'd;—
I was left a trampled orphan, and a selfish uncle's ward.

Or to burst all links of habit—there to wander far away,
On from island unto island at the gateways of the day.

Larger constellations burning, mellow moons and happy skies,
Breadths of tropic shade and palms in cluster, knots of Paradise.

Never comes the trader, never floats an European flag,
Slides the bird o'er lustrous woodland, swings the trailer from the crag;

LOCKSLEY HALL

Droops the heavy-blossom'd bower, hangs the heavy-fruited tree—
Summer isles of Eden lying in dark-purple spheres of sea.

There methinks would be enjoyment more than in this march of mind,
In the steamship, in the railway, in the thoughts that shake mankind.

There the passions cramp'd no longer shall have scope and breathing space;
I will take some savage woman, she shall rear my dusky race.

Iron jointed, supple-sinew'd, they shall dive, and they shall run,
Catch the wild goat by the hair, and hurl their lances in the sun;

Whistle back the parrot's call, and leap the rainbows of the brooks,
Not with blinded eyesight poring over miserable books—

Fool, again the dream, the fancy! but I *know* my words are wild,
But I count the gray barbarian lower than the Christian child.

I, to herd with narrow foreheads, vacant of our glorious gains,
Like a beast with lower pleasures, like a beast with lower pains!

Mated with a squalid savage—what to me were sun or clime?
I the heir of all the ages, in the foremost files of time—

I that rather held it better men should perish one by one,
Than that earth should stand at gaze like Joshua's moon in Ajalon!

Not in vain the distance beacons. Forward, forward let us range,
Let the great world spin for ever down the ringing grooves of change.

Thro' the shadow of the globe we sweep into the younger day:
Better fifty years of Europe than a cycle of Cathay.

Mother-Age (for mine I knew not) help me as when life
    begun:
Rift the hills, and roll the waters, flash the lightnings, weigh
    the Sun.

O, I see the crescent promise of my spirit hath not set.
Ancient founts of inspiration well thro' all my fancy yet.

Howsoever these things be, a long farewell to Locksley Hall!
Now for me the woods may wither, now for me the roof-tree
    fall.

Comes a vapor from the margin, blackening over heath and
    holt,
Cramming all the blast before it, in its breast a thunderbolt.

Let it fall on Locksley Hall, with rain or hail, or fire or snow;
For the mighty wind arises, roaring seaward, and I go.

GODIVA

I waited for the train at Coventry;
I hung with grooms and porters on the bridge,
To watch the three tall spires; and there I shaped
The city's ancient legend into this:—
    Not only we, the latest seed of Time,
New men, that in the flying of a wheel
Cry down the past, not only we, that prate
Of rights and wrongs, have loved the people well,
And loathed to see them over-tax'd; but she
Did more, and underwent, and overcame,
The woman of a thousand summers back,
Godiva, wife to that grim Earl, who ruled
In Coventry: for when he laid a tax
Upon his town, and all the mothers brought
Their children, clamoring, "If we pay, we starve!"
She sought her lord, and found him, where he strode
About the hall, among his dogs, alone,
His beard a foot below him, and his hair

GODIVA

A yard behind. She told him of their tears,
And pray'd him, "If they pay this tax, they starve."
Whereat he stared, replying, half-amazed,
"You would not let your little finger ache
For such as *these?*"—"But I would die," said she.
He laugh'd, and swore by Peter and by Paul:
Then fillip'd at the diamond in her ear;
"Oh ay, ay, ay, you talk!"—"Alas!" she said,
"But prove me what it is I would not do."
And from a heart as rough as Esau's hand,
He answer'd, "Ride you naked thro' the town,
And I repeal it"; and nodding, as in scorn,
He parted, with great strides among his dogs.

So left alone, the passions of her mind,
As winds from all the compass shift and blow,
Made war upon each other for an hour,
Till pity won. She sent a herald forth,
And bade him cry, with sound of trumpet, all
The hard condition; but that she would loose
The people: therefore, as they loved her well,
From then till noon no foot should pace the street,
No eye look down, she passing; but that all
Should keep within, door shut, and window barr'd.

Then fled she to her inmost bower, and there
Unclasp'd the wedded eagles of her belt,
The grim Earl's gift; but ever at a breath
She linger'd, looking like a summer moon
Half-dipt in cloud: anon she shook her head,
And shower'd the rippled ringlets to her knee;
Unclad herself in haste; adown the stair
Stole on; and, like a creeping sunbeam, slid
From pillar unto pillar, until she reach'd
The gateway; there she found her palfrey trapt
In purple blazon'd with armorial gold.

Then she rode forth, clothed on with chastity:
The deep air listen'd round her as she rode,
And all the low wind hardly breathed for fear.
The little wide-mouth'd heads upon the spout
Had cunning eyes to see: the barking cur
Made her cheek flame: her palfrey's footfall shot
Like horrors thro' her pulses: the blind walls
Were full of chinks and holes; and overhead
Fantastic gables, crowding, stared: but she

Not less thro' all bore up, till, last, she saw
The white-flower'd elder-thicket from the field
Gleam thro' the Gothic archway in the wall.

Then she rode back, clothed on with chastity:
And one low churl, compact of thankless earth,
The fatal byword of all years to come,
Boring a little auger-hole in fear,
Peep'd—but his eyes, before they had their will,
Were shrivell'd into darkness in his head,
And dropt before him. So the Powers, who wait
On noble deeds, cancell'd a sense misused;
And she, that knew not, pass'd: and all at once,
With twelve great shocks of sound, the shameless noon
Was clash'd and hammer'd from a hundred towers,
One after one: but even then she gain'd
Her bower; whence reissuing, robed and crown'd,
To meet her lord, she took the tax away
And built herself an everlasting name.

THE DAY-DREAM

Prologue

O LADY FLORA, let me speak:
    A pleasant hour has passed away
While, dreaming on your damask cheek,
    The dewy sister-eyelids lay.
As by the lattice you reclined,
    I went thro' many wayward moods
To see you dreaming—and, behind,
    A summer crisp with shining woods.
And I too dream'd, until at last
    Across my fancy, brooding warm,
The reflex of a legend past,
    And loosely settled into form.
And would you have the thought I had,
    And see the vision that I saw,
Then take the broidery-frame, and add
    A crimson to the quaint Macaw,
And I will tell it. Turn your face,
    Nor look with that too-earnest eye—
The rhymes are dazzled from their place,
    And order'd words asunder fly.

THE DAY-DREAM

The Sleeping Palace

I

The varying year with blade and sheaf
   Clothes and reclothes the happy plains,
Here rests the sap within the leaf,
   Here stays the blood along the veins.
Faint shadows, vapors lightly curl'd,
   Faint murmurs from the meadows come,
Like hints and echoes of the world
   To spirits folded in the womb.

II

Soft lustre bathes the range of urns
   On every slanting terrace-lawn.
The fountain to his place returns
   Deep in the garden lake withdrawn.
Here droops the banner on the tower,
   On the hall-hearths the festal fires,
The peacock in his laurel bower,
   The parrot in his gilded wires.

III

Roof-haunting martins warm their eggs:
   In these, in those the life is stay'd.
The mantles from the golden pegs
   Droop sleepily: no sound is made,
Not even of a gnat that sings.
   More like a picture seemeth all
Than those old portraits of old kings,
   That watch the sleepers from the wall.

IV

Here sits the Butler with a flask
   Between his knees, half-drain'd; and there
The wrinkled steward at his task,
   The maid-of-honor blooming fair;
The page has caught her hand in his:
   Her lips are sever'd as to speak:
His own are pouted to a kiss:
   The blush is fix'd upon her cheek.

V

Till all the hundred summers pass,
  The beams, that thro' the Oriel shine,
Make prisms in every carven glass,
  And beaker brimm'd with noble wine.
Each baron at the banquet sleeps,
  Grave faces gather'd in a ring.
His state the king reposing keeps.
  He must have been a jovial king.

VI

All round a hedge upshoots, and shows
  At distance like a little wood;
Thorns, ivies, woodbine, mistletoes,
  And grapes with bunches red as blood;
All creeping plants, a wall of green
  Close-matted, burr and brake and brier,
And glimpsing over these, just seen,
  High up, the topmost palace spire.

VII

When will the hundred summers die,
  And thought and time be born again,
And newer knowledge, drawing nigh,
  Bring truth that sways the soul of men?
Here all things in their place remain,
  As all were order'd, ages since.
Come, Care and Pleasure, Hope and Pain,
  And bring the fated fairy Prince.

The Sleeping Beauty

I

YEAR after year unto her feet,
  She lying on her couch alone,
Across the purple coverlet,
  The maiden's jet-black hair has grown,
On either side her tranced form
  Forth streaming from a braid of pearl:
The slumbrous light is rich and warm,
  And moves not on the rounded curl.

THE DAY-DREAM

II

The silk star-broider'd coverlid
  Unto her limbs itself doth mould
Languidly ever; and, amid
  Her full black ringlets downward roll'd,
Glows forth each softly-shadow'd arm
  With bracelets of the diamond bright:
Her constant beauty doth inform
  Stillness with love, and day with light.

III

She sleeps: her breathings are not heard
  In palace chambers far apart.
The fragrant tresses are not stirr'd
  That lie upon her charmed heart.
She sleeps: on either hand upswells
  The gold-fringed pillow lightly prest:
She sleeps, nor dreams, but ever dwells
  A perfect form in perfect rest.

The Arrival

I

ALL precious things, discover'd late,
  To those that seek them issue forth;
For love in sequel works with fate,
  And draws the veil from hidden worth.
He travels far from other skies—
  His mantle glitters on the rocks—
A fairy Prince, with joyful eyes,
  And lighter-footed than the fox.

II

The bodies and the bones of those
  That strove in other days to pass,
Are wither'd in the thorny close,
  Or scatter'd blanching on the grass.
He gazes on the silent dead:
  "They perish'd in their daring deeds."
This proverb flashes thro' his head,
  "The many fail: the one succeeds."

III

He comes, scarce knowing what he seeks:
    He breaks the hedge: he enters there:
The color flies into his cheeks:
    He trusts to light on something fair;
For all his life the charm did talk
    About his path, and hover near
With words of promise in his walk,
    And whisper'd voices at his ear.

IV

More close and close his footsteps wind:
    The Magic Music in his heart
Beats quick and quicker, till he find
    The quiet chamber far apart.
The spirit flutters like a lark,
    He stoops—to kiss her—on his knee.
"Love, if thy tresses be so dark,
    How dark those hidden eyes must be!"

The Revival

I

A TOUCH, a kiss! the charm was snapt.
    There rose a noise of striking clocks,
And feet that ran, and doors that clapt,
    And barking dogs, and crowing cocks;
A fuller light illumined all,
    A breeze thro' all the garden swept,
A sudden hubbub shook the hall,
    And sixty feet the fountain leapt.

II

The hedge broke in, the banner blew,
    The butler drank, the steward scrawl'd,
The fire shot up, the martin flew,
    The parrot scream'd, the peacock squall'd,
The maid and page renew'd their strife,
    The palace bang'd, and buzz'd and clackt,
And all the long-pent stream of life
    Dash'd downward in a cataract.

III

And last with these the king awoke,
  And in his chair himself uprear'd,
And yawn'd, and rubb'd his face, and spoke,
  "By holy rood, a royal beard!
How say you? we have slept, my lords.
  My beard has grown into my lap."
The barons swore, with many words,
  'Twas but an after-dinner's nap.

IV

"Pardy," return'd the king, "but still
  My joints are somewhat stiff or so.
My lord, and shall we pass the bill
  I mention'd half an hour ago?"
The chancellor, sedate and vain,
  In courteous words return'd reply:
But dallied with his golden chain,
  And, smiling, put the question by.

The Departure

I

AND on her lover's arm she leant,
  And round her waist she felt it fold,
And far across the hills they went
  In that new world which is the old:
Across the hills, and far away
  Beyond this utmost purple rim,
And deep into the dying day
  The happy princess follow'd him.

II

"I'd sleep another hundred years,
  O love, for such another kiss;"
"O wake for ever, love," she hears,
  "O love, 'twas such as this and this."
And o'er them many a sliding star,
  And many a merry wind was borne,
And, stream'd thro' many a golden bar,
  The twilight melted into morn.

III

"O eyes long laid in happy sleep!"
    "O happy sleep, that lightly fled!"
"O happy kiss, that woke thy sleep!"
    "O love, thy kiss would wake the dead!"
And o'er them many a flowing range
    Of vapor buoy'd the crescent-bark,
And, rapt thro' many a rosy change,
    The twilight died into the dark.

IV

"A hundred summers! can it be?
    And whither goest thou, tell me where?"
"O seek my father's court with me,
    For there are greater wonders there."
And o'er the hills, and far away
    Beyond their utmost purple rim,
Beyond the night, across the day,
    Thro' all the world she follow'd him.

Moral

I

So, Lady Flora, take my lay,
    And if you find no moral there,
Go, look in any glass and say,
    What moral is in being fair.
Oh, to what uses shall we put
    The wildweed flower that simply blows?
And is there any moral shut
    Within the bosom of the rose?

II

But any man that walks the mead,
    In bud or blade, or bloom, may find,
According as his humors lead,
    A meaning suited to his mind.
And liberal applications lie
    In Art like Nature, dearest friend;
So 'twere to cramp its use, if I
    Should hook it to some useful end.

THE DAY-DREAM

L'Envoi

I

You shake your head. A random string
   Your finer female sense offends.
Well—were it not a pleasant thing
   To fall asleep with all one's friends;
To pass with all our social ties
   To silence from the paths of men;
And every hundred years to rise
   And learn the world and sleep again;
To sleep thro' terms of mighty wars,
   And wake on science grown to more,
On secrets of the brain, the stars,
   As wild as aught of fairy lore;
And all that else the years will show,
   The Poet-forms of stronger hours,
The vast Republics that may grow,
   The Federations and the Powers;
Titanic forces taking birth
   In divers seasons, divers climes;
For we are Ancients of the earth,
   And in the morning of the times.

II

So sleeping, so aroused from sleep
   Thro' sunny decades new and strange,
Or gay quinquenniads would we reap
   The flower and quintessence of change.

III

Ah, yet would I—and would I might!
   So much your eyes my fancy take—
Be still the first to leap to light
   That I might kiss those eyes awake!
For, am I right, or am I wrong,
   To choose your own you did not care;
You'd have *my* moral from the song,
   And I will take my pleasure there:
And, am I right or am I wrong,

My fancy, ranging thro' and thro',
   To search a meaning for the song,
     Perforce will still revert to you;
   Nor finds a closer truth than this
     All-graceful head, so richly curl'd,
   And evermore a costly kiss
     The prelude to some brighter world.

IV

For since the time when Adam first
     Embraced his Eve in happy hour,
And every bird of Eden burst
     In carol, every bud to flower,
What eyes, like thine, have waken'd hopes,
     What lips, like thine, so sweetly join'd?
Where on the double rosebud droops
     The fulness of the pensive mind;
Which all too dearly self-involved,
     Yet sleeps a dreamless sleep to me;
A sleep by kisses undissolved,
     That lets thee neither hear nor see:
But break it. In the name of wife,
     And in the rights that name may give,
Are clasp'd the moral of thy life,
     And that for which I care to live.

Epilogue

So, Lady Flora, take my lay,
   And, if you find a meaning there,
O whisper to your glass, and say,
   "What wonder, if he thinks me fair?"
What wonder I was all unwise,
   To shape the song for your delight
Like long-tail'd birds of Paradise
   That float thro' Heaven, and cannot light?
Or old-world trains, upheld at court
   By Cupid-boys of blooming hue—
But take it—earnest wed with sport,
   And either sacred unto you.

Amphion

My father left a park to me,
  But it is wild and barren,
A garden too with scarce a tree,
  And waster than a warren:
Yet say the neighbors when they call,
  It is not bad but good land,
And in it is the germ of all
  That grows within the woodland.

O had I lived when song was great
  In days of old Amphion,
And ta'en my fiddle to the gate,
  Nor cared for seed or scion!
And had I lived when song was great
  And legs of trees were limber,
And ta'en my fiddle to the gate,
  And fiddled in the timber!

'Tis said he had a tuneful tongue,
  Such happy intonation,
Wherever he sat down and sung
  He left a small plantation;
Wherever in a lonely grove
  He set up his forlorn pipes,
The gouty oak began to move,
  And flounder into hornpipes.

The mountain stirr'd its bushy crown,
  And, as tradition teaches,
Young ashes pirouetted down
  Coquetting with young beeches;
And briony-vine and ivy-wreath
  Ran forward to his rhyming,
And from the valleys underneath
  Came little copses climbing.

The linden broke her ranks and rent
  The woodbine wreaths that bind her,
And down the middle, buzz! she went
  With all her bees behind her:

The poplars, in long order due,
  With cypress promenaded,
The shock-head willows two and two
  By rivers gallopaded.

Came wet-shod alder from the wave,
  Came yews, a dismal coterie;
Each pluck'd his one foot from the grave,
  Poussetting with a sloe-tree:
Old elms came breaking from the vine,
  The vine stream'd out to follow,
And, sweating rosin, plump'd the pine
  From many a cloudy hollow.

And wasn't it a sight to see,
  When, ere his song was ended,
Like some great landslip, tree by tree,
  The country-side descended;
And shepherds from the mountain-eaves
  Look'd down, half-pleased, half-frighten'd,
As dash'd about the drunken leaves
  The random sunshine lighten'd!

Oh, nature first was fresh to men,
  And wanton without measure;
So youthful and so flexile then,
  You moved her at your pleasure.
Twang out, my fiddle! shake the twigs!
  And make her dance attendance;
Blow, flute, and stir the stiff-set sprigs,
  And scirrhous roots and tendons.

'Tis vain! in such a brassy age
  I could not move a thistle;
The very sparrows in the hedge
  Scarce answer to my whistle;
Or at the most, when three-parts-sick
  With strumming and with scraping,
A jackass heehaws from the rick,
  The passive oxen gaping.

But what is that I hear? a sound
  Like sleepy counsel pleading;
O Lord!—'tis in my neighbor's ground,
  The modern Muses reading.

They read Botanic Treatises,
  And Works on Gardening thro' there,
And Methods of transplanting trees
  To look as if they grew there.

The wither'd Misses! how they prose
  O'er books of travell'd seamen,
And show you slips of all that grows
  From England to Van Diemen.
They read in arbors clipt and cut,
  And alleys, faded places,
By squares of tropic summer shut
  And warm'd in crystal cases.

But these, tho' fed with careful dirt,
  Are neither green nor sappy;
Half-conscious of the garden-squirt,
  The spindlings look unhappy.
Better to me the meanest weed
  That blows upon its mountain,
The vilest herb that runs to seed
  Beside its native fountain.

And I must work thro' months of toil,
  And years of cultivation,
Upon my proper patch of soil
  To grow my own plantation.
I'll take the showers as they fall,
  I will not vex my bosom:
Enough if at the end of all
  A little garden blossom.

St. Agnes' Eve

Deep on the convent-roof the snows
  Are sparkling to the moon:
My breath to heaven like vapor goes:
  May my soul follow soon!
The shadows of the convent-towers
  Slant down the snowy sward,
Still creeping with the creeping hours
  That lead me to my Lord:

Make Thou my spirit pure and clear
　As are the frosty skies,
Or this first snowdrop of the year
　That in my bosom lies.
As these white robes are soil'd and dark,
　To yonder shining ground;
As this pale taper's earthly spark,
　To yonder argent round;
So shows my soul before the Lamb,
　My spirit before Thee;
So in mine earthly house I am,
　To that I hope to be.
Break up the heavens, O Lord! and far,
　Thro' all yon starlight keen,
Draw me, thy bride, a glittering star,
　In raiment white and clean.

He lifts me to the golden doors;
　The flashes come and go;
All heaven bursts her starry floors,
　And strows her lights below,
And deepens on and up! the gates
　Roll back, and far within
For me the Heavenly Bridegroom waits,
　To make me pure of sin.
The sabbaths of Eternity,
　One sabbath deep and wide—
A light upon the shining sea—
　The Bridegroom with his bride!

Sir Galahad

My good blade carves the casques of men,
　My tough lance thrusteth sure,
My strength is as the strength of ten,
　Because my heart is pure.
The shattering trumpet shrilleth high,
　The hard brands shiver on the steel,
The splinter'd spear-shafts crack and fly,
　The horse and rider reel:

SIR GALAHAD

They reel, they roll in clanging lists,
   And when the tide of combat stands,
Perfume and flowers fall in showers,
   That lightly rain from ladies' hands.

How sweet are looks that ladies bend
   On whom their favors fall!
For them I battle till the end,
   To save from shame and thrall:
But all my heart is drawn above,
   My knees are bow'd in crypt and shrine:
I never felt the kiss of love,
   Nor maiden's hand in mine.
More bounteous aspects on me beam,
   Me mightier transports move and thrill;
So keep I fair thro' faith and prayer
   A virgin heart in work and will.

When down the story crescent goes,
   A light before me swims,
Between dark stems the forest glows,
   I hear a noise of hymns:
Then by some secret shrine I ride;
   I hear a voice but none are there;
The stalls are void, the doors are wide,
   The tapers burning fair.
Fair gleams the snowy altar-cloth,
   The silver vessels sparkle clean,
The shrill bell rings, the censer swings,
   And solemn chants resound between.

Sometimes on lonely mountan-meres
   I find a magic bark;
I leap on board: no helmsman steers:
   I float till all is dark.
A gentle sound, an awful light!
   Three angels bear the holy Grail:
With folded feet, in stoles of white,
   On sleeping wings they sail.
Ah, blessed vision! blood of God!
   My spirit beats her mortal bars,
As down dark tides the glory slides,
   And star-like mingles with the stars.

When on my goodly charger borne
 Thro' dreaming towns I go,
The cock crows ere the Christmas morn,
 The streets are dumb with snow.
The tempest crackles on the leads,
 And, ringing, springs from brand and mail;
But o'er the dark a glory spreads,
 And gilds the driving hail.
I leave the plain, I climb the height;
 No branchy thicket shelter yields;
But blessed forms in whistling storms
 Fly o'er waste fens and windy fields.

A maiden knight—to me is given
 Such hope, I know not fear;
I yearn to breathe the airs of heaven
 That often meet me here.
I muse on joy that will not cease,
 Pure spaces clothed in living beams,
Pure lilies of eternal peace,
 Whose odors haunt my dreams;
And, striken by an angel's hand,
 This mortal armor that I wear,
This weight and size, this heart and eyes,
 Are touch'd, are turn'd to finest air.

The clouds are broken in the sky,
 And thro' the mountain-walls
A rolling organ-harmony
 Swells up, and shakes and falls.
Then move the trees, the copses nod,
 Wings flutter, voices hover clear:
"O just and faithful knight of God!
 Ride on! the prize is near."
So pass I hostel, hall, and grange;
 By bridge and ford, by park and pale,
All-arm'd I ride, whate'er betide,
 Until I find the holy Grail.

Edward Gray

Sweet Emma Moreland of yonder town
  Met me walking on yonder way,
"And have you lost your heart?" she said;
  "And are you married yet, Edward Gray?"

Sweet Emma Moreland spoke to me;
  Bitterly weeping I turn'd away:
"Sweet Emma Moreland, love no more
  Can touch the heart of Edward Gray.

"Ellen Adair she loved me well,
  Against her father's and mother's will:
To-day I sat for an hour and wept,
  By Ellen's grave, on the windy hill.

"Shy she was, and I thought her cold;
  Thought her proud, and fled over the sea;
Fill'd I was with folly and spite,
  When Ellen Adair was dying for me.

"Cruel, cruel the words I said!
  Cruelly came they back to-day:
'You're too slight and fickle,' I said,
  'To trouble the heart of Edward Gray.'

"There I put my face in the grass—
  Whisper'd, 'Listen to my despair:
I repent me of all I did:
  Speak a little, Ellen Adair!'

"Then I took a pencil, and wrote
  On the mossy stone, as I lay,
'Here lies the body of Ellen Adair;
  And here the heart of Edward Gray!'

"Love may come, and love may go,
  And fly, like a bird, from tree to tree;
But I will love no more, no more,
  Till Ellen Adair come back to me.

"Bitterly wept I over the stone:
  Bitterly weeping I turn'd away:
There lies the body of Ellen Adair!
  And there the heart of Edward Gray!"

WILL WATERPROOF'S LYRICAL MONOLOGUE

MADE AT THE COCK

O PLUMP head-waiter at The Cock,
  To which I most resort,
How goes the time? 'Tis five o'clock.
  Go fetch a pint of port:
But let it not be such as that
  You set before chance-comers,
But such whose father-grape grew fat
  On Lusitanian summers.

No vain libation to the Muse,
  But may she still be kind,
And whisper lovely words, and use
  Her influence on the mind,
To make me write my random rhymes,
  Ere they be half-forgotten;
Nor add and alter, many times,
  Till all be ripe and rotten.

I pledge her, and she comes and dips
  Her laurel in the wine,
And lays it thrice upon my lips,
  These favor'd lips of mine;
Until the charm have power to make
  New lifeblood warm the bosom,
And barren commonplaces break
  In full and kindly blossom.

I pledge her silent at the board;
  Her gradual fingers steal
And touch upon the master-chord
  Of all I felt and feel.

Old wishes, ghosts of broken plans,
   And phantom hopes assemble;
And that child's heart within the man's
   Begins to move and tremble.

Thro' many an hour of summer suns,
   By many pleasant ways,
Against its fountain upward runs
   The current of my days:
I kiss the lips I once have kiss'd;
   The gas-light wavers dimmer;
And softly, thro' a vinous mist,
   My college friendships glimmer.

I grow in worth, and wit, and sense,
   Unboding critic-pen,
Or that eternal want of pence,
   Which vexes public men,
Who hold their hands to all, and cry
   For that which all deny them—
Who sweep the crossings, wet or dry.
   And all the world go by them.

Ah yet, tho' all the world forsake,
   Tho' fortune clip my wings,
I will not cramp by heart, nor take
   Half-views of men and things.
Let Whig and Tory stir their blood;
   There must be stormy weather;
But for some true result of good
   All parties work together.

Let there be thistles, there are grapes;
   If old things, there are new;
Ten thousand broken lights and shapes,
   Yet glimpses of the true.
Let raffs be rife in prose and rhyme,
   We lack not rhymes and reasons,
As on this whirligig of Time
   We circle with the seasons.

This earth is rich in man and maid;
  With fair horizons bound:
This whole wide earth of light and shade
  Comes out a perfect round.
High over roaring Temple-bar,
  And set in Heaven's third story,
I look at all things as they are,
  But thro' a kind of glory.

Head-waiter, honor'd by the guest
  Half-mused, or reeling ripe,
The pint, you brought me, was the best
  That ever came from pipe.
But tho' the port surpasses praise,
  My nerves have dealt with stiffer.
Is there some magic in the place?
  Or do my peptics differ?

For since I came to live and learn,
  No pint of white or red
Had ever half the power to turn
  This wheel within my head,
Which bears a season'd brain about,
  Unsubject to confusion,
Tho' soak'd and saturate, out and out,
  Thro' every convolution.

For I am of a numerous house,
  With many kinsmen gay,
Where long and largely we carouse
  As who shall say me nay:
Each month, a birth-day coming on,
  We drink defying trouble,
Or sometimes two would meet in one,
  And then we drank it double;

Whether the vintage, yet unkept,
  Had relish fiery-new,
Or elbow-deep in sawdust, slept,
  As old as Waterloo;

Or stow'd, when classic Canning died,
   In musty bins and chambers,
Had cast upon its crusty side
   The gloom of ten Decembers.

The Muse, the jolly Muse, it is!
   She answer'd to my call,
She changes with that mood or this,
   Is all-in-all to all:
She lit the spark within my throat,
   To make my blood run quicker,
Used all her fiery will, and smote
   Her life into the liquor.

And hence this halo lives about
   The waiter's hands, that reach
To each his perfect pint of stout,
   His proper chop to each.
He looks not like the common breed
   That with the napkin dally;
I think he came like Ganymede,
   From some delightful valley.

The Cock was of a larger egg
   Than modern poultry drop,
Stept forward on a firmer leg,
   And cramm'd a plumper crop;
Upon an ampler dunghill trod,
   Crow'd lustier late and early,
Sipt wine from silver, praising God,
   And raked in golden barley.

A private life was all his joy,
   Till in a court he saw
A something-pottle-bodied boy
   That knuckled at the taw:
He stoop'd and clutch'd him, fair and good,
   Flew over roof and casement:
His brothers of the weather stood
   Stock-still for sheer amazement.

But he, by farmstead, thorpe and spire,
   And follow'd with acclaims,
A sign to many a staring shire
   Came crowing over Thames.
Right down by smoky Paul's they bore,
   Till, where the street grows straiter,
One fix'd for ever at the door,
   And one became head-waiter.

But whither would my fancy go?
   How out of place she makes
The violet of a legend blow
   Among the chops and steaks!
'Tis but a steward of the can,
   One shade more plump than common;
As just and mere a serving-man
   As any born of woman.

I ranged too high: what draws me down
   Into the common day?
Is it the weight of that half-crown,
   Which I shall have to pay?
For, something duller than at first,
   Nor wholly comfortable,
I sit, my empty glass reversed,
   And thrumming on the table:

Half fearful that, with self at strife,
   I take myself to task;
Lest of the fulness of my life
   I leave an empty flask:
For I had hope, by something rare
   To prove myself a poet:
But, while I plan and plan, my hair
   Is gray before I know it.

So fares it since the years began,
   Till they be gather'd up;
The truth, that flies the flowing can,
   Will haunt the vacant cup:

WILL WATERPROOF'S LYRICAL MONOLOGUE

And others' follies teach us not,
    Nor much their wisdom teaches;
And most, of sterling worth, is what
    Our own experience preaches.

Ah, let the rusty theme alone!
    We know not what we know.
But for my pleasant hour, 'tis gone;
    'Tis gone, and let it go.
'Tis gone: a thousand such have slipt
    Away from my embraces,
And fall'n into the dusty crypt
    Of darken'd forms and faces.

Go, therefore, thou! thy betters went
    Long since, and came no more;
With peals of genial clamor sent
    From many a tavern-door,
With twisted quirks and happy hits,
    From misty men of letters;
The tavern-hours of mighty wits—
    Thine elders and thy betters.

Hours, when the Poet's words and looks
    Had yet their native glow:
Nor yet the fear of little books
    Had made him talk for show;
But, all his vast heart sherris-warm'd,
    He flash'd his random speeches,
Ere days, that deal in ana, swarm'd
    His literary leeches.

So mix for ever with the past,
    Like all good things on earth!
For should I prize thee, couldst thou last,
    At half thy real worth?
I hold it good, good things should pass:
    With time I will not quarrel:
It is but yonder empty glass
    That makes me maudlin-moral.

Head-waiter of the chop-house here,
  To which I most resort,
I too must part: I hold thee dear
  For this good pint of port.
For this, thou shalt from all things suck
  Marrow of mirth and laughter;
And wheresoe'er thou move, good luck
  Shall fling her old shoe after.

But thou wilt never move from hence,
  The sphere thy fate allots:
Thy latter days increased with pence
  Go down among the pots:
Thou battenest by the greasy gleam
  In haunts of hungry sinners,
Old boxes, larded with the steam
  Of thirty thousand dinners.

We fret, we fume, would shift our skins,
  Would quarrel with our lot;
Thy care is, under polish'd tins,
  To serve the hot-and-hot;
To come and go, and come again,
  Returning like the pewit,
And watch'd by silent gentlemen,
  That trifle with the cruet.

Live long, ere from thy topmost head
  The thick-set hazel dies;
Long, ere the hateful crow shall tread
  The corners of thine eyes:
Live long, nor feel in head or chest
  Our changeful equinoxes,
Till mellow Death, like some late guest,
  Shall call thee from the boxes.

But when he calls, and thou shalt cease
  To pace the gritted floor,
And, laying down an unctuous lease
  Of life, shalt earn no more;
No carved cross-bones, the types of Death,
  Shall show thee past to Heaven:
But carved cross-pipes, and, underneath,
  A pint-pot neatly graven.

Lady Clare

It was the time when lilies blow,
    And clouds are highest up in air,
Lord Ronald brought a lily-white doe
    To give his cousin, Lady Clare.

I trow they did not part in scorn:
    Lovers long-betroth'd were they:
They too will wed the morrow morn:
    God's blessing on the day!

"He does not love me for my birth,
    Nor for my lands so broad and fair;
He loves me for my own true worth,
    And that is well," said Lady Clare.

In there came old Alice the nurse,
    Said, "Who was this that went from thee?"
"It was my cousin," said Lady Clare,
    "To-morrow he weds with me."

"O God be thank'd!" said Alice the nurse,
    "That all comes round so just and fair:
Lord Ronald is heir of all your lands,
    And you are *not* the Lady Clare."

"Are ye out of your mind, my nurse, my nurse?"
    Said Lady Clare, "that ye speak so wild?"
"As God's above," said Alice the nurse,
    "I speak the truth: you are my child.

"The old Earl's daughter died at my breast;
    I speak the truth, as I live by bread!
I buried her like my own sweet child,
    And put my child in her stead."

"Falsely, falsely have ye done,
    O mother," she said, "if this be true,
To keep the best man under the sun
    So many years from his due."

"Nay now, my child," said Alice the nurse,
  "But keep the secret for your life,
And all you have will be Lord Ronald's,
  When you are man and wife."

"If I'm a beggar born," she said,
  "I will speak out, for I dare not lie.
Pull off, pull off, the brooch of gold,
  And fling the diamond necklace by."

"Nay now, my child," said Alice the nurse,
  "But keep the secret all ye can."
She said, "Not so: but I will know
  If there be any faith in man."

"Nay now, what faith?" said Alice the nurse,
  "The man will cleave unto his right."
"And he shall have it," the lady replied,
  "Tho' I should die to-night."

"Yet give one kiss to your mother dear!
  Alas, my child, I sinn'd for thee."
"O mother, mother, mother," she said,
  "So strange it seems to me.

"Yet here's a kiss for my mother dear,
  My mother dear, if this be so,
And lay your hand upon my head,
  And bless me, mother, ere I go."

She clad herself in a russet gown,
  She was no longer Lady Clare:
She went by dale, and she went by down,
  With a single rose in her air.

The lily-white doe Lord Ronald had brought
  Leapt up from where she lay,
Dropt her head in the maiden's hand,
  And follow'd her all the way.

Down stept Lord Ronald from his tower:
  "O Lady Clare, you shame your worth!
Why come you drest like a village maid,
  That are the flower of the earth?"

LADY CLARE

"If I come drest like a village maid,
  I am but as my fortunes are:
I am a beggar born," she said,
  "And not the Lady Clare."

"Play me no tricks," said Lord Ronald,
  "For I am yours in word and in deed.
Play me no tricks," said Lord Ronald,
  "Your riddle is hard to read."

O and proudly stood she up!
  Her heart within her did not fail:
She look'd into Lord Ronald's eyes,
  And told him all her nurse's tale.

He laugh'd a laugh of merry scorn:
  He turn'd and kiss'd her where she stood:
"If you are not the heiress born,
  And I," said he, "the next in blood—

"If you are not the heiress born,
  And I," said he, "the lawful heir,
We two will wed to-morrow morn,
  And you shall still be Lady Clare."

THE CAPTAIN

A LEGEND OF THE NAVY

HE that only rules by terror
  Doeth grievous wrong.
Deep as Hell I count his error.
  Let him hear my song.
Brave the Captain was: the seamen
  Made a gallant crew,
Gallant sons of English freemen,
  Sailors bold and true.
But they hated his oppression,
  Stern he was and rash;
So for every light transgression
  Doom'd them to the lash.
Day by day more harsh and cruel
  Seem'd the Captain's mood.

Secret wrath like smother'd fuel
  Burnt in each man's blood.
Yet he hoped to purchase glory,
  Hoped to make the name
Of his vessel great in story,
  Wheresoe'er he came.
So they past by capes and islands,
  Many a harbor-mouth,
Sailing under palmy highlands
  Far within the South.
On a day when they were going
  O'er the lone expanse,
In the north, her canvas flowing,
  Rose a ship of France.
Then the Captain's color heighten'd,
  Joyful came his speech:
But a cloudy gladness lighten'd
  In the eyes of each.
"Chase," he said: the ship flew forward,
  And the wind did blow;
Stately, lightly, went she Norward,
  Till she near'd the foe.
Then they look'd at him they hated,
  Had what they desired:
Mute with folded arms they waited—
  Not a gun was fired.
But they heard the foeman's thunder
  Roaring out their doom;
All the air was torn in sunder,
  Crashing went the boom,
Spars were splinter'd, decks were shatter'd,
  Bullets fell like rain;
Over mast and deck were scatter'd
  Blood and brains of men.
Spars were splinter'd; decks were broken:
  Every mother's son—
Down they dropt—no word was spoken—
  Each beside his gun.
On the decks as they were lying,
  Were their faces grim.
In their blood, as they lay dying,
  Did they smile on him.
Those, in whom he had reliance

For his noble name,
With one smile of still defiance
   Sold him unto shame.
Shame and wrath his heart confounded,
   Pale he turn'd and red,
Till himself was deadly wounded
   Falling on the dead.
Dismal error! fearful slaughter!
   Years have wander'd by,
Side by side beneath the water
   Crew and Captain lie;
There the sunlit ocean tosses
   O'er them mouldering,
And the lonely seabird crosses
   With one waft of the wing.

THE LORD OF BURLEIGH

IN her ear he whispers gayly,
   "If my heart by signs can tell,
Maiden, I have watch'd thee daily,
   And I think thou lov'st me well."
She replies, in accents fainter,
   "There is none I love like thee."
He is but a landscape-painter,
   And a village maiden she.
He to lips, that fondly falter,
   Presses his without reproof:
Leads her to the village altar,
   And they leave her father's roof.
"I can make no marriage present:
   Little can I give my wife.
Love will make our cottage pleasant,
   And I love thee more than life."
They by parks and lodges going
   See the lordly castles stand:
Summer woods, about them blowing,
   Made a murmur in the land.
From deep thought himself he rouses,
   Says to her that loves him well,
"Let us see these handsome houses
   Where the wealthy nobles dwell."

So she goes by him attended,
   Hears him lovingly converse,
Sees whatever fair and splendid
   Lay betwixt his home and hers;
Parks with oak and chestnut shady,
   Parks and order'd gardens great,
Ancient homes of lord and lady,
   Built for pleasure and for state.
All he shows her makes him dearer:
   Evermore she seems to gaze
On that cottage growing nearer,
   Where they twain will spend their days.
O but she will love him truly!
   He shall have a cheerful home;
She will order all things duly,
   When beneath his roof they come.
Thus her heart rejoices greatly,
   Till a gateway she discerns
With armorial bearings stately,
   And beneath the gate she turns;
Sees a mansion more majestic
   Than all those she saw before:
Many a gallant gay domestic
   Bows before him at the door.
And they speak in gentle murmur,
   When they answer to his call,
While he treads with footsteps firmer,
   Leading on from hall to hall.
And, while now she wonders blindly,
   Nor the meaning can divine,
Proudly turns he round and kindly,
   "All of this is mine and thine."
Here he lives in state and bounty,
   Lord of Burleigh, fair and free,
Not a lord in all the county
   Is so great a lord as he.
All at once the color flushes
   Her sweet face from brow to chin:
As it were with shame she blushes,
   And her spirit changed within.
Then her countenance all over
   Pale again as death did prove:
But he clasp'd her like a lover,

And he cheer'd her soul with love.
So she strove against her weakness,
　　Tho' at times her spirit sank:
Shaped her heart with woman's meekness
　　To all duties of her rank:
And a gentle consort made he,
　　And her gentle mind was such
That she grew a noble lady,
　　And the people loved her much.
But a trouble weigh'd upon her,
　　And perplex'd her, night and morn,
With the burthen of an honor
　　Unto which she was not born.
Faint she grew, and ever fainter,
　　And she murmur'd, "Oh, that he
Were once more that landscape-painter,
　　Which did win my heart from me!"
So she droop'd and droop'd before him,
　　Fading slowly from his side:
Three fair children first she bore him,
　　Then before her time she died.
Weeping, weeping late and early,
　　Walking up and pacing down,
Deeply mourn'd the Lord of Burleigh,
　　Burleigh-house by Stamford-town.
And he came to look upon her,
　　And he look'd at her and said,
"Bring the dress and put it on her,
　　That she wore when she was wed."
Then her people, softly treading,
　　Bore to earth her body, drest
In the dress that she was wed in,
　　That her spirit might have rest.

The Voyage

I

We left behind the painted buoy
　　That tosses at the harbor-mouth;
And madly danced our hearts with joy,
　　As fast we fleeted to the South:

How fresh was every sight and sound
  On open main or winding shore!
We knew the merry world was round,
  And we might sail for evermore.

II

Warm broke the breeze against the brow,
  Dry sang the tackle, sang the sail:
The Lady's-head upon the prow
  Caught the shrill salt, and sheer'd the gale.
The broad seas swell'd to meet the keel,
  And swept behind; so quick the run,
We felt the good ship shake and reel,
  We seem'd to sail into the Sun!

III

How oft we saw the Sun retire,
  And burn the threshold of the night,
Fall from his Ocean-lane of fire,
  And sleep beneath his pillar'd light!
How oft the purple-skirted robe
  Of twilight slowly downward drawn,
As thro' the slumber of the globe
  Again we dash'd into the dawn!

IV

New stars all night above the brim
  Of waters lighten'd into view;
They climb'd as quickly, for the rim
  Changed every moment as we flew.
Far ran the naked moon across
  The houseless ocean's heaving field,
Or flying shone, the silver boss
  Of her own halo's dusky shield;

V

The peaky islet shifted shapes,
  High towns on hills were dimly seen,
We past long lines of Northern capes
  And dewy Northern meadows green.

THE VOYAGE

We came to warmer waves, and deep
  Across the boundless east we drove,
Where those long swells of breaker sweep
  The nutmeg rocks and isles of clove.

VI

By peaks that flamed, or, all in shade,
  Gloom'd the low coast and quivering brine
With ashy rains, that spreading made
  Fantastic plume or sable pine;
By sands and steaming flats, and floods
  Of mighty mouth, we scudded fast,
And hills and scarlet-mingled woods
  Glow'd for a moment as we past.

VII

O hundred shores of happy climes,
  How swiftly stream'd ye by the bark!
At times the whole sea burn'd, at times
  With wakes of fire we tore the dark;
At times a carven craft would shoot
  From havens hid in fairy bowers,
With naked limbs and flowers and fruit,
  But we nor paused for fruit nor flowers.

VIII

For one fair Vision ever fled
  Down the waste waters day and night,
And still we follow'd where she led,
  In hope to gain upon her flight.
Her face was evermore unseen,
  And fixt upon the far sea-line;
But each man murmur'd, "O my Queen,
  I follow till I make thee mine."

IX

And now we lost her, now she gleam'd
  Like Fancy made of golden air,
Now nearer to the prow she seem'd
  Like Virtue firm, like Knowledge fair,

Now high on waves that idly burst
    Like Heavenly Hope she crown'd the sea,
And now, the bloodless point reversed,
    She bore the blade of Liberty.

X

And only one among us—him
    We pleased not—he was seldom pleased:
He saw not far: his eyes were dim:
    But ours he swore were all diseased.
"A ship of fools," he shriek'd in spite,
    "A ship of fools," he sneer'd and wept.
And overboard one stormy night
    He cast his body, and on we swept.

XI

And never sail of ours was furl'd,
    Nor anchor dropt at eve or morn;
We lov'd the glories of the world,
    But laws of nature were our scorn.
For blasts would rise and rave and cease,
    But whence were those that drove the sail
Across the whirlwind's heart of peace,
    And to and thro' the counter gale?

XII

Again to colder climes we came,
    For still we follow'd where she led:
Now mate is blind and captain lame,
    And half the crew are sick or dead,
But, blind or lame or sick or sound,
    We follow that which flies before:
We know the merry world is round,
    And we may sail for evermore.

SIR LAUNCELOT AND QUEEN GUINEVERE

A FRAGMENT

LIKE souls that balance joy and pain,
With tears and smiles from heaven again
The maiden Spring upon the plain
Came in a sun-lit fall of rain.

SIR LAUNCELOT AND QUEEN GUINEVERE

In crystal vapor everywhere
Blue isles of heaven laugh'd between,
And far, in forest-deeps unseen,
The topmost elm-tree gather'd green
    From draughts of balmy air.

Sometimes the linnet piped his song:
Sometimes the throstle whistled strong:
Sometimes the sparhawk, wheel'd along,
Hush'd all the groves from fear of wrong:
    By grassy capes with fuller sound
In curves the yellowing river ran,
And drooping chestnut-buds began
To spread into the perfect fan,
    Above the teeming ground.

Then, in the boyhood of the year,
Sir Launcelot and Queen Guinevere
Rode thro' the coverts of the deer,
With blissful treble ringing clear.
    She seem'd a part of joyous Spring:
A gown of grass-green silk she wore,
Buckled with golden clasps before;
A light-green tuft of plumes she bore
    Closed in a golden ring.

Now on some twisted ivy-net,
Now by some tinkling rivulet,
In mosses mixt with violet
Her cream-white mule his pastern set:
    And fleeter now she skimm'd the plains
Than she whose elfin prancer springs
By night to eery warblings,
When all the glimmering moorland rings
    With jingling bridle-reins.

As she fled fast thro' sun and shade,
The happy winds upon her play'd,
Blowing the ringlet from the braid:
She look'd so lovely, as she sway'd

The rein with dainty finger-tips,
A man had given all other bliss,
And all his wordly worth for this,
To waste his whole heart in one kiss
    Upon her perfect lips.

A Farewell

Flow down, cold rivulet, to the sea,
    Thy tribute wave deliver:
No more by thee my steps shall be,
    For ever and for ever.

Flow, softly flow, by lawn and lea,
    A rivulet then a river:
No where by thee my steps shall be,
    For ever and for ever.

But here will sigh thine alder tree,
    And here thine aspen shiver;
And here by thee will hum the bee,
    For ever and for ever.

A thousand suns will stream on thee,
    A thousand moons will quiver;
But not by thee my steps shall be,
    For ever and for ever.

The Beggar Maid

Her arms across her breast she laid;
    She was more fair than words can say:
Bare-footed came the beggar maid
    Before the king Cophetua.
In robe and crown the king stept down,
    To meet and greet her on her way;
"It is no wonder," said the lords,
    "She is more beautiful than day."

As shines the moon in clouded skies,
  She in her poor attire was seen:
One praised her ankles, one her eyes,
  One her dark hair and lovesome mien.
So sweet a face, such angel grace,
  In all that land had never been:
Cophetua sware a royal oath:
  "This beggar maid shall be my queen!"

THE EAGLE

FRAGMENT

He clasps the crag with crooked hands;
Close to the sun in lonely lands,
Ring'd with the azure world, he stands.

The wrinkled sea beneath him crawls;
He watches from his mountain walls,
And like a thunderbolt he falls.

Move eastward, happy earth, and leave
  Yon orange sunset waning slow;
From fringes of the faded eve,
  O, happy planet, eastward go;
Till over thy dark shoulder glow
  Thy silver sister-world, and rise
To glass herself in dewy eyes
That watch me from the glen below.

Ah, bear me with thee, smoothly borne,
  Dip forward under starry light,
And move me to my marriage-morn,
  And round again to happy night.

Come not, when I am dead,
  To drop thy foolish tears upon my grave,
To trample round my fallen head,
  And vex the unhappy dust thou wouldst not save.
There let the wind sweep and the plover cry;
      But thou, go by.

Child, if it were thine error or thy crime
  I care no longer, being all unblest:
Wed whom thou wilt, but I am sick of Time,
  And I desire to rest.
Pass on, weak heart, and leave me where I lie:
  Go by, go by.

The Letters

I

Still on the tower stood the vane,
  A black yew gloom'd the stagnant air,
I peer'd athwart the chancel pane
  And saw the altar cold and bare.
A clog of lead was round my feet,
  A band of pain across my brow;
"Cold altar, Heaven and earth shall meet
  Before you hear my marriage vow."

II

I turn'd and humm'd a bitter song
  That mock'd the wholesome human heart,
And then we met in wrath and wrong,
  We met, but only meant to part.
Full cold my greeting was and dry;
  She faintly smiled, she hardly moved;
I saw with half-unconscious eye
  She wore the colors I approved.

III

She took the little ivory chest,
  With half a sigh she turn'd the key,
Then raised her head with lips comprest,
  And gave my letters back to me.
And gave the trinkets and the rings,
  My gifts, when gifts of mine could please;
As looks a father on the things
  Of his dead son, I look'd on these.

IV

She told me all her friends had said;
　　I raged against the public liar;
She talk'd as if her love were dead,
　　But in my words were seeds of fire.
"No more of love; your sex is known:
　　I never will be twice deceived.
Henceforth I trust the man alone,
　　The woman cannot be believed.

V

"Thro' slander, meanest spawn of Hell—
　　And women's slander is the worst,
And you, whom once I lov'd so well,
　　Thro' you, my life will be accurst."
I spoke with heart, and heat and force,
　　I shook her breast with vague alarms—
Like torrents from a mountain source
　　We rush'd into each other's arms.

VI

We parted: sweetly gleam'd the stars,
　　And sweet the vapor-braided blue,
Low breezes fann'd the belfry bars,
　　As homeward by the church I drew.
The very graves appear'd to smile,
　　So fresh they rose in shadow'd swells;
"Dark porch," I said, "and silent aisle,
　　There comes a sound of marriage bells.

The Vision of Sin

I

I HAD a vision when the night was late:
A youth came riding toward a palace-gate.
He rode a horse with wings, that would have flown,
But that his heavy rider kept him down.
And from the palace came a child of sin,
And took him by the curls, and led him in,

Where sat a company with heated eyes,
Expecting when a fountain should arise:
A sleepy light upon their brows and lips—
As when the sun, a crescent of eclipse,
Dreams over lake and lawn, and isles and capes—
Suffused them, sitting, lying, languid shapes,
By heaps of gourds, and skins of wine, and piles of grapes.

II

Then methought I heard a mellow sound,
Gathering up from all the lower ground;
Narrowing in to where they sat assembled
Low voluptuous music winding trembled,
Wov'n in circles: they that heard it sigh'd,
Panted hand-in-hand with faces pale,
Swung themselves, and in low tones replied;
Till the fountain spouted, showering wide
Sleet of diamond-drift and pearly hail;
Then the music touch'd the gates and died;
Rose again from where it seem'd to fail,
Storm'd in orbs of song, a growing gale;
Till thronging in and in, to where they waited,
As 'twere a hundred-throated nightingale,
The strong tempestuous treble throbb'd and palpitated;
Ran into its giddiest whirl of sound,
Caught the sparkles, and in circles,
Purple gauzes, golden hazes, liquid mazes,
Flung the torrent rainbow round:
Then they started from their places,
Moved with violence, changed in hue,
Caught each other with wild grimaces,
Half-invisible to the view,
Wheeling with precipitate paces
To the melody, till they flew,
Hair, and eyes, and limbs, and faces,
Twisted hard in fierce embraces,
Like to Furies, like to Graces,
Dash'd together in blinding dew:
Till, kill'd with some luxurious agony,
The nerve-dissolving melody
Flutter'd headlong from the sky.

THE VISION OF SIN

III

And then I look'd up toward a mountain-tract,
That girt the region with high cliff and lawn:
I saw that every morning, far withdrawn
Beyond the darkness and the cataract,
God made Himself an awful rose of dawn,
Unheeded: and detaching, fold by fold,
From those still heights, and, slowly drawing near,
A vapor heavy, hueless, formless, cold,
Came floating on for many a month and year,
Unheeded: and I thought I would have spoken,
And warn'd that madman ere it grew too late:
But, as in dreams, I could not. Mine was broken,
When that cold vapor touch'd the palace gate,
And link'd again. I saw within my head
A gray and gap-tooth'd man as lean as death,
Who slowly rode across a wither'd heath,
And lighted at a ruin'd inn, and said:

IV

"Wrinkled ostler, grim and thin!
   Here is custom come your way;
Take my brute, and lead him in,
   Stuff his ribs with mouldy hay.

"Bitter barmaid, waning fast!
   See that sheets are on my bed;
What! the flower of life is past:
   It is long before you wed.

"Slip-shod waiter, lank and sour,
   At the Dragon on the heath!
Let us have a quiet hour,
   Let us hob-and-nob with Death.

"I am old, but let me drink;
   Bring me spices, bring me wine;
I remember, when I think,
   That my youth was half divine.

"Wine is good for shrivell'd lips,
  When a blanket wraps the day,
When the rotten woodland drips,
  And the leaf is stamp'd in clay.

"Sit thee down, and have no shame,
  Cheek by jowl, and knee by knee:
What care I for any name?
  What for order or degree?

"Let me screw thee up a peg:
  Let me loose thy tongue with wine:
Callest thou that thing a leg?
  Which is thinnest? thine or mine?

"Thou shalt not be saved by works:
  Thou hast been a sinner too:
Ruin'd trunks on wither'd forks,
  Empty scarecrows, I and you!

"Fill the cup, and fill the can:
  Have a rouse before the morn:
Every moment dies a man,
  Every moment one is born.

"We are men of ruin'd blood;
  Therefore comes it we are wise.
Fish are we that love the mud,
  Rising to no fancy-flies.

"Name and fame! to fly sublime
  Thro' the courts, the camps, the schools,
Is to be the ball of Time,
  Bandied by the hands of fools.

"Friendship!—to be two in one—
  Let the canting liar pack!
Well I know, when I am gone,
  How she mouths behind my back.

"Virtue!—to be good and just—
  Every heart, when sifted well,
Is a clot of warmer dust,
  Mix'd with cunning sparks of hell.

THE VISION OF SIN

"O! we two as well can look
  Whited thought and cleanly life
As the priest, above his book
  Leering at his neighbor's wife.

"Fill the cup, and fill the can:
  Have a rouse before the morn:
Every moment dies a man,
  Every moment one is born.

"Drink, and let the parties rave:
  They are fill'd with idle spleen;
Rising, falling, like a wave,
  For they know not what they mean

"He that roars for liberty
  Faster binds a tyrant's power;
And the tyrant's cruel glee
  Forces on the freer hour.

"Fill the can, and fill the cup:
  All the windy ways of men
Are but dust that rises up,
  And is lightly laid again.

"Greet her with applausive breath,
  Freedom, gayly doth she tread;
In her right a civic wreath,
  In her left a human head.

"No, I love not what is new;
  She is of an ancient house:
And I think we know the hue
  Of that cap upon her brows.

"Let her go! her thirst she slakes
  Where the bloody conduit runs,
Then her sweetest meal she makes
  On the first-born of her sons.

"Drink to lofty hopes that cool—
  Visions of a perfect State:
Drink we, last, the public fool,
  Frantic love and frantic hate.

"Chant me now some wicked stave,
  Till thy drooping courage rise,
And the glow-worm of the grave
  Glimmer in thy rheumy eyes.

"Fear not thou to loose thy tongue;
  Set thy hoary fancies free;
What is loathsome to the young
  Savors well to thee and me.

"Change, reverting to the years,
  When thy nerves could understand
What there is in loving tears,
  And the warmth of hand in hand.

"Tell me tales of thy first love—
  April hopes, the fools of chance;
Till the graves begin to move,
  And the dead begin to dance.

"Fill the can, and fill the cup:
  All the windy ways of men
Are but dust that rises up,
  And is lightly laid again.

"Trooping from their mouldy dens
  The chap-fallen circle spreads:
Welcome, fellow-citizens,
  Hollow hearts and empty heads!

"You are bones, and what of that?
  Every face, however full,
Padded round with flesh and fat,
  Is but modell'd on a skull.

"Death is king, and Vivat Rex!
  Tread a measure on the stones,
Madam—if I know your sex,
  From the fashion of your bones

"No, I cannot praise the fire
  In your eye—nor yet your lip:
All the more do I admire
  Joints of cunning workmanship.

"Lo! God's likeness—the ground-plan—
  Neither modell'd, glazed, nor framed:
Buss me, thou rough sketch of man,
  Far too naked to be shamed!

"Drink to Fortune, drink to Chance,
  While we keep a little breath!
Drink to heavy Ignorance!
  Hob-and-nob with brother Death!

"Thou art mazed, the night is long,
  And the longer night is near:
What! I am not all as wrong
  As a bitter jest is dear.

"Youthful hopes, by scores, to all,
  When the locks are crisp and curl'd;
Unto me my maudlin gall
  And my mockeries of the world.

"Fill the cup and fill the can:
  Mingle madness, mingle scorn!
Dregs of life, and lees of man:
  Yet we will not die forlorn."

V

The voice grew faint: there came a further change:
Once more uprose the mystic mountain-range:
Below were men and horses pierced with worms,
And slowly quickening into lower forms;
By shards and scurf of salt, and scum of dross,
Old plash of rains, and refuse patch'd with moss.
Then some one spake: "Behold! it was a crime
Of sense avenged by sense that wore with time."
Another said: "The crime of sense became
The crime of malice, and is equal blame."
And one: "He had not wholly quench'd his power;
A little grain of conscience made him sour."
At last I heard a voice upon the slope
Cry to the summit, "Is there any hope?"
To which an answer peal'd from that high land,
But in a tongue no man could understand;
And on the glimmering limit far withdrawn
God made Himself an awful rose of dawn.

To ———,

AFTER READING A LIFE AND LETTERS

"Cursed be he that moves my bones."
Shakespeare's Epitaph.

You might have won the Poet's name,
  If such be worth the winning now,
  And gain'd a laurel for your brow
Of sounder leaf than I can claim;

But you have made the wiser choice,
  A life that moves to gracious ends
  Thro' troops of unrecording friends,
A deedful life, a silent voice:

And you have miss'd the irreverent doom
  Of those that wear the Poet's crown:
  Hereafter, neither knave nor clown
Shall hold their orgies at your tomb.

For now the Poet cannot die,
  Nor leave his music as of old,
  But round him ere he scarce be cold
Begins the scandal and the cry:

"Proclaim the faults he would not show:
  Break lock and seal: betray the trust:
  Keep nothing sacred: tis but just
The many-headed beast should know."

Ah shameless! for he did but sing
  A song that pleased us from its worth;
  No public life was his on earth,
No blazon'd statesman he, nor king.

He gave the people of his best:
  His worst he kept, his best he gave.
  My Shakespeare's curse on clown and knave
Who will not let his ashes rest!

Who make it seem more sweet to be
   The little life of bank and brier,
   The bird that pipes his lone desire
And dies unheard within his tree,

Than he that warbles long and loud
   And drops at Glory's temple-gates,
   For whom the carrion vulture waits
To tear his heart before the crowd!

To E. L., on His Travels in Greece

Illyrian woodlands, echoing falls
   Of water, sheets of summer glass,
   The long divine Peneïan pass,
The vast Akrokeraunian walls,

Tomohrit, Athos, all things fair,
   With such a pencil, such a pen,
   You shadow forth to distant men,
I read and felt that I was there:

And trust me while I turn'd the page,
   And track'd you still on classic ground,
   I grew in gladness till I found
My spirits in the golden age.

For me the torrent ever pour'd
   And glisten'd—here and there alone
   The broad-limb'd Gods at random thrown
By fountain-urns;—and Naiads oar'd

A glimmering shoulder under gloom
   Of cavern pillars; on the swell
   The silver lily heaved and fell;
And many a slope was rich in bloom

From him that on the mountain lea
   By dancing rivulets fed his flocks
   To him who sat upon the rocks,
And fluted to the morning sea.

Break, break, break,
  On thy cold gray stones, O Sea!
And I would that my tongue could utter
  The thoughts that arise in me.

O well for the fisherman's boy,
  That he shouts with his sister at play!
O well for the sailor lad,
  That he sings in his boat on the bay!

And the stately ships go on
  To their haven under the hill;
But O for the touch of a vanish'd hand,
  And the sound of a voice that is still!

Break, break, break,
  At the foot of thy crags, O Sea!
But the tender grace of a day that is dead
  Will never come back to me.

THE POET'S SONG

The rain had fallen, the Poet arose,
  He pass'd by the town and out of the street,
A light wind blew from the gates of the sun,
  And waves of shadow went over the wheat,
And he sat him down in a lonely place,
  And chanted a melody loud and sweet,
That made the wild-swan pause in her cloud,
  And the lark drop down at his feet.

The swallow stopt as he hunted the bee,
  The snake slipt under a spray,
The wild hawk stood with the down on his beak,
  And stared, with his foot on the prey,
And the nightingale thought, "I have sung many songs,
  But never a one so gay,
For he sings of what the world will be
  When the years have died away."

The Brook

Here, by this brook, we parted; I to the East
And he for Italy—too late—too late:
One whom the strong sons of the world despise;
For lucky rhymes to him were scrip and share,
And mellow metres more than cent for cent;
Nor could he understand how money breeds,
Thought it a dead thing; yet himself could make
The thing that is not as the thing that is.
O had he lived! In our schoolbooks we say,
Of those that held their heads above the crowd,
They flourish'd then or then; but life in him
Could scarce be said to flourish, only touch'd
On such a time as goes before the leaf,
When all the wood stands in a mist of green,
And nothing perfect: yet the brook he loved,
For which, in branding summers of Bengal,
Or ev'n the sweet half-English Neilgherry air
I panted, seems, as I re-listen to it,
Prattling the primrose fancies of the boy,
To me that loved him; for "O brook," he says,
"O babbling brook," says Edmund in his rhyme,
"Whence come you?" and the brook, why not? replies.

>I come from haunts of coot and hern,
>   I make a sudden sally,
>And sparkle out among the fern,
>   To bicker down a valley.

>By thirty hills I hurry down,
>   Or slip between the ridges,
>By twenty thorps, a little town,
>   And half a hundred bridges.

>Till last by Philip's farm I flow
>   To join the brimming river,
>For men may come and men may go,
>   But I go on for ever.

"Poor lad, he died at Florence, quite worn out,
Travelling to Naples. There is Darnley bridge,
It has more ivy; there the river; and there
Stands Philip's farm where brook and river meet.

>   I chatter over stony ways,
>   In little sharps and trebles,
>   I bubble into eddying bays,
>   I babble on the pebbles.
>
>   With many a curve my banks I fret
>   By many a field and fallow,
>   And many a fairy foreland set
>   With willow-weed and mallow.
>
>   I chatter, chatter, as I flow
>   To join the brimming river,
>   For men may come and men may go,
>   But I go on for ever.

"But Philip chatter'd more than brook or bird;
Old Philip; all about the fields you caught
His weary daylong chirping, like the dry
High-elbow'd grigs that leap in summer grass.

>   I wind about, and in and out,
>   With here a blossom sailing,
>   And here and there a lusty trout,
>   And here and there a grayling,
>
>   And here and there a foamy flake
>   Upon me, as I travel
>   With many a silvery waterbreak
>   Above the golden gravel,
>
>   And draw them all along, and flow
>   To join the brimming river,
>   For men may come and men may go,
>   But I go on for ever.

"O darling Katie Willows, his one child!
A maiden of our century, yet most meek;
A daughter of our meadows, yet not coarse;
Straight, but as lissome as a hazel wand;
Her eyes a bashful azure, and her hair
In gloss and hue the chestnut, when the shell
Divides threefold to show the fruit within.

"Sweet Katie, once I did her a good turn,
Her and her far-off cousin and betrothed,
James Willows, of one name and heart with her.
For here I came, twenty years back—the week
Before I parted with poor Edmund, crost
By that old bridge which, half in ruins then,

THE BROOK

Still makes a hoary eyebrow for the gleam
Beyond it, where the waters marry—crost,
Whistling a random bar of Bonny Doon,
And push'd at Philip's garden-gate. The gate,
Half-parted from a weak and scolding hinge,
Stuck; and he clamor'd from a casement, 'Run'
To Katie somewhere in the walks below,
'Run, Katie!' Katie never ran: she moved
To meet me, winding under woodbine bowers,
A little flutter'd, with her eyelids down,
Fresh apple-blossom, blushing for a boon.

"What was it? less of sentiment than sense
Had Katie; not illiterate; nor of those
Who dabbling in the fount of fictive tears,
And nursed by mealy-mouth'd philanthropies,
Divorce the Feeling from her mate the Deed.

"She told me. She and James had quarrell'd. Why?
What cause of quarrel? None, she said, no cause;
James had no cause: but when I prest the cause,
I learnt that James had flickering jealousies
Which anger'd her. Who anger'd James? I said.
But Katie snatch'd her eyes at once from mine,
And sketching with her slender pointed foot
Some figure like a wizard pentagram
On garden gravel, let my query pass
Unclaim'd, in flushing silence, till I ask'd
If James were coming. 'Coming every day,'
She answer'd, 'ever longing to explain,
But evermore her father came across
With some long-winded tale, and broke him short;
And James departed vext with him and her.'
How could I help her? 'Would I—was it wrong?'
(Claspt hands and that petitionary grace
Of sweet seventeen subdued me ere she spoke)
'O would I take her father for one hour,
For one half-hour, and let him talk to me!'
And even while she spoke, I saw where James
Made toward us, like a wader in the surf,
Beyond the brook, waist-deep in meadow-sweet.

"O Katie, what I suffer'd for your sake!
For in I went, and call'd old Philip out
To show the farm: full willingly he rose:
He led me thro' the short sweet-smelling lanes
Of his wheat-suburb, babbling as he went.
He praised his land, his horses, his machines;
He praised his ploughs, his cows, his hogs, his dogs;
He praised his hens, his geese, his guinea-hens;
His pigeons, who in session on their roofs
Approved him, bowing at their own deserts:
Then from the plaintive mother's teat he took
Her blind and shuddering puppies, naming each,
And naming those, his friends, for whom they were:
Then crost the common into Darnley chase
To show Sir Arthur's deer. In copse and fern
Twinkled the innumerable ear and tail.
Then, seated on a serpent-rooted beech,
He pointed out a pasturing colt, and said:
'That was the four-year-old I sold the Squire.'
And there he told a long long-winded tale
Of how the Squire had seen the colt at grass,
And how it was the thing his daughter wish'd,
And how he sent the bailiff to the farm
To learn the price, and what the price he ask'd,
And how the bailiff swore that he was mad,
But he stood firm; and so the matter hung;
He gave them line: and five days after that
He met the bailiff at the Golden Fleece,
Who then and there had offer'd something more,
But he stood firm; and so the matter hung;
He knew the man; the colt would fetch its price;
He gave them line: and how by chance at last
(It might be May or April, he forgot,
The last of April or the first of May)
He found the bailiff riding by the farm,
And, talking from the point, he drew him in,
And there he mellow'd all his heart with ale,
Until they closed a bargain, hand in hand.

"Then, while I breathed in sight of haven, he,
Poor fellow, could he help it? recommenced,
And ran thro' all the coltish chronicle,
Wild Will, Black Bess, Tantivy, Tallyho,

Reform, White Rose, Bellerophon, the Jilt,
Arbaces, and Phenomenon, and the rest,
Till, not to die a listener, I arose,
And with me Philip, talking still; and so
We turn'd our foreheads from the falling sun,
And following our own shadows thrice as long
As when they follow'd us from Philip's door,
Arrived, and found the sun of sweet content
Re-risen in Katie's eyes, and all things well.

> I steal by lawns and grassy plots,
>   I slide by hazel covers;
> I move the sweet forget-me-nots
>   That grow for happy lovers.
>
> I slip, I slide, I gloom, I glance,
>   Among my skimming swallows;
> I make the netted sunbeam dance
>   Against my sandy shallows.
>
> I murmur under moon and stars
>   In brambly wildernesses;
> I linger by my shingly bars;
>   I loiter round my cresses;
>
> And out again I curve and flow
>   To join the brimming river,
> For men may come and men may go,
>   But I go on for ever.

Yes, men may come and go; and these are gone,
All gone. My dearest brother, Edmund, sleeps,
Not by the well-known stream and rustic spire,
But unfamiliar Arno, and the dome
Of Brunelleschi; sleeps in peace: and he,
Poor Philip, of all his lavish waste of words
Remains the lean P. W. on his tomb:
I scraped the lichen from it: Katie walks
By the long wash of Australasian seas
Far off, and holds her head to other stars,
And breathes in converse seasons. All are gone."

So Lawrence Aylmer, seated on a stile
In the long hedge, and rolling in his mind
Old waifs of rhyme, and bowing o'er the brook
A tonsured head in middle age forlorn,
Mused, and was mute. On a sudden a low breath

Of tender air made tremble in the hedge
The fragile bindweed-bells and briony rings;
And he look'd up. There stood a maiden near,
Waiting to pass. In much amaze he stared
On eyes a bashful azure, and on hair
In gloss and hue the chestnut, when the shell
Divides threefold to show the fruit within:
Then, wondering, ask'd her "Are you from the farm?"
"Yes," answer'd she. "Pray stay a little: pardon me;
What do they call you?" "Katie." "That were strange.
What surname?" "Willows." "No!" "That is my name."
"Indeed!" and here he look'd so self-perplext,
That Katie laugh'd, and laughing blush'd, till he
Laugh'd also, but as one before he wakes,
Who feels a glimmering strangeness in his dream.
Then looking at her; "Too happy, fresh and fair,
Too fresh and fair in our sad world's best bloom,
To be the ghost of one who bore your name
About these meadows, twenty years ago."

"Have you not heard?" said Katie, "we came back.
We bought the farm we tenanted before.
Am I so like her? so they said on board.
Sir, if you knew her in her English days,
My mother, as it seems you did, the days
That most she loves to talk of, come with me.
My brother James is in the harvest-field:
But she—you will be welcome—O, come in!"

Sea Dreams

A CITY clerk, but gently born and bred;
His wife, an unknown artist's orphan child—
One babe was theirs, a Margaret, three years old:
They, thinking that her clear germander eye
Droopt in the giant-factoried city-gloom,
Came, with a month's leave given them, to the sea:
For which his gains were dock'd, however small:
Small were his gains, and hard his work; besides,
Their slender household fortunes (for the man
Had risk'd his little) like the little thrift,
Trembled in perilous places o'er a deep:

SEA DREAMS

And oft, when sitting all alone, his face
Would darken, as he cursed his credulousness,
And that one unctuous mouth which lured him, rogue,
To buy strange shares in some Peruvian mine.
Now seaward-bound for health they gain'd a coast,
All sand and cliff and deep-inrunning cave,
At close of day; slept, woke, and went the next,
The Sabbath, pious variers from the church,
To chapel; where a heated pulpiteer,
Not preaching simple Christ to simple men,
Announced the coming doom, and fulminated
Against the scarlet woman and her creed;
For sideways up he swung his arms, and shriek'd
"Thus, thus with violence," ev'n as if he held
The Apocalyptic millstone, and himself
Were that great Angel; "Thus with violence
Shall Babylon be cast into the sea;
Then comes the close." The gentlehearted wife
Sat shuddering at the ruin of a world;
He at his own: but when the wordy storm
Had ended, forth they came and paced the shore,
Ran in and out the long sea-framing caves,
Drank the large air, and saw, but scarce believed
(The sootflake of so many a summer still
Clung to their fancies) that they saw, the sea.
So now on sand they walk'd, and now on cliff,
Lingering about the thymy promontories,
Till all the sails were darken'd in the west,
And rosed in the east: then homeward and to bed:
Where she, who kept a tender Christian hope,
Haunting a holy text, and still to that
Returning, as the bird returns, at night,
"Let not the sun go down upon your wrath,"
Said, "Love, forgive him:" but he did not speak;
And silenced by that silence lay the wife,
Remembering her dear Lord who died for all,
And musing on the little lives of men,
And how they mar this little by their feuds.

But while the two were sleeping, a full tide
Rose with ground-swell, which, on the foremost rocks
Touching, upjetted in spirts of wild sea-smoke,
And scaled in sheets of wasteful foam, and fell

In vast sea-cataracts—ever and anon
Dead claps of thunder from within the cliffs
Heard thro' the living roar. At this the babe,
Their Margaret cradled near them, wail'd and woke
The mother, and the father suddenly cried,
"A wreck, a wreck!" then turn'd, and groaning said,

"Forgive! How many will say, 'forgive,' and find
A sort of absolution in the sound
To hate a little longer! No; the sin
That neither God nor man can well forgive,
Hypocrisy, I saw it in him at once.
Is it so true that second thoughts are best?
Not first, and third, which are a riper first?
Too ripe, too late! they come too late for use.
Ah love, there surely lives in man and beast
Something divine to warn them of their foes:
And such a sense, when first I fronted him,
Said, 'Trust him not;' but after when I came
To know him more, I lost it, knew him less;
Fought with what seem'd my own uncharity;
Sat at his table; drank his costly wines;
Made more and more allowance for his talk;
Went further, fool! and trusted him with all,
All my poor scrapings from a dozen years
Of dust and deskwork: there is no such mine,
None; but a gulf of ruin, swallowing gold,
Not making. Ruin'd! ruin'd! the sea roars
Ruin: a fearful night!"

"Not fearful; fair,"
Said the good wife, "if every star in heaven
Can make it fair: you do but hear the tide.
Had you ill dreams?"

"O yes," he said, "I dream'd
Of such a tide swelling toward the land,
And I from out the boundless outer deep
Swept with it to the shore, and enter'd one
Of those dark caves that run beneath the cliffs.
I thought the motion of the boundless deep
Bore thro' the cave, and I was heaved upon it
In darkness: then I saw one lovely star

SEA DREAMS

Larger and larger. 'What a world,' I thought,
'To live in!' but in moving on I found
Only the landward exit of the cave,
Bright with the sun upon the stream beyond:
And near the light a giant woman sat,
All over earthy, like a piece of earth,
A pickaxe in her hand: then out I slipt
Into a land all sun and blossom, trees
As high as heaven, and every bird that sings:
And here the night-light flickering in my eyes
Awoke me."

"That was then your dream," she said,
"Not sad, but sweet."

"So sweet, I lay," said he,
"And mused upon it, drifting up the stream
In fancy, till I slept again, and pieced
The broken vision; for I dream'd that still
The motion of the great deep bore me on,
And that the woman walk'd upon the brink:
I wonder'd at her strength, and ask'd her of it:
'It came,' she said, 'by working in the mines:'
O then to ask her of my shares, I thought;
And ask'd; but not a word; she shook her head.
And then the motion of the current ceased,
And there was rolling thunder; and we reach'd
A mountain, like a wall of burs and thorns;
But she with her strong feet up the hill
Trod out a path: I follow'd; and at top
She pointed seaward: there a fleet of glass,
That seem'd a fleet of jewels under me,
Sailing along before a gloomy cloud
That not one moment ceased to thunder, past
In sunshine: right across its track there lay,
Down in the water, a long reef of gold,
Or what seem'd gold: and I was glad at first
To think that in our often-ransack'd world
Still so much gold was left; and then I fear'd
Lest the gay navy there should splinter on it,
And fearing waved my arm to warn them off;
An idle signal, for the brittle fleet
(I thought I could have died to save it) near'd,

Touch'd, clink'd, and clash'd, and vanish'd, and I woke,
I heard the clash so clearly. Now I see
My dream was Life; the woman honest Work;
And my poor venture but a fleet of glass
Wreck'd on a reef of visionary gold."

"Nay," said the kindly wife to comfort him,
"You raised your arm, you tumbled down and broke
The glass with little Margaret's medicine in it;
And, breaking that, you made and broke your dream:
A trifle makes a dream, a trifle breaks."

"No trifle," groan'd the husband; "yesterday
I met him suddenly in the street, and ask'd
That which I ask'd the woman in my dream.
Like her, he shook his head. 'Show me the books!'
He dodged me with a long and loose account.
'The books, the books!' but he, he could not wait,
Bound on a matter he of life and death:
When the great Books (see Daniel seven and ten)
Were open'd, I should find he meant me well;
And then began to bloat himself, and ooze
All over with the fat affectionate smile
That makes the widow lean. 'My dearest friend,
Have faith, have faith! We live by faith,' said he;
'And all things work together for the good
Of those'—it makes me sick to quote him—last
Gript my hand hard, and with God-bless-you went.
I stood like one that had received a blow:
I found a hard friend in his loose accounts,
A loose one in the hard grip of his hand,
A curse in his God-bless-you: then my eyes
Pursued him down the street, and far away,
Among the honest shoulders of the crowd,
Read rascal in the motions of his back,
And scoundrel in the supple-sliding knee."

"Was he so bound, poor soul?" said the good wife;
"So are we all: but do not call him, love,
Before you prove him, rogue, and proved, forgive.
His gain is loss; for he that wrongs his friend
Wrongs himself more, and ever bears about
A silent court of justice in his breast,

SEA DREAMS

Himself the judge and jury, and himself
The prisoner at the bar, ever condemn'd:
And that drags down his life: then comes what comes
Hereafter: and he meant, he said he meant,
Perhaps he meant, or partly meant, you well."

" 'With all his conscience and one eye askew'—
Love, let me quote these lines, that you may learn
A man is likewise counsel for himself,
Too often, in that silent court of yours—
'With all his conscience and one eye askew,
So false, he partly took himself for true;
Whose pious talk, when most his heart was dry,
Made wet the crafty crowsfoot round his eye;
Who, never naming God except for gain,
So never took that useful name in vain,
Made Him his catspaw and the Cross his tool,
And Christ the bait to trap his dupe and fool;
Nor deeds of gifts, but gifts of grace he forged,
And snake-like slimed his victim ere he gorged;
And oft at Bible meetings, o'er the rest
Arising, did his holy oily best,
Dropping the too rough H in Hell and Heaven,
To spread the Word by which himself had thriven.'
How like you this old satire?"

"Nay," she said,
"I loathe it: he had never kindly heart,
Nor ever cared to better his own kind,
Who first wrote satire, with no pity in it.
But will you hear *my* dream, for I had one
That altogether went to music? Still
It awed me."

Then she told it, having dream'd
Of that same coast.

—But round the North, a light,
A belt, it seem'd, of luminous vapor, lay,
And ever in it a low musical note
Swell'd up and died; and, as it swell'd, a ridge
Of breaker issued from the belt, and still
Grew with the growing note, and when the note

Had reach'd a thunderous fullness, on those cliffs
Broke, mixt with awful light (the same as that
Living within the belt) whereby she saw
That all those lines of cliffs were cliffs no more,
But huge cathedral fronts of every age,
Grave, florid, stern, as far as eye could see,
One after one: and then the great ridge drew,
Lessening to the lessening music, back,
And past into the belt and swell'd again
Slowly to music: ever when it broke
The statues, king or saint, or founder fell;
Then from the gaps and chasms of ruin left
Came men and women in dark clusters round,
Some crying, "Set them up! they shall not fall!"
And others, "Let them lie, for they have fall'n."
And still they strove and wrangled: and she grieved
In her strange dream, she knew not why, to find
Their wildest wailings never out of tune
With that sweet note; and ever as their shrieks
Ran highest up the gamut, that great wave
Returning, while none mark'd it, on the crowd
Broke, mixt with awful light, and show'd their eyes
Glaring, with passionate looks, and swept away
The men of flesh and blood, and men of stone,
To the waste deeps together.

        "Then I fixt
My wistful eyes on two fair images,
Both crown'd with stars and high among the stars,—
The Virgin Mother standing with her child
High up on one of those dark minster-fronts—
Till she began to totter, and the child
Clung to the mother, and sent out a cry
Which mixt with little Margaret's, and I woke,
And my dream awed me:—well—but what are dreams?
Yours came but from the breaking of a glass,
And mine but from the crying of a child."

 "Child? No!" said he, "but this tide's roar, and his,
Our Boanerges with his threats of doom,
And loud-lung'd Antibabylonianisms
 (Altho' I grant but little music there)
Went both to make your dream: but if there were
A music harmonizing our wild cries,

SEA DREAMS

Sphere-music such as that you dream'd about,
Why, that would make our passions far too like
The discords dear to the musician. No—
One shriek of hate would jar all the hymns of heaven:
True Devils with no ear, they howl in tune
With nothing but the Devil!"

                                            " 'True' indeed!
One out of our town, but later by an hour
Here than ourselves, spoke with me on the shore;
While you were running down the sands, and made
The dimpled flounce of the sea-furbelow flap,
Good man, to please the child. She brought strange news.
Why were you silent when I spoke to-night?
I had set my heart on your forgiving him
Before you knew. We *must* forgive the dead."

  "Dead! who is dead?"

                                       "The man your eye pursued.
A little after you had parted with him,
He suddenly dropt dead of heart-disease."

"Dead? he? of heart-disease? what heart had he
To die of? dead?"

                          "Ah, dearest, if there be
A devil in man, there is an angel too,
And if he did that wrong you charge him with,
His angel broke his heart. But your rough voice
(You spoke so loud) has roused the child again.
Sleep, little birdie, sleep! will she not sleep
Without her 'little birdie'? well then, sleep,
And I will sing you, 'birdie.' "

                                           Saying this,
The woman half turn'd round from him she loved,
Left him one hand, and reaching thro' the night
Her other, found (for it was close beside)
And half-embraced the basket cradlehead
With one soft arm, which, like the pliant bough
That moving moves the nest and nestling, sway'd
The cradle, while she sang this baby song.

What does little birdie say
In her nest at peep of day?
Let me fly, says little birdie,
Mother, let me fly away.
Birdie, rest a little longer,
Till the little wings are stronger.
So she rests a little longer,
Then she flies away.

What does little baby say,
In her bed at peep of day?
Baby says, like little birdie,
Let me rise and fly away.
Baby, sleep a little longer,
Till the little limbs are stronger.
If she sleeps a little longer,
Baby too shall fly away.

"She sleeps: let us too, let all evil, sleep.
He also sleeps—another sleep than ours.
He can do no more wrong: forgive him, dear,
And I shall sleep the sounder!"

          Then the man,
"His deeds yet live, the worst is yet to come.
Yet let your sleep for this one night be sound:
I do forgive him!"

         "Thanks, my love," she said,
"Your own will be the sweeter," and they slept.

LUCRETIUS

LUCILIA, wedded to Lucretius, found
Her master cold; for when the morning flush
Of passion and the first embrace had died
Between them, tho' he lov'd her none the less,
Yet often when the woman heard his foot
Return from pacings in the field, and ran
To greet him with a kiss, the master took
Small notice, or austerely, for—his mind
Half buried in some weightier argument,

Or fancy, borne perhaps upon the rise
And long roll of the Hexameter—he past
To turn and ponder those three hundred scrolls
Left by the Teacher, whom he held divine.
She brook'd it not; but wrathful, petulant,
Dreaming some rival, sought and found a witch
Who brew'd the philtre which had power, they said,
To lead an errant passion home again.
And this, at times, she mingled with his drink,
And this destroy'd him; for the wicked broth
Confused the chemic labor of the blood,
And tickling the brute brain within the man's
Made havoc among those tender cells, and check'd
His power to shape: he loathed himself; and once
After a tempest woke upon a morn
That mock'd him with returning calm, and cried:

"Storm in the night! for thrice I heard the rain
Rushing; and once the flash of a thunderbolt—
Methought I never saw so fierce a fork—
Struck out the streaming mountainside, and show'd
A riotous confluence of watercourses
Blanching and billowing in a hollow of it,
Where all but yester-eve was dusty-dry.

"Storm, and what dreams, ye holy Gods, what dreams!
For thrice I waken'd after dreams. Perchance
We do but recollect the dreams that come
Just ere the waking: terrible! for it seem'd
A void was made in Nature; all her bonds
Crack'd; and I saw the flaring atom-streams
And torrents of her myriad universe,
Ruining along the illimitable inane,
Fly on to clash together again, and make
Another and another frame of things
For ever: that was mine, my dream, I knew it—
Of and belonging to me, as the dog
With inward yelp and restless forefoot plies
His function of the woodland: but the next!
I thought that all the blood by Sylla shed
Came driving rainlike down again on earth,
And where it dash'd the reddening meadow, sprang
No dragon warriors from Cadmean teeth,

For these I thought my dream would show to me,
But girls, Hetairai, curious in their art,
Hired animalisms, vile as those that made
The mulberry-faced Dictator's orgies worse
Than aught they fable of the quiet Gods.
And hands they mixt, and yell'd and round me drove
In narrowing circles till I yell'd again
Half-suffocated, and sprang up, and saw—
Was it the first beam of my latest day?

"Then, then, from utter gloom stood out the breasts,
The breasts of Helen, and hoveringly a sword
Now over and now under, now direct,
Pointed itself to pierce, but sank down shamed
At all that beauty; and as I stared, a fire,
The fire that left a roofless Ilion,
Shot out of them, and scorch'd me that I woke.

"Is this thy vengeance, holy Venus, thine,
Because I would not one of thine own doves,
Not ev'n a rose, were offer'd to thee? thine,
Forgetful how my rich procemion makes
Thy glory fly along the Italian field,
In lays that will outlast thy Deity?

"Deity? nay, thy worshippers. My tongue
Trips, or I speak profanely. Which of these
Angers thee most, or angers thee at all?
Not if thou be'st of those who, far aloof
From envy, hate and pity, and spite and scorn,
Live the great life which all our greatest fain
Would follow, center'd in eternal calm.

"Nay, if thou canst, O Goddess, like ourselves
Touch, and be touch'd, then would I cry to thee
To kiss thy Mavors, roll thy tender arms
Round him, and keep him from the lust of blood
That makes a steaming slaughterhouse of Rome.

"Ay, but I meant not thee; I meant not her,
Whom all the pines of Ida shook to see
Slide from that quiet heaven of hers, and tempt
The Trojan, while his neat-herds were abroad;

Nor her that o'er her wounded hunter wept
Her Deity false in human-amorous tears;
Nor whom her beardless apple-arbiter
Decided fairest. Rather, O ye Gods,
Poet-like, as the great Sicilian called
Calliope to grace his golden verse—
Ay, and this Kypris also—did I take
That popular name of thine to shadow forth
The all-generating powers and genial heat
Of Nature, when she strikes thro' the thick blood
Of cattle, and light is large, and lambs are glad
Nosing the mother's udder, and the bird
Makes his heart voice amid the blaze of flowers:
Which things appear the work of mighty Gods.

"The Gods! and if I go, *my* work is left
Unfinish'd—*if* I go. The Gods, who haunt
The lucid interspace of world and world,
Where never creeps a cloud, or moves a wind,
Nor ever falls the least white star of snow,
Nor ever lowest roll of thunder moans,
Nor sound of human sorrow mounts to mar
Their sacred everlasting calm! and such,
Not all so fine, nor so divine a calm,
Not such, nor all unlike it, man may gain
Letting his own life go. The Gods, the Gods!
If all be atoms, how then should the Gods
Being atomic not be dissoluble,
Not follow the great law? My master held
That Gods there are, for all men so believe.
I prest my footsteps into his, and meant
Surely to lead my Memmius in a train
Of flowery clauses onward to the proof
That Gods there are, and deathless.
  Mean? I meant?
I have forgotten what I meant: my mind
Stumbles, and all my faculties are lamed.

"Look where another of our Gods, the Sun,
Apollo, Delius, or of older use
All-seeing Hyperion—what you will—
Has mounted yonder; since he never sware,
Except his wrath were wreak'd on wretched man,

That he would only shine among the dead
Hereafter; tales! for never yet on earth
Could dead flesh creep, or bits of roasting ox
Moan round the spit—nor knows he what he sees;
King of the East altho' he seem, and girt
With song and flame and fragrance, slowly lifts
His golden feet on those empurpled stairs
That climb into the windy halls of heaven:
And here he glances on an eye newborn,
And gets for greeting but a wail of pain;
And here he stays upon a freezing orb
That fain would gaze upon him to the last;
And here upon a yellow eyelid fall'n
And closed by those who mourn a friend in vain,
Not thankful that his troubles are no more.
And me, altho' his fire is on my face
Blinding, he sees not, nor at all can tell
Whether I mean this day to end myself,
Or lend an ear to Plato where he says,
That men like soldiers may not quit the post
Allotted by the Gods: but he that holds
The Gods are careless, wherefore need he care
Greatly for them, nor rather plunge at once,
Being troubled, wholly out of sight, and sink
Past earthquake—ay, and gout and stone, that break
Body toward death, and palsy, death-in life,
And wretched age—and worst disease of all,
These prodigies of myriad nakednesses,
And twisted shapes of lust, unspeakable,
Abominable, strangers at my hearth
Not welcome, harpies miring every dish,
The phantom husks of something foully done,
And fleeting thro' the boundless universe,
And blasting the long quiet of my breast
With animal heat and dire insanity?

"How should the mind, except it loved them, clasp
These idols to herself? or do they fly
Now thinner, and now thicker, like the flakes
In a fall of snow, and so press in, perforce
Of multitude, as crowds that in an hour
Of civic tumult jam the doors, and bear
The keepers down, and throng, their rags and they

The basest, far into that council-hall
Where sit the best and stateliest of the land?

"Can I not fling this horror off me again,
Seeing with how great ease Nature can smile,
Balmier and nobler from her bath of storm,
At random ravage? and how easily
The mountain there has cast his cloudy slough,
Now towering o'er him in serenest air,
A mountain o'er a mountain,—ay, and within
All hollow as the hopes and fears of men?

"But who was he, that in the garden snared
Picus and Faunus, rustic Gods? a tale
To laugh at—more to laugh at in myself—
Nor look! what is it? there? yon arbutus
Totters; a noiseless riot underneath
Strikes through the wood, sets all the tops quivering—
The mountain quickens into Nymph and Faun;
And here an Oread—how the sun delights
To glance and shift about her slippery sides,
And rosy knees and supple roundedness,
And budded bosom-peaks—who this way runs
Before the rest—A satyr, a satyr, see,
Follows; but him I proved impossible;
Twy-natured is no nature: yet he draws
Nearer and nearer, and I scan him now
Beastlier than any phantom of his kind
That ever butted his rough brother-brute
For lust or lusty blood or provender:
I hate, abhor, spit, sicken at him; and she
Loathes him as well; such a precipitate heel,
Fledged as it were with Mercury's ankle-wing,
Whirls her to me: but will she fling herself,
Shameless upon me? Catch her, goat-foot: nay,
Hide, hide them, million-myrtled wilderness,
And cavern-shadowing laurels, hide! do I wish—
What?—that the bush were leafless? or to whelm
All of them in one massacre? O ye Gods,
I know you careless, yet, behold, to you
From childly wont and ancient use I call—
I thought I lived securely as yourselves—
No lewdness, narrowing envy, monkey-spite,

No madness of ambition, avarice, none:
No larger feast than under plane or pine
With neighbors laid along the grass, to take
Only such cups as left us friendly-warm,
Affirming each his own philosophy—
Nothing to mar the sober majesties
Of settled, sweet, Epicurean life.
But now it seems some unseen monster lays
His vast and filthy hands upon my will,
Wrenching it backward into his; and spoils
My bliss in being; and it was not great;
For save when shutting reasons up in rhythm,
Or Heliconian honey in living words,
To make a truth less harsh, I often grew
Tired of so much within our little life,
Or of so little in our little life—
Poor little life that toddles half an hour
Crown'd with a flower or two, and there an end—
And since the nobler pleasure seem to fade,
Why should I, beastlike as I find myself,
Not manlike end myself?—our privilege—
What beast has heart to do it? And what man,
What Roman would be dragg'd in triumph thus?
Not I; not he, who bears one name with her
Whose death-blow struck the dateless doom of kings,
When, brooking not the Tarquin in her veins,
She made her blood in sight of Collatine
And all his peers, flushing the guiltless air,
Spout from the maiden fountain in her heart.
And from it sprang the Commonwealth, which breaks
As I am breaking now!

                        "And therefore now
Let her, that is the womb and tomb of all,
Great Nature, take, and forcing far apart
Those blind beginnings that have made me man,
Dash them anew together at her will
Thro' all her cycles—into man once more,
Or beast or bird or fish, or opulent flower:
But till this cosmic order everywhere
Shatter'd into one earthquake in one day
Cracks all to pieces,—and that hour perhaps
Is not so far when momentary man

Shall seem no more a something to himself,
But he, his hopes and hates, his homes and fanes,
And even his bones long laid within the grave,
The very sides of the grave itself shall pass,
Vanishing, atom and void, atom and void,
Into the unseen for ever,—till that hour,
My golden work in which I told a truth
That stays the rolling Ixionian wheel,
And numbs the Fury's ringlet-snake, and plucks
The mortal soul from out immortal hell,
Shall stand: ay, surely: then it fails at last
And perishes as I must; for O Thou,
Passionless bride, divine Tranquillity,
Yearn'd after by the wisest of the wise,
Who fail to find thee, being as thou art
Without one pleasure and without one pain,
Howbeit I know thou surely must be mine
Or soon or late, yet out of season, thus
I woo thee roughly, for thou carest not
How roughly men may woo thee so they win—
Thus—thus: the soul flies out and dies in the air."

With that he drove the knife into his side:
She heard him raging, heard him fall; ran in,
Beat breast, tore hair, cried out upon herself
As having fail'd in duty to him, shriek'd
That she but meant to win him back, fell on him
Clasp'd, kiss'd him, wail'd: he answer'd, "Care not thou!
Thy duty? What is duty? Fare thee well!"

ODE ON THE DEATH OF THE DUKE OF WELLINGTON

PUBLISHED IN 1852

I

BURY the Great Duke
  With an empire's lamentation,
Let us bury the Great Duke
  To the noise of the mourning of a mighty nation,
Mourning when their leaders fall,
Warriors carry the warrior's pall,
And sorrow darkens hamlet and hall.

II

Where shall we lay the man whom we deplore?
Here, in streaming London's central roar.
Let the sound of those he wrought for,
And the feet of those he fought for,
Echo round his bones for evermore.

III

Lead out the pageant: sad and slow,
As fits an universal woe,
Let the long long procession go,
And let the sorrowing crowd about it grow,
And let the mournful martial music blow;
The last great Englishman is low.

IV

Mourn, for to us he seems the last,
Remembering all his greatness in the Past.
No more in soldier fashion will he greet
With lifted hand the gazer in the street.
O friends, our chief state-oracle is mute:
Mourn for the man of long-enduring blood,
The statesman-warrior, moderate, resolute,
Whole in himself, a common good.
Mourn for the man of amplest influence,
Yet clearest of ambitious crime,
Our greatest yet with least pretence,
Great in council and great in war,
Foremost captain of his time,
Rich in saving common-sense,
And, as the greatest only are,
In his simplicity sublime.
O good gray head which all men knew,
O voice from which their omens all men drew,
O iron nerve to true occasion true,
O fall'n at length that tower of strength
Which stood four-square to all the winds that blew!
Such was he whom we deplore.
The long self-sacrifice of life is o'er.
The great World-victor's victor will be seen no more.

V

All is over and done:
Render thanks to the Giver,
England, for thy son.
Let the bell be toll'd.
Render thanks to the Giver,
And render him to the mould.
Under the cross of gold
That shines over city and river,
There he shall rest for ever
Among the wise and the bold.
Let the bell be toll'd:
And a reverent people behold
The towering car, the sable steeds:
Bright let it be with its blazon'd deeds,
Dark in its funeral fold.
Let the bell be toll'd:
And a deeper knell in the heart be knoll'd;
And the sound of the sorrowing anthem roll'd
Thro' the dome of the golden cross;
And the volleying cannon thunder his loss;
He knew their voices of old.
For many a time in many a clime
His captain's-ear has heard them boom
Bellowing victory, bellowing doom:
When he with those deep voices wrought,
Guarding realms and kings from shame;
With those deep voices our dead captain taught
The tyrant, and asserts his claim
In that dread sound to the great name
Which he has worn so pure of blame,
In praise and in dispraise the same,
A man of well-attemper'd frame.
O civic muse, to such a name,
To such a name for ages long,
To such a name,
Preserve a broad approach of fame,
And ever-echoing avenues of song.

VI

Who is he that cometh, like an honor'd guest,
With banner and with music, with soldier and with priest,

With a nation weeping, and breaking on my rest?
Mighty Seaman, this is he
Was great by land as thou by sea.
Thine island loves thee well, thou famous man,
The greatest sailor since our world began.
Now, to the roll of muffled drums,
To thee the greatest soldier comes;
For this is he
Was great by land as thou by sea;
His foes were thine; he kept us free;
O give him welcome, this is he
Worthy of our gorgeous rites,
And worthy to be laid by thee;
For this is England's greatest son,
He that gain'd a hundred fights,
Nor ever lost an English gun:
This is he that far away
Against the myriads of Assaye
Clash'd with his fiery few and won;
And underneath another sun,
Warring on a later day,
Round affrighted Lisbon drew
The treble works, the vast designs
Of his labor'd rampart-lines,
Where he greatly stood at bay,
Whence he issued forth anew,
And ever great and greater grew,
Beating from the wasted vines
Back to France her banded swarms,
Back to France with countless blows,
Till o'er the hills her eagles flew
Beyond the Pyrenean pines,
Follow'd up in valley and glen
With blare of bugle, clamor of men,
Roll of cannon and clash of arms,
And England pouring on her foes.
Such a war had such a close.
Again their ravening eagle rose
In anger, wheel'd on Europe-shadowing wings,
And barking for the thrones of kings;
Till one that sought but Duty's iron crown
On that loud Sabbath shook the spoiler down;
A day of onsets of despair!

DEATH OF THE DUKE OF WELLINGTON

Dash'd on every rocky square
Their surging charges foam'd themselves away;
Last, the Prussian trumpet blew;
Thro' the long-tormented air
Heaven flash'd a sudden jubilant ray,
And down we swept and charged and overthrew.
So great a soldier taught us there,
What long-enduring hearts could do
In that world earthquake, Waterloo!
Mighty Seaman, tender and true,
And pure as he from taint of craven guile,
O saviour of the silver-coasted isle,
O shaker of the Baltic and the Nile
If aught of things that here befall
Touch a spirit among things divine,
If love of country move thee there at all,
Be glad, because his bones are laid by thine!
And thro' the centuries let a people's voice
In full acclaim,
A people's voice,
The proof and echo of all human fame,
A people's voice, when they rejoice
At civic revel and pomp and game,
Attest their great commander's claim
With honor, honor, honor, honor to him,
Eternal honor to his name.

VII

A people's voice! we are a people yet.
Tho' all men else their nobler dreams forget,
Confused by brainless mobs and lawless Powers;
Thank Him who isled us here, and roughly set
His Briton in blown seas and storming showers,
We have a voice, with which to pay the debt
Of boundless love and reverence and regret
To those great men who fought, and kept it ours.
And keep it ours, O God, from brute control;
O Statesmen, guard us, guard the eye, the soul
Of Europe, keep our noble England whole,
And save the one true seed of freedom sown
Betwixt a people and their ancient throne,
That sober freedom out of which there springs
Our loyal passion for our temperate kings;

For, saving that, ye help to save mankind
Till public wrong be crumbled into dust,
And drill the raw world for the march of mind,
Till crowds at length be sane and crowns be just.
But wink no more in slothful overtrust.
Remember him who led your hosts;
He bade you guard the sacred coasts.
Your cannons moulder on the seaward wall;
His voice is silent in your council-hall
For ever; and whatever tempests lour
For ever silent; even if they broke
In thunder, silent; yet remember all
He spoke among you, and the Man who spoke;
Who never sold the truth to serve the hour,
Nor palter'd with Eternal God for power;
Who let the turbid streams of rumor flow
Thro' either babbling world of high and low;
Whose life was work, whose language rife
With rugged maxims hewn from life;
Who never spoke against a foe;
Whose eighty winters freeze with one rebuke
All great self-seekers trampling on the right:
Truth-teller was our England's Alfred named;
Truth-lover was our English Duke;
Whatever record leap to light
He never shall be shamed.

VIII

Lo, the leader in these glorious wars
Now to glorious burial slowly borne,
Follow'd by the brave of other lands,
He, on whom from both her open hands
Lavish Honor shower'd all her stars,
And affluent Fortune emptied all her horn.
Yea, let all good things await
Him who cares not to be great,
But as he saves or serves the state.
Not once or twice in our rough island-story,
The path of duty was the way to glory;
He that walks it, only thirsting
For the right, and learns to deaden
Love of self, before his journey closes,
He shall find the stubborn thistle bursting

Into glossy purples, which outredden
All voluptuous garden-roses.
Not once or twice in our fair island-story,
The path of duty was the way to glory:
He, that ever following her commands,
On with toil of heart and knees and hands,
Thro' the long gorge to the far light has won
His path upward, and prevail'd,
Shall find the toppling crags of Duty scaled
Are close upon the shining tablelands
To which our God Himself is moon and sun.
Such was he: his work is done.
But while the races of mankind endure,
Let his great example stand
Colossal, seen of every land,
And keep the soldier firm, the statesman pure:
Till in all lands and thro' all human story
The path of duty be the way to glory:
And let the land whose hearts he saved from shame
For many and many an age proclaim
At civic revel and pomp and game,
And when the long-illumined cities flame,
Their ever-loyal iron leader's fame,
With honor, honor, honor, honor to him,
Eternal honor to his name.

IX

Peace, his triumph will be sung
By some yet unmoulded tongue
Far on in summers that we shall not see:
Peace, it is a day of pain
For one about whose patriarchal knee
Late the little children clung:
O peace, it is a day of pain
For one, upon whose hand and heart and brain
Once the weight and fate of Europe hung.
Ours the pain, be his the gain!
More than is of man's degree
Must be with us, watching here
At this, our great solemnity.
Whom we see not we revere;
We revere, and we refrain
From talk of battles loud and vain,

And brawling memories all too free
For such a wise humility
As befits a solemn fane:
We revere, and while we hear
The tides of Music's golden sea
Setting toward eternity,
Uplifted high in heart and hope are we,
Until we doubt not that for one so true
There must be other nobler work to do
Than when he fought at Waterloo,
And Victor he must ever be.
For tho' the Giant Ages heave the hill
And break the shore, and evermore
Make and break, and work their will;
Tho' world on world in myriad myriads roll
Round us, each with different powers,
And other forms of life than ours,
What know we greater than the soul?
On God and Godlike men we build our trust.
Hush, the Dead March wails in the people's ears:
The dark crowd moves, and there are sobs and tears:
The black earth yawns: the mortal disappears;
Ashes to ashes, dust to dust;
He is gone who seem'd so great.—
Gone; but nothing can bereave him
Of the force he made his own
Being here, and we believe him
Something far advanced in State,
And that he wears a truer crown
Than any wreath that man can weave him.
Speak no more of his renown,
Lay your earthly fancies down,
And in the vast cathedral leave him.
God accept him, Christ receive him.

THE CHARGE OF THE LIGHT BRIGADE

I

HALF a league, half a league,
Half a league onward,
All in the valley of Death
Rode the six hundred.

THE CHARGE OF THE LIGHT BRIGADE

"Forward, the Light Brigade!
Charge for the guns," he said:
Into the valley of Death
  Rode the six hundred.

II

"Forward, the Light Brigade!"
Was there a man dismay'd?
Not tho' the soldier knew
  Some one had blunder'd:
Theirs not to make reply,
Theirs not to reason why,
Theirs but to do and die:
Into the valley of Death
  Rode the six hundred.

III

Cannon to right of them,
Cannon to left of them,
Cannon in front of them
  Volley'd and thunder'd;
Storm'd at with shot and shell,
Boldly they rode and well,
Into the jaws of Death,
Into the mouth of Hell
  Rode the six hundred.

IV

Flash'd all their sabres bare,
Flash'd as they turn'd in air
Sabring the gunners there,
Charging an army, while
  All the world wonder'd:
Plunged in the battery-smoke
Right thro' the line they broke;
Cossack and Russian
Reel'd from the sabre-stroke
  Shatter'd and sunder'd.
Then they rode back, but not,
  Not the six hundred.

V

Cannon to right of them,
Cannon to left of them,
Cannon behind them
   Volley'd and thunder'd;
Storm'd at with shot and shell,
While horse and hero fell,
They that had fought so well
Came thro' the jaws of Death,
Back from the mouth of Hell,
All that was left of them,
   Left of six hundred.

VI

When can their glory fade?
O the wild charge they made!
   All the world wonder'd.
Honor the charge they made!
Honor the Light Brigade,
   Noble six hundred!

THE GRANDMOTHER

I

AND Willy, my eldest-born, is gone, you say, little Anne?
Ruddy and white, and strong on his legs, he looks like a man.
And Willy's wife his written: she never was over-wise,
Never the wife for Willy: he wouldn't take my advice.

II

For, Annie, you see, her father was not the man to save,
Hadn't a head to manage, and drank himself into his grave.
Pretty enough, very pretty! but I was against it for one.
Eh!—but he wouldn't hear me—and Willy, you say, is gone.

III

Willy, my beauty, my eldest-born, the flower of the flock;
Never a man could fling him: for Willy stood like a rock.
"Here's a leg for a babe of a week!" says doctor; and he would
   be bound,
There was not his like that year in twenty parishes round.

THE GRANDMOTHER

IV

Strong of his hands, and strong on his legs, but still of his tongue!
I ought to have gone before him: I wonder he went so young.
I cannot cry for him, Annie: I have not long to stay;
Perhaps I shall see him the sooner, for he lived far away.

V

Why do you look at me, Annie? you think I am hard and cold;
But all my children have gone before me, I am so old:
I cannot weep for Willy, nor can I weep for the rest;
Only at your age, Annie, I could have wept with the best.

VI

For I remember a quarrel I had with your father, my dear,
All for a slanderous story, that cost me many a tear.
I mean your grandfather, Annie: it cost me a world of woe,
Seventy years ago, my darling, seventy years ago.

VII

For Jenny, my cousin, had come to the place, and I knew right well
That Jenny had tript in her time: I knew, but I would not tell.
And she to be coming and slandering me, the base little liar!
But the tongue is a fire as you know, my dear, the tongue is a fire.

VIII

And the parson made it his text that week, and he said likewise,
That a lie which is half a truth is ever the blackest of lies,
That a lie which is all a lie may be met and fought with outright,
But a lie which is part a truth is a harder matter to fight.

IX

And Willy had not been down to the farm for a week and a day;
And all things look'd half-dead, tho' it was the middle of May.
Jenny, to slander me, who knew what Jenny had been!
But soiling another, Annie, will never make one's self clean.

X

And I cried myself well-nigh blind, and all of an evening late
I climb'd to the top of the garth, and stood by the road at the gate.
The moon like a rick on fire was rising over the dale,
And whit, whit, whit, in the bush beside me chirrupt the nightingale.

XI

All of a sudden he stopt: there past by the gate of the farm,
Willy,—he didn't see me,—and Jenny hung on his arm.
Out into the road I started, and spoke I scarce knew how;
Ah, there's no fool like the old one—it makes me angry now.

XII

Willy stood up like a man, and look'd the thing that he meant;
Jenny, the viper, made me a mocking curtsey and went.
And I said, "Let us part: in a hundred years it'll all be the same,
You cannot love me at all, if you love not my good name."

XIII

And he turn'd, and I saw his eyes all wet, in the sweet moonshine:
"Sweetheart, I love you so well that your good name is mine.
And what do I care for Jane, let her speak of you well or ill;
But marry me out of hand: we two shall be happy still."

XIV

"Marry you, Willy!" said I, "but I needs must speak my mind,
And I fear you'll listen to tales, be jealous and hard and unkind."
But he turn'd and claspt me in his arms, and answer'd, "No, love, no;"
Seventy years ago, my darling, seventy years ago.

XV

So Willy and I were wedded: I wore a lilac gown;
And the ringers rang with a will, and he gave the ringers a crown.
But the first that ever I bare was dead before he was born,
Shadow and shine is life, little Annie, flower and thorn.

XVI

That was the first time, too, that ever I thought of death.
There lay the sweet little body that never had drawn a breath.
I had not wept, little Annie, not since I had been a wife;
But I wept like a child that day, for the babe had fought for his life.

XVII

His dear little face was troubled, as if with anger or pain:
I look'd at the still little body—his trouble had all been in vain.
For Willy I cannot weep, I shall see him another morn:
But I wept like a child for the child that was dead before he was born.

XVIII

But he cheer'd me, my good man, for he seldom said me nay:
Kind, like a man, was he; like a man, too, would have his way:
Never jealous—not he: we had many a happy year;
And he died, and I could not weep—my own time seem'd so near.

XIX

But I wish'd it had been God's will that I, too, then could have died:
I began to be tired a little, and fain had slept at his side.
And that was ten years back, or more, if I don't forget:
But as to the children, Annie, they're all about me yet.

XX

Pattering over the boards, my Annie who left me at two,
Patter she goes, my own little Annie, an Annie like you:
Pattering over the boards, she comes and goes at her will,
While Harry is in the five-acre and Charlie ploughing the hill.

XXI

And Harry and Charlie, I hear them too—they sing to their team:
Often they come to the door in a pleasant kind of a dream.
They come and sit by my chair, they hover about my bed—
I am not always certain if they be alive or dead.

XXII

And yet I know for a truth, there's none of them left alive;
For Harry went at sixty, your father at sixty-five:
And Willy, my eldest-born, at nigh threescore and ten;
I knew them all as babies, and now they're elderly men.

XXIII

For mine is a time of peace, it is not often I grieve;
I am oftener sitting at home in my father's farm at eve:
And the neighbors come and laugh and gossip, and so do I;
I find myself often laughing at things that have long gone by.

XXIV

To be sure the preacher says, our sins should make us sad:
But mine is a time of peace, and there is Grace to be had;
And God, not man, is the Judge of us all when life shall cease
And in this Book, little Annie, the message is one of Peace.

XXV

And age is a time of peace, so it be free from pain,
And happy has been my life; but I would not live it again.
I seem to be tired a little, that's all, and long for rest;
Only at your age, Annie, I could have wept with the best.

XXVI

So Willy has gone, my beauty, my eldest-born, my flower;
But how can I weep for Willy, he has but gone for an hour,—
Gone for a minute, my son, from this room into the next;
I, too, shall go in a minute. What time have I to be vext?

XXVII

And Willy's wife has written, she never was over-wise.
Get me my glasses, Annie: thank God that I keep my eyes.
There is but a trifle left you, when I shall have past away.
But stay with the old woman now: you cannot have long to
    stay.

Northern Farmer

OLD STYLE

I

Wheer 'asta beän saw long and meä liggin' 'ere aloän?
Noorse? thoort nowt o' a noorse: whoy, Doctor's abeän an' agoän:
Says that I moänt 'a naw moor aäle: but I beänt a fool:
Git ma my aäle, fur I beänt a-gooin' to breäk my rule.

II

Doctors, they knaws nowt, fur a says what's nawways true:
Naw soort o' koind o' use to saäy the things that a do.
I've 'ed my point o' aäle ivry noight sin' I beän 'ere,
An' I've 'ed my quart ivry market-noight for foorty year.

III

Parson's a beän loikewoise, an' a sittin' ere o' my bed.
"The amoighty's a taäkin o' you to 'issén, my friend," a said,
An' a towd ma my sins, an's toithe were due, an' I gied it in hond;
I done moy duty boy 'um, as I 'a done boy the lond.

IV

Larn'd a ma' beä. I reckons I 'annot sa mooch to larn.
But a cast oop, thot a did, 'boot Bessy Marris's barne.
Thaw a knaws I hallus voäted wi' Squoire an' choorch an' staäte,
An' i' the woost o' toimes I wur niver agin the raäte.

V

An' I hallus coom'd to's choorch afoor moy Sally wur deäd,
An' 'eerd 'um a bummin' awaäy loike a buzzard-clock[1] ower my 'eäd,
An' I niver knaw'd whot a meän'd but I thowt a 'ad summut to saäy,
An' I thowt a said whot a owt to 'a said an' I coom'd awaäy.

---
[1] Cockchafer.

VI

Bessy Marris's barne! tha knaws she laäid it to meä.
Mowt a bean, maphap, for she wur a bad un, sheä.
'Siver, I kep 'um, I kep 'um, my lass, tha mun understond;
I done moy duty boy 'um as I 'a done boy the lond.

VII

But Parson a cooms an' a goos, an' a says it eäsy an' freeä
"The amoighty's a taäkin o' you to 'issén, my friend," says 'eä.
I weänt saäy men be loiars, thaw summum said it in 'aäste:
But 'e reäds wonn sarmin a weeäk, an' I 'a stubb'd Thurnaby waäste.

VIII

D'ya moind the waäste, my lass? naw, naw, tha was not born then;
Theer wur a boggle in it, I often 'eerd 'um mysen;
Moäst loike a butter-bump,[1] fur I 'eerd 'um aboot an' aboot,
[1] Bittern.
But I stubb'd 'um oop wi' the lot, an' raäved an' rembled 'um oot.

IX

Keäper's it wur; fo' they fun 'um theer a-laäid of 'is faäce
Doon i' the woild 'enemies[2] afoor I coom'd to the plaäce.
Noäks or Thimbleby—toäner 'ed shot 'um as deäd as a naäil.
Noäks wur 'ang'd for it oop at 'soize—but git ma my aäle.

X

Dubbut loook at the waäste: theer warn't not feeäd for a cow
Nowt at all but bracken an' fuzz, an' loook at it now—
Warnt worth nowt a haäcre, an' now theer's lots o' feeäd,
Fourscoor yows upon it an' some on it doon i' seeäd.

XI

Nobbut a bit on it's left, an' I meän'd to 'a stubb'd it at fall,
Done it ta-year I meän'd, an' runn'd plow thruff it an' all,
If godamoighty an' parson 'ud nobbut let me aloän,
Meä, wi' haäte oonderd haäcre o' Squoire's an' lond o' my oän.

[2] Anemones.

XII

Do godamoighty knaw what a's doing a-taäkin' o' meä?
I beänt wonn as saws 'ere a beän an' yonder a peä;
An' Squoire 'ull be sa mad an' all—a' dear a' dear!
And I 'a managed for Squoire coom Michaelmas thutty year.

XIII

A mowt 'a taäen owd Joänes, as 'ant nor a 'aäpoth o' sense,
Or a mowt 'a taäen young Robins—a niver mended a fence:
But godamoighty a moost taäke meä an' taäke ma now
Wi' aäf the cows to cauve an' Thurnaby hoälms to plow!

XIV

Loook 'ow quoloty smoiles when they seeäs ma a passin' boy,
Says to thessén naw doubt "what a man a beä sewer-loy!"
Fur they knaws what I beän to Squoire sin fust a coom'd to the
   'All;
I done moy duty by Squoire an' I done moy duty boy hall.

XV

Squoire's i' Lunnon, an' summun I reckons 'ull 'a to wroite,
For whoä's to howd the lond ater meä thot muddles ma quoit;
Sartin-sewer I beä, thot a weänt niver give it to Joänes,
Naw, nor a moänt to Robins—a niver rembles the stoäns.

XVI

But summun 'ull come ater meä mayhap wi' 'is kittle o' steäm
Huzzin' an' maäzin' the blessed feälds wi' the Divil's oän teäm.
Sin' I mun doy I mun doy, thaw loife they says is sweet,
But sin' I mun doy I mun doy, for I couldn abeär to see it.

XVII

What atta stannin' theer fur, an' doesn bring ma the aäle?
Doctor's a 'toättler, lass, an a's hallus i' the owd taäle;
I weänt breäk rules fur Doctor, a knaws naw moor nor a floy;
Git ma my aäle I tell tha, an' if I mun doy I mun doy.

NORTHERN FARMER

NEW STYLE

I

Dosn't thou 'ear my 'erse's legs, as they canters awaäy?
Proputty, proputty, proputty—that's what I 'ears 'em saäy.
Proputty, proputty, proputty—Sam, thou's an ass for thy paaïns:
Theer's moor sense i' one o' 'is legs nor in all thy braaïns.

II

Woä—theer's a craw to pluck wi' tha, Sam: yon's parson's 'ouse—
Dosn't thou knaw that a man mun be eäther a man or a mouse?
Time to think on it then; for thou'll be twenty to weeäk.[1]
Proputty, proputty—woä then woä—let ma 'ear mysén speäk.

III

Me an' thy muther, Sammy, 'as beän a-talkin' o' thee;
Thou's beän talkin' to muther, an' she beän a tellin' it me.
Thou'll not marry for munny—thou's sweet upo' parson's lass—
Noä—thou'll marry for luvv—an' we boäth on us thinks tha an ass.

IV

Seeä'd her todaäy goä by—Saäint's daäy—they was ringing the bells.
She's a beauty thou thinks—an' soä is scoors o' gells,
Them as 'as munny an' all—wot's a beauty?—the flower as blaws.
But proputty, proputty sticks, an' proputty, proputty graws.

V

Do'ant be stunt:[2] taäke time: I knaws what maäkes tha sa mad.
Warn't I craäzed fur the lasses mysén when I wur a lad?
But I knaw'd a Quaäker feller as often 'as towd ma this:
"Doänt thou marry for munny, but goä wheer munny is!"

[1] This week.
[2] Obstinate.

VI

An' I went wheer munny war: an' thy muther coom to 'and,
Wi' lots o' munny laaïd by, an' a nicetish bit o' land.
Maäybe she warn't a beauty—I niver giv it a thowt—
But warn't she as good to cuddle an' kiss as a lass as 'ant nowt?

VII

Parson's lass 'ant nowt, an' she weänt 'a nowt when 'e's deäd,
Mun be a guvness, lad, or summut, and addle[3] her breäd:
Why? fur 'e's nobbut a curate, an' weänt niver git naw 'igher;
An' 'e maäde the bed as 'e ligs on afoor 'e coom'd to the shire.

VIII

An thin 'e coom'd to the parish wi' lots o' Varsity debt,
Stook to his taaïl they did, an' 'e 'ant got shut on 'em yet.
An' 'e ligs on 'is back i' the grip, wi' noän to lend 'im a shove,
Woorse nor a far-welter'd[4] yowe: fur, Sammy, 'e married fur luvv.

IX

Luvv? what's luvv? thou can luvv thy lass an' 'er munny too,
Maakin' 'em goä togither as they've good right to do.
Could'n I luvv thy muther by cause o' 'er munny laaïd by?
Naäy—fur I luvv'd 'er a vast sight moor fur it: reäson why.

X

Ay an' thy muther says thou wants to marry the lass,
Cooms of a gentleman burn: an' we boäth on us thinks tha an ass.
Woä then, proputty, wiltha?—an ass as near as mays nowt[5]—
Woä then, wiltha? dangtha!—the bees is as fell as owt.[6]

XI

Breäk me a bit o' the esh for his 'eäd, lad, out o' the fence!
Gentleman burn! what's gentleman burn? is it shillins an' pence?
Proputty, proputty's ivrything 'ere, an', Sammy, I'm blest
If it isn't the saäme oop yonder, fur them as 'as it's the best.

---

[3] Earn.
[4] Or fow-welter'd,—said of a sheep lying on its back in the furrow.
[5] Makes nothing.
[6] The flies are as fierce as anything.

XII

Tis'n them as 'as munny as breäks into 'ouses an' steäls,
Them as 'as coäts to their backs an' taäkes their regular meäls.
Noä, but it's them as niver knaws wheer a meäl's to be 'ad.
Taäke my word for it, Sammy, the poor in a loomp is bad.

XIII

Them or thir feythers, tha sees, mun 'a beän a laäzy lot,
Fur work mun 'a gone to the gittin' whiniver munny was got.
Feyther 'ad ammost nowt; leastways 'is munny was 'id.
But 'e tued an' moil'd 'issén deäd, an 'e died a good un, 'e did.

XIV

Look thou theer wheer Wrigglesby beck cooms out by the 'ill
Feyther run oop to the farm, an' I runs oop to the mill;
An' I'll run oop to the brig, an' that thou'll live to see;
And if thou marries a good un I'll leäve the land to thee.

XV

Thim's my noätions, Sammy, wheerby I means to stick;
But if thou marries a bad un, I'll leave the land to Dick.—
Coom oop, proputty, proputty—that's what I 'ears 'im saäy—
Proputty, proputty, proputty—canter an' canter awaäy.

The Daisy

WRITTEN AT EDINBURGH

O LOVE, what hours were thine and mine,
In lands of palm and southern pine;
  In lands of palm, of orange-blossom,
Of olive, aloe, and maize and vine.

What Roman strength Turbìa show'd
In ruin, by the mountain road;
  How like a gem, beneath, the city
Of little Monaco, basking, glow'd.

How richly down the rocky dell
The torrent vineyard streaming fell
  To meet the sun and sunny waters,
That only heaved with a summer swell.

THE DAISY

What slender campanili grew
By bays, the peacock's neck in hue;
   Where, here and there, on sandy beaches
A milky-bell'd amaryllis blew.

How young Columbus seem'd to rove,
Yet present in his natal grove,
   Now watching high on mountain cornice,
And steering, now, from a purple cove,

Now pacing mute by ocean's rim;
Till, in a narrow street and dim,
   I stay'd the wheels at Cogoletto,
And drank, and loyally drank to him.

Nor knew we well what pleased us most,
Not the clipt palm of which they boast;
   But distant color, happy hamlet,
A moulder'd citadel on the coast,

Or tower, or high hill-convent, seen
A light amid its olives green;
   Or olive-hoary cape in ocean;
Or rosy blossom in hot ravine,

Where oleanders flush'd the bed
Of silent torrents, gravel-spread;
   And, crossing, oft we saw the glisten
Of ice, far up on a mountain head.

We loved that hall, tho' white and cold,
Those niched shapes of noble mould,
   A princely people's awful princes,
The grave, severe Genovese of old.

At Florence too what golden hours,
In those long galleries, were ours;
   What drives about the fresh Cascinè,
Or walks in Boboli's ducal bowers.

In bright vignettes, and each complete,
Of tower or duomo, sunny-sweet,
   Or palace, how the city glitter'd,
Thro' cypress avenues, at our feet.

But when we crost the Lombard plain
Remember what a plague of rain;
   Of rain at Reggio, rain at Parma;
At Lodi, rain, Piacenza, rain.

And stern and sad (so rare the smiles
Of sunlight) look'd the Lombard piles;
   Porch-pillars on the lion resting,
And sombre, old, colonnaded aisles.

O Milan, O the chanting quires,
The giant windows' blazon'd fires,
   The height, the space, the gloom, the glory!
A mount of marble, a hundred spires!

I climb'd the roofs at break of day;
Sun-smitten Alps before me lay.
   I stood among the silent statues,
And statued pinnacles, mute as they.

How faintly-flush'd, how phantom-fair,
Was Monte Rosa, hanging there
   A thousand shadowy-pencill'd valleys
And snowy dells in a golden air.

Remember how we came at last
To Como; shower and storm and blast
   Had blown the lake beyond his limit,
And all was flooded; and how we past

From Como, when the light was gray,
And in my head, for half the day,
   The rich Virgilian rustic measure
Of Lari Maxume, all the way,

Like ballad-burthen music, kept,
As on The Lariano crept
   To that fair port below the castle
Of Queen Theodolind, where we slept;

Or hardly slept, but watch'd awake
A cypress in the moonlight shake,
   The moonlight touching o'er a terrace
One tall Agavè above the lake.

What more? we took our last adieu,
And up the snowy Splugen drew,
  But ere we reach'd the highest summit
I pluck'd a daisy, I gave it you.

It told of England then to me,
And now it tells of Italy.
  O love, we two shall go no longer
To lands of summer across the sea;

So dear a life your arms enfold
Whose crying is a cry for gold:
  Yet here to-night in this dark city,
When ill and weary, alone and cold,

I found, tho' crush'd to hard and dry,
This nursling of another sky
  Still in the little book you lent me,
And where you tenderly laid it by:

And I forgot the clouded Forth,
The gloom that saddens Heaven and Earth.
  The bitter east, the misty summer
And gray metropolis of the North.

Perchance, to lull the throbs of pain,
Perchance, to charm a vacant brain,
  Perchance, to dream you still beside me,
My fancy fled to the South again.

To the Rev. F. D. Maurice

January, 1854

Come, when no graver cares employ,
Godfather, come and see your boy:
  Your presence will be sun in winter,
Making the little one leap for joy.

For, being of that honest few,
Who give the Fiend himself his due,
  Should eighty-thousand college-councils
Thunder "Anathema," friend, at you;

Should all our churchmen foam in spite
At you, so careful of the right,
   Yet one lay-hearth would give you welcome
(Take it and come) to the Isle of Wight;

Where, far from noise and smoke of town,
I watch the twilight falling brown
   All round a careless-order'd garden
Close to the ridge of a noble down.

You'll have no scandal while you dine,
But honest talk and wholesome wine,
   And only hear the magpie gossip
Garrulous under a roof of pine:

For groves of pine on either hand,
To break the blast of winter, stand;
   And further on, the hoary Channel
Tumbles a billow on chalk and sand;

Where, if below the milky steep
Some ship of battle slowly creep,
   And on thro' zones of light and shadow
Glimmer away to the lonely deep.

We might discuss the Northern sin
Which made a selfish war begin;
   Dispute the claims, arrange the chances;
Emperor, Ottoman, which shall win:

Or whether war's avenging rod
Shall lash all Europe into blood;
   Till you should turn to dearer matters,
Dear to the man that is dear to God;

How best to help the slender store,
How mend the dwellings, of the poor;
   How gain in life, as life advances,
Valor and charity more and more.

Come, Maurice, come: the lawn as yet
Is hoar with rime, or spongy-wet;
   But when the wreath of March has blossom'd,
Crocus, anemone, violet,

Or later, pay one visit here,
For those are few we hold as dear;
    Nor pay but one, but come for many,
Many and many a happy year.

WILL

I

O well for him whose will is strong!
He suffers, but he will not suffer long;
He suffers, but he cannot suffer wrong:
For him nor moves the loud world's random mock,
Nor all Calamity's hugest waves confound,
Who seems a promontory of rock,
That, compass'd round with turbulent sound,
In middle ocean meets the surging shock,
Tempest-buffeted, citadel-crown'd.

II

But ill for him who, bettering not with time,
Corrupts the strength of heaven-descended Will,
And ever weaker grows thro' acted crime,
Or seeming-genial venial fault,
Recurring and suggesting still!
He seems as one whose footsteps halt,
Toiling in immeasurable sand,
And o'er a weary sultry land,
Far beneath a blazing vault,
Sown in a wrinkle in the monstrous hill,
The city sparkles like a grain of salt.

In the Valley of Cauteretz

All along the valley, stream that flashest white,
Deepening thy voice with the deepening of the night,
All along the valley, where thy waters flow,
I walk'd with one I loved two and thirty years ago.
All along the valley, while I walk'd to-day,

The two and thirty years were a mist that rolls away;
For all along the valley, down thy rocky bed,
Thy living voice to me was as the voice of the dead,
And all along the valley, by rock and cave and tree,
The voice of the dead was a living voice to me.

IN THE GARDEN AT SWAINSTON

NIGHTINGALES warbled without,
    Within was weeping for thee:
Shadows of three dead men
    Walk'd in the walks with me,
    Shadows of three dead men and
        thou wast one of the three.

Nightingales sang in his woods:
    The Master was far away:
Nightingales warbled and sang
    Of a passion that lasts but a day;
    Still in the house in his coffin the
        Prince of courtesy lay.

Two dead men have I known
    In courtesy like to thee:
Two dead men have I loved
    With a love that ever will be:
    Three dead men have I loved, and
        thou art last of the three.

THE FLOWER

ONCE in a golden hour
    I cast to earth a seed.
Up there came a flower,
    The people said, a weed.

To and fro they went
    Thro' my garden-bower,
And muttering discontent
    Cursed me and my flower.

Then it grew so tall
  It wore a crown of light,
But thieves from o'er the wall
  Stole the seed by night.

Sow'd it far and wide
  By every town and tower,
Till all the people cried,
  "Splendid is the flower."

Read my little fable:
  He that runs may read.
Most can raise the flowers now,
  For all have got the seed.

And some are pretty enough,
  And some are poor indeed;
And now again the people
  Call it but a weed.

Requiescat

Fair is her cottage in its place,
  Where yon broad water sweetly, slowly glides.
It sees itself from thatch to base
  Dream in the sliding tides.

And fairer she, but ah how soon to die!
  Her quiet dream of life this hour may cease.
Her peaceful being slowly passes by
  To some more perfect peace.

The Sailor Boy

He rose at dawn and, fired with hope,
  Shot o'er the seething harbor-bar,
And reach'd the ship and caught the rope,
  And whistled to the morning star.

And while he whistled long and loud
    He heard a fierce mermaiden cry,
"O boy, tho' thou art young and proud,
    I see the place where thou wilt lie.

"The sands and yeasty surges mix
    In caves about the dreary bay,
And on thy ribs the limpet sticks,
    And in thy heart the scrawl shall play."

"Fool," he answer'd, "death is sure
    To those that stay and those that roam,
But I will nevermore endure
    To sit with empty hands at home.

"My mother clings about my neck,
    My sisters crying, 'Stay for shame;'
My father raves of death and wreck,
    They are all to blame, they are all to blame.

"God help me! save I take my part
    Of danger on the roaring sea,
A devil rises in my heart,
    Far worse than any death to me."

The Islet

"Whither, O whither, love, shall we go,
    For a score of sweet little summers or so?"
The sweet little wife of the singer said,
On the day that follow'd the day she was wed,
"Whither, O whither, love, shall we go?"
And the singer shaking his curly head
Turn'd as he sat, and struck the keys
There at his right with a sudden crash,
Singing, "And shall it be over the seas
With a crew that is neither rude nor rash,
But a bevy of Eroses apple-cheek'd,
In a shallop of crystal ivory-beak'd,
With a satin sail of a ruby glow,
To a sweet little Eden on earth that I know,
A mountain islet pointed and peak'd;

THE ISLET

Waves on a diamond shingle dash,
Cataract brooks to the ocean run,
Fairily-delicate palaces shine
Mixt with myrtle and clad with vine,
And overstream'd and silvery-streak'd
With many a rivulet high against the Sun
The facets of the glorious mountain flash
Above the valleys of palm and pine."
"Thither, O thither, love, let us go."

"No, no, no!
For in all that exquisite isle, my dear,
There is but one bird with a musical throat,
And his compass is but of a single note,
That it makes one weary to hear."

"Mock me not! mock me not! love, let us go."

"No, love, no.
For the bud ever breaks into bloom on the tree,
And a storm never wakes on the lonely sea,
And a worm is there in the lonely wood,
That pierces the liver and blackens the blood;
And makes it a sorrow to be."

CHILD–SONGS

I

THE CITY CHILD

DAINTY little maiden, whither would you wander?
  Whither from this pretty home, the home where mother dwells?
"Far and far away," said the dainty little maiden,
"All among the gardens, auriculas, anemones,
  Roses and lilies and Canterbury-bells."

Dainty little maiden, whither would you wander?
  Whither from this pretty house, this city-house of ours?
"Far and far away," said the dainty little maiden,
"All among the meadows, the clover and the clematis,
  Daisies and kingcups and honeysuckle-flowers."

II

Minnie and Winnie

Minnie and Winnie
 Slept in a shell.
Sleep, little ladies!
 And they slept well.

Pink was the shell within,
 Silver without;
Sounds of the great sea
 Wander'd about.

Sleep, little ladies!
 Wake not soon!
Echo on echo
 Dies to the moon.

Two bright stars
 Peep'd into the shell.
"What are they dreaming of?
 Who can tell?"

Started a green linnet
 Out of the croft;
Wake, little ladies,
 The sun is aloft!

The Spiteful Letter

Here, it is here, the close of the year,
 And with it a spiteful letter.
My name in song has done him much wrong,
 For himself has done much better.

O little bard, is your lot so hard,
 If men neglect your pages?
I think not much of yours or of mine,
 I hear the roll of the ages.

THE SPITEFUL LETTER

Rhymes and rhymes in the range of the times!
  Are mine for the moment stronger?
Yet hate me not, but abide your lot,
  I last but a moment longer.

This faded leaf, our names are as brief;
  What room is left for a hater?
Yet the yellow leaf hates the greener leaf,
  For it hangs one moment later.

Greater than I—is that your cry?
  And men will live to see it.
Well—if it be so—so it is, you know;
  And if it be so, so be it.

Brief, brief is a summer leaf,
  But this is the time of hollies.
O hollies and ivies and evergreens,
  How I hate the spites and the follies!

LITERARY SQUABBLES

AH God! the petty fools of rhyme
  That shriek and sweat in pigmy wars
Before the stony face of Time,
  And look'd at by the silent stars:

Who hate each other for a song,
  And do their little best to bite
And pinch their brethren in the throng,
  And scratch the very dead for spite:

And strain to make an inch of room
  For their sweet selves, and cannot hear
The sullen Lethe rolling doom
  On them and theirs and all things here:

When one small touch of Charity
  Could lift them nearer God-like state
Than if the crowned Orb should cry
  Like those who cried Diana great:

And I too, talk, and lose the touch
　　　I talk of. Surely, after all,
　The noblest answer unto such
　　　Is perfect stillness when they brawl.

The Victim

I

A plague upon the people fell,
　A famine after laid them low,
Then thorpe and byre arose in fire,
　For on them brake the sudden foe;
So thick they died the people cried,
　"The Gods are moved against the land."
The Priest in horror about his altar
　To Thor and Odin lifted a hand:
　　　"Help us from famine
　　　And plague and strife!
　　　What would you have of us?
　　　Human life?
　　　Were it our nearest,
　　　Were it our dearest,
　　　(Answer, O answer)
　　　We give you his life."

II

But still the foeman spoil'd and burn'd,
　And cattle died, and deer in wood,
And bird in air, and fishes turn'd
　And whiten'd all the rolling flood;
And dead men lay all over the way,
　Or down in a furrow scathed with flame:
And ever and aye the Priesthood moan'd,
　Till at last it seem'd that an answer came.
　　　"The King is happy
　　　In child and wife;
　　　Take you his dearest,
　　　Give us a life."

III

The Priest went out by heath and hill;
  The King was hunting in the wild;
They found the mother sitting still;
  She cast her arms about the child.
The child was only eight summers old,
  His beauty still with his years increased,
His face was ruddy, his hair was gold,
  He seem'd a victim due to the priest.
    The Priest beheld him,
    And cried with joy,
    "The Gods have answer'd:
    We give them the boy."

IV

The King return'd from out the wild,
  He bore but little game in hand;
The mother said, "They have taken the child
  To spill his blood and heal the land:
The land is sick, the people diseased,
  And blight and famine on all the lea:
The holy Gods, they must be appeased,
  So I pray you tell the truth to me.
    They have taken our son,
    They will have his life.
    Is *he* your dearest?
    Or I, the wife?"

V

The King bent low, with hand on brow,
  He stay'd his arms upon his knee:
"O wife, what use to answer now?
  For now the Priest has judged for me."
The King was shaken with holy fear;
  "The Gods," he said, "would have chosen well;
Yet both are near, and both are dear,
  And which the dearest I cannot tell!"
    But the Priest was happy,
    His victim won:
    "We have his dearest,
    His only son!"

VI

The rites prepared, the victim bared,
  The knife uprising toward the blow
To the altar-stone she sprang alone,
  "Me, not my darling, no!"
He caught her away with a sudden cry;
  Suddenly from him brake his wife,
And shrieking "*I* am his dearest, I—
  I am his dearest!" rush'd on the knife.
    And the Priest was happy,
    "O, Father Odin,
    We give you a life.
    Which was his nearest?
    Who was his dearest?
    The Gods have answer'd;
    We give them the wife!"

WAGES

GLORY of warrior, glory of orator, glory of song,
  Paid with a voice flying by to be lost on an endless sea—
Glory of Virtue, to fight, to struggle, to right the wrong—
  Nay, but she aim'd not at glory, no lover of glory she:
Give her the glory of going on, and still to be.

The wages of sin is death: if the wages of Virtue be dust,
  Would she have heart to endure for the life of the worm and
    the fly?
She desires no isles of the blest, no quiet seats of the just,
  To rest in a golden grove, or to bask in a summer sky:
Give her the wages of going on, and not to die.

THE HIGHER PANTHEISM

THE sun, the moon, the stars, the seas, the hills and the plains—
Are not these, O Soul, the Vision of Him who reigns?

Is not the Vision He? tho' He be not that which He seems?
Dreams are true while they last, and do we not live in dreams?

THE HIGHER PANTHEISM

Earth, these solid stars, this weight of body and limb,
Are they not sign and symbol of thy division from Him?

Dark is the world to thee: thyself art the reason why;
For is He not all but thou, that hast power to feel "I am I"?

Glory about thee, without thee; and thou fulfillest thy doom
Making Him broken gleams, and a stifled splendor and gloom.

Speak to Him thou for He hears, and Spirit with Spirit can
    meet—
Closer is He than breathing, and nearer than hands and feet.

God is law, say the wise; O Soul, and let us rejoice,
For if He thunder by law the thunder is yet His voice.

Law is God, say some: no God at all, says the fool;
For all we have power to see is a straight staff bent in a pool;

And the ear of man cannot hear, and the eye of man cannot
    see:
But if we could see and hear, this Vision—were it not He?

The Voice and the Peak

I

The voice and the Peak
    Far over summit and lawn,
The lone glow and long roar
    Green-rushing from the rosy thrones of dawn!

II

All night have I heard the voice
    Rave over the rocky bar,
But thou wert silent in heaven,
    Above thee glided the star.

III

Hast thou no voice, O Peak,
    That standest high above all?
"I am the voice of the Peak,
    I roar and rave for I fall.

IV

"A thousand voices go
  To North, South, East, and West;
They leave the heights and are troubled,
  And moan and sink to their rest.

V.

"The fields are fair beside them,
  The chestnut towers in his bloom;
But they—they feel the desire of the deep—
  Fall, and follow their doom.

VI

"The deep has power on the height,
  And the height has power on the deep;
They are raised for ever and ever,
  And sink again into sleep."

VII

Not raised for ever and ever,
  But when their cycle is o'er,
The valley, the voice, the peak, the star
  Pass, and are found no more.

VIII

The Peak is high and flush'd
  At his highest with sunrise fire;
The Peak is high, and the stars are high,
  And the thought of a man is higher.

IX

A deep below the deep,
  And a height beyond the height!
Our hearing is not hearing,
  And our seeing is not sight.

X

The voice and the Peak
  Far into heaven withdrawn,
The lone glow and long roar
  Green-rushing from the rosy thrones of dawn!

A Dedication

Dear, near and true—no truer Time himself
Can prove you, tho' he makes you evermore
Dearer and nearer, as the rapid of life
Shoots to the fall—take this and pray that he
Who wrote it, honoring your sweet faith in him,
May trust himself; and after praise and scorn,
As one who feels the immeasurable world,
Attain the wise indifference of the wise;
And after Autumn past—if left to pass
His autumn into seeming-leafless days—
Draw toward the long frost and longest night,
Wearing his wisdom lightly, like the fruit
Which in our winter woodland looks a flower.[1]

Flower in the crannied wall,
I pluck you out of the crannies,
I hold you here, root and all, in my hand,
Little flower—but *if* I could understand
What you are, root and all, and all in all,
I should know what God and man is.

[1] The fruit of the Spindle-tree (*Euonymus Europæus*).

IDYLLS OF THE KING

Dedication

THESE to His Memory—since he held them dear,
Perchance as finding here unconsciously
Some image of himself—I dedicate,
I dedicate, I consecrate with tears—
These Idylls.

                And indeed He seems to me
Scarce other than my king's ideal knight,
"Who reverenced his conscience as his king;
Whose glory was, redressing human wrong;
Who spake no slander, no, nor listen'd to it;
Who loved one only and who clave to her—"
Her—over all whose realms to their last isle,
Commingled with the gloom of imminent war,
The shadow of His loss drew like eclipse,
Darkening the world. We have lost him: he is gone:
We know him now: all narrow jealousies
Are silent; and we see him as he moved,
How modest, kindly, all-accomplish'd, wise,
With what sublime repression of himself,
And in what limits, and how tenderly;
Not swaying to this faction or to that;
Not making his high place the lawless perch
Of wing'd ambitions, nor a vantage-ground
For pleasure, but thro' all this tract of years
Wearing the white flower of a blameless life,
Before a thousand peering littlenesses,
In that fierce light which beats upon a throne,
And blackens every blot: for where is he,
Who dares foreshadow for an only son
A lovelier life, a more unstain'd, than his?
Or how should England dreaming of *his* sons
Hope more for these than some inheritance
Of such a life, a heart, a mind as thine,

Thou noble Father of her Kings to be,
Laborious for her people and her poor—
Voice in the rich dawn of an ampler day—
Far-sighted summoner of War and Waste
To fruitful strifes and rivalries of peace—
Sweet nature gilded by the gracious gleam
Of letters, dear to Science, dear to Art,
Dear to thy land and ours, a Prince indeed,
Beyond all titles, and a household name,
Hereafter, thro' all times, Albert the Good.

  Break not, O woman's heart, but still endure;
Break not, for thou art Royal, but endure,
Remembering all the beauty of that star
Which shone so close beside Thee that ye made
One light together, but his past and leaves
The Crown a lonely splendor.

                        May all love,
His love, unseen but felt, o'ershadow Thee,
The love of all Thy sons encompass Thee,
The love of all Thy daughters cherish Thee,
The love of all thy people comfort Thee,
Till God's love set Thee at his side again!

The Coming of Arthur

LEODOGRAN, the King of Cameliard,
Had one fair daughter, and none other child;
And she was fairest of all flesh on earth,
Guinevere, and in her his one delight.

  For many a petty king ere Arthur came
Ruled in this isle, and ever waging war
Each upon other, wasted all the land;
And still from time to time the heathen host
Swarm'd overseas, and harried what was left.
And so there grew great tracts of wilderness,
Wherein the beast was ever more and more,
But man was less and less, till Arthur came.
For first Aurelius lived and fought and died,
And after him King Uther fought and died,
But either fail'd to make the kingdom one.
And after these King Arthur for a space,

And thro' the puissance of his Table Round,
Drew all their petty princedoms under him,
Their king and head, and made a realm, and reign'd.

And thus the land of Cameliard was waste,
Thick with wet woods, and many a beast therein,
And none or few to scare or chase the beast;
So that wild dog, and wolf and boar and bear
Came night and day, and rooted in the fields,
And wallow'd in the gardens of the King.
And ever and anon the wolf would steal
The children and devour, but now and then,
Her own brood lost or dead, lent her fierce teat
To human sucklings; and the children, housed
In her foul den, there at their meat would growl,
And mock their foster-mother on four feet,
Till, straighten'd, they grew up to wolf-like men,
Worse than the wolves. And King Leodogran
Groan'd for the Roman legions here again,
And Cæsar's eagle: then his brother king,
Urien, assail'd him: last a heathen horde,
Reddening the sun with smoke and earth with blood,
And on the spike that split the mother's heart
Spitting the child, brake on him, till, amazed,
He knew not whither he should turn for aid.

But—for he heard of Arthur newly crown'd,
Tho' not without an uproar made by those
Who cried, "He is not Uther's son"—the King
Sent to him, saying, "Arise, and help us thou!
For here between the man and beast we die."

And Arthur yet had done no deed of arms,
But heard the call, and came: and Guinevere
Stood by the castle walls to watch him pass;
But since he neither wore on helm or shield
The golden symbol of his kinglihood,
But rode a simple knight among his knights,
And many of these in richer arms than he,
She saw him not, or mark'd not, if she saw,
One among many, tho' his face was bare.
But Arthur, looking downward as he past,
Felt the light of her eyes into his life

Smite on the sudden, yet rode on, and pitch'd
His tents beside the forest. Then he drave
The heathen; after, slew the beast, and fell'd
The forest, letting in the sun, and made
Broad pathways for the hunter and the knight
And so return'd.

          For while he linger'd there,
A doubt that ever smoulder'd in the hearts
Of those great Lords and Barons of his realm
Flash'd forth and into war: for most of these,
Colleaguing with a score of petty kings,
Made head against him, crying, "Who is he
That he should rule us? who hath proven him
King Uther's son? for lo! we look at him,
And find nor face nor bearing, limbs nor voice,
Are like to those of Uther whom we knew.
This is the son of Gorloïs, not the King;
This is the son of Anton, not the King."

  And Arthur, passing thence to battle, felt
Travail, and throes and agonies of the life,
Desiring to be join'd with Guinevere;
And thinking as he rode, "Her father said
That there between the man and beast they die
Shall I not lift her from this land of beasts
Up to my throne, and side by side with me?
What happiness to reign a lonely king,
Vext—O ye stars that shudder over me,
O earth that soundest hollow under me,
Vext with waste dreams? for saving I be join'd
To her that is the fairest under heaven,
I seem as nothing in the mighty world,
And cannot will my will, nor work my work
Wholly, nor make myself in mine own realm
Victor and lord. But were I join'd with her,
Then might we live together as one life,
And reigning with one will in everything
Have power in this dark land to lighten it,
And power on this dead world to make it live."

   Thereafter—as he speaks who tells the tale—
When Arthur reach'd a field-of-battle bright

With pitch'd pavilions of his foe, the world
Was all so clear about him, that he saw
The smallest rock far on the faintest hill,
And even in high day the morning star.
So when the King had set his banner broad,
At once from either side, with trumpet-blast,
And shouts, and clarions shrilling unto blood,
The long-lanced battle let their horses run,
And now the Barons and the kings prevail'd,
And now the King, as here and there that war
Went swaying; but the Powers who walk the world
Made lightnings and great thunders over him,
And dazed all eyes, till Arthur by main might,
And mightier of his hands with every blow,
And leading all his knighthood threw the kings
Carádos, Urien, Cradlemont of Wales,
Claudias, and Clariance of Northumberland,
The King Brandagoras of Latangor,
With Anguisant of Erin, Morganore,
And Lot of Orkney. Then, before a voice
As dreadful as the shout of one who sees
To one who sins, and deems himself alone
And all the world asleep, they swerved and brake
Flying, and Arthur call'd to stay the brands
That hack'd among the flyers, "Ho! they yield!"
So like a painted battle the war stood
Silenced, the living quiet as the dead,
And in the heart of Arthur joy was lord.
He laugh'd upon his worrior whom he loved
And honor'd most. "Thou dost not doubt me King,
So well thine arm hath wrought for me to-day."
"Sir and my liege," he cried, "the fire of God
Descends upon thee in the battle-field:
I know thee for my King!" Whereat the two,
For each had warded either in the fight,
Sware on the field of death a deathless love.
And Arthur said, "Man's word is God in man:
Let chance what will, I trust thee to the death."

Then quickly from the foughten field he sent
Ulfius, and Brastias, and Bedivere,

His new-made knights, to King Leodogran,
Saying, "If I in aught have served thee well,
Give me thy daughter Guinevere to wife."

  Whom when he heard, Leodogran in heart
Debating—"How should I that am a king,
However much he holp me at my need,
Give my one daughter saving to a king,
And a king's son?"—lifted his voice, and call'd
A hoary man, his chamberlain, to whom
He trusted all things, and of him required
His counsel: "Knowest thou aught of Arthur's birth?"

  Then spake the hoary chamberlain and said,
"Sir King, there be but two old men that know:
And each is twice as old as I; and one
Is Merlin, the wise man that ever served
King Uther thro' his magic art; and one
Is Merlin's master (so they call him) Bleys,
Who taught him magic; but the scholar ran
Before the master, and so far, that Bleys
Laid magic by, and sat him down, and wrote
All things and whatsoever Merlin did
In one great annal-book, where after years
Will learn the secret of our Arthur's birth."

  To whom the King Leodogran replied,
"O friend, had I been holpen half as well
By this King Arthur as by thee to-day,
Then beast and man had had their share of me:
But summon here before us yet once more
Ulfius, and Brastias, and Bedivere."

  Then, when they came before him, the King said,
"I have seen the cuckoo chased by lesser fowl,
And reason in the chase: but wherefore now
Do these your lords stir up the heat of war,
Some calling Arthur born of Gorloïs,
Others of Anton? Tell me, ye yourselves,
Hold ye this Arthur for King Uther's son?"

And Ulfius and Brastius answer'd, "Ay."
Then Bedivere, the first of all his knights
Knighted by Arthur at his crowning, spake—
For bold in heart and act and word was he,
Whenever slander breathed against the King—

"Sir, there be many rumors on this head:
For there be those who hate him in their hearts,
Call him baseborn, and since his ways are sweet,
And theirs are bestial, hold him less than man:
And there be those who deem him more than man,
And dream he dropt from heaven, but my belief
In all this matter—so ye care to learn—
Sir, for ye know that in King Uther's time
The prince and warrior Gorloïs, he that held
Tintagil castle by the Cornish sea,
Was wedded with a winsome wife, Ygerne:
And daughters had she borne him,—one whereof,
Lot's wife, the Queen of Orkney, Bellicent,
Hath ever like a loyal sister cleaved
To Arthur,—but a son she had not borne.
And Uther cast upon her eyes of love:
But she, a stainless wife to Gorloïs,
So loathed the bright dishonor of his love,
That Gorloïs and King Uther went to war:
And overthrown was Gorloïs and slain.
Then Uther in his wrath and heat besieged
Ygerne within Tintagil, where her men,
Seeing the mighty swarm about their walls,
Left her and fled, and Uther enter'd in,
And there was none to call to but himself.
So, compass'd by the power of the King,
Enforced she was to wed him in her tears,
And with a shameful swiftness: afterward,
Not many moons, King Uther died himself,
Moaning and wailing for an heir to rule
After him, lest the realm should go to wrack.
And that same night, the night of the new year,
By reason of the bitterness and grief
That vext his mother, all before his time
Was Arthur born, and all as soon as born
Deliver'd at a secret postern-gate
To Merlin, to be holden far apart

Until his hour should come; because the lords
Of that fierce day were as the lords of this,
Wild beasts, and surely would have torn the child
Piecemeal among them, had they known; for each
But sought to rule for his own self and hand,
And many hated Uther for the sake
Of Gorloïs. Wherefore Merlin took the child,
And gave him to Sir Anton, an old knight
And ancient friend of Uther; and his wife
Nursed the young prince, and rear'd him with her own;
And no man knew. And ever since the lords
Have foughten like wild beasts among themselves,
So that the realm has gone to wrack: but now,
This year, when Merlin (for his hour had come)
Brought Arthur forth, and set him in the hall,
Proclaiming, 'Here is Uther's heir, your king,'
A hundred voices cried, 'Away with him
No king of ours! a son of Gorloïs he,
Or else the child of Anton, and no king,
Or else baseborn.' Yet Merlin thro' his craft,
And while the people clamor'd for a king,
Had Arthur crown'd; but after, the great lords
Banded, and so brake out in open war."

Then while the King debated with himself
If Arthur were the child of shamefulness,
Or born the son of Gorloïs, after death,
Or Uther's son, and born before his time,
Or whether there were truth in anything
Said by these three, there came to Cameliard,
With Gawain and young Modred, her two sons,
Lot's wife, the Queen of Orkney, Bellicent;
Whom as he could, not as he would, the King
Made feast for, saying, as they sat at meat,

"A doubtful throne is ice on summer seas.
Ye come from Arthur's court. Victor his men
Report him! Yea, but ye—think ye this king—
So many those that hate him, and so strong,
So few his knights, however brave they be—
Hath body enow to hold his foemen down?"

"O King," she cried, "and I will tell thee: few,
Few, but all brave, all of one mind with him;
For I was near him when the savage yells
Of Uther's peerage died, and Arthur sat
Crown'd on the daïs, and his warriors cried,
'Be thou the king, and we will work thy will
Who love thee.' Then the King in low deep tones,
And simple words of great authority,
Bound them by so strait vows to his own self,
That when they rose, knighted from kneeling, some
Were pale as at the passing of a ghost,
Some flush'd, and others dazed, as one who wakes
Half-blinded at the coming of a light.

"But when he spake and cheer'd his Table Round
With large divine and comfortable words
Beyond my tongue to tell thee—I beheld
From eye to eye thro' all their Order flash
A momentary likeness of the King:
And ere it left their faces, thro' the cross
And those around it and the Crucified,
Down from the casement over Arthur, smote
Flame-color, vert and azure, in three rays,
One falling upon each of three fair queens,
Who stood in silence near his throne, the friends
Of Arthur, gazing on him, tall, with bright
Sweet faces, who will help him at his need.

"And there I saw mage Merlin, whose vast wit
And hundred winters are but as the hands
Of loyal vassals toiling for their liege.

"And near him stood the Lady of the Lake,
Who knows a subtler magic than his own—
Clothed in white samite, mystic, wonderful.
She gave the King his huge cross-hilted sword,
Whereby to drive the heathen out: a mist
Of incense curl'd about her, and her face
Wellnigh was hidden in the minster gloom;
But there was heard among the holy hymns
A voice as of the waters, for she dwells
Down in a deep, calm, whatsoever storms

May shake the world, and when the surface rolls,
Hath power to walk the waters like our Lord.

"There likewise I beheld Excalibur
Before him at his crowning borne, the sword
That rose from out the bosom of the lake,
And Arthur row'd across and took it—rich
With jewels, elfin Urim, on the hilt,
Bewildering heart and eye—the blade so bright
That men are blinded by it—on one side,
Graven in the oldest tongue of all this world,
'Take me,' but turn the blade and ye shall see,
And written in the speech ye speak yourself,
'Cast me away!' And sad was Arthur's face
Taking it, but old Merlin counsell'd him,
'Take thou and strike! the time to cast away
Is yet far-off.' So this great brand the king
Took, and by this will beat his foemen down."

Thereat Leodogran rejoiced, but thought
To sift his doubtings to the last, and ask'd,
Fixing full eyes of question on her face,
"The swallow and the swift are near akin,
But thou art closer to this noble prince,
Being his own dear sister;" and she said,
"Daughter of Gorloïs and Ygerne am I;"
"And therefore Arthur's sister?" ask'd the King.
She answer'd, "These be secret things," and sign'd
To those two sons to pass and let them be.
And Gawain went, and breaking into song
Sprang out, and follow'd by his flying hair
Ran like a colt, and leapt at all he saw:
But Modred laid his ear beside the doors,
And there half-heard; the same that afterward
Struck for the throne, and striking found his doom.

And then the Queen made answer, "What know I?
For dark my mother was in eyes and hair,
And dark in hair and eyes am I; and dark
Was Gorloïs, yea and dark was Uther too,
Wellnigh to blackness; but this King is fair
Beyond the race of Britons and of men.
Moreover, always in my mind I hear

A cry from out the dawning of my life,
A mother weeping, and I hear her say,
'O that ye had some brother, pretty one,
To guard thee on the rough ways of the world.' "

"Ay," said the King, "and hear ye such a cry?
But when did Arthur chance upon thee first?"

"O King!" she cried, "and I will tell thee true:
He found me first when yet a little maid:
Beaten I had been for a little fault
Whereof I was not guilty; and out I ran
And flung myself down on a bank of heath,
And hated this fair world and all therein,
And wept, and wish'd that I were dead; and he—
I know not whether of himself he came,
Or brought by Merlin, who, they say, can walk
Unseen at pleasure—he was at my side
And spake sweet words, and comforted my heart,
And dried my tears, being a child with me.
And many a time he came, and evermore
As I grew greater grew with me; and sad
At times he seem'd, and sad with him was I,
Stern too at times, and then I loved him not,
But sweet again, and then I loved him well.
And now of late I see him less and less,
But those first days had golden hours for me,
For then I surely thought he would be king.

"But let me tell thee now another tale:
For Bleys, our Merlin's master, as they say,
Died but of late, and sent his cry to me,
To hear him speak before he left his life.
Shrunk like a fairy changeling lay the mage;
And when I enter'd told me that himself
And Merlin ever served about the King,
Uther, before he died; and on the night
When Uther in Tintagil past away
Moaning and wailing for an heir, the two
Left the still King, and passing forth to breathe,
Then from the castle gateway by the chasm
Descending thro' the dismal night—a night
In which the bounds of heaven and earth were lost—

Beheld, so high upon the dreary deeps
It seem'd in heaven, a ship, the shape thereof
A dragon wing'd, and all from stem to stern
Bright with a shining people on the decks,
And gone as soon as seen. And then the two
Dropt to the cove, and watch'd the great sea fall,
Wave after wave, each mightier than the last,
Till last, a ninth one, gathering half the deep
And full of voices, slowly rose and plunged
Roaring, and all the wave was in a flame:
And down the wave and in the flame was borne
A naked babe, and rode to Merlin's feet,
Who stoopt and caught the babe, and cried 'The King!
Here is an heir for Uther!' And the fringe
Of that great breaker, sweeping up the strand,
Lash'd at the wizard as he spake the word,
And all at once round him rose in fire,
So that the child and he were clothed in fire.
And presently thereafter follow'd calm,
Free sky and stars: 'And this same child,' he said,
'Is he who reigns; nor could I part in peace
Till this were told.' And saying this the seer
Went thro' the strait and dreadful pass of death,
Not ever to be question'd any more
Save on the further side; but when I met
Merlin, and ask'd him if these things were truth—
The shining dragon and the naked child
Descending in the glory of the seas—
He laugh'd as is his wont, and answer'd me
In riddling triplets of old time, and said:

" 'Rain, rain, and sun! a rainbow in the sky!
A young man will be wiser by and by;
An old man's wit may wander ere he die.

Rain, rain, and sun! a rainbow on the lea!
And truth is this to me, and that to thee;
And truth or clothed or naked let it be.

Rain, sun, and rain! and the free blossom blows:
Sun, rain, and sun! and where is he who knows?
From the great deep to the great deep he goes.'

"So Merlin riddling anger'd me; but thou
Fear not to give this King thine only child,

Guinevere: so great bards of him will sing
Hereafter; and dark sayings from of old
Ranging and ringing thro' the minds of men,
And echo'd by old folk beside their fires
For comfort after their wage-work is done,
Speak of the King; and Merlin in our time
Hath spoken also, not in jest, and sworn
Tho' men may wound him that he will not die,
But pass, again to come; and then or now
Utterly smite the heathen underfoot,
Till these and all men hail him for their king."

She spake and King Leodogran rejoiced,
But musing "Shall I answer yea or nay?"
Doubted, and drowsed, nodded and slept, and saw,
Dreaming, a slope of land that ever grew,
Field after field, up to a height, the peak
Haze-hidden, and thereon a phantom king,
Now looming, and now lost; and on the slope
The sword rose, the hind fell, the herd was driven,
Fire glimpsed; and all the land from roof and rick,
In drifts of smoke before a rolling wind,
Stream'd to the peak, and mingled with the haze
And made it thicker; while the phantom king
Sent out at times a voice; and here or there
Stood one who pointed toward the voice, the rest
Slew on and burnt, crying, "No king of ours,
No son of Uther, and no king of ours;"
Till with a wink his dream was changed, the haze
Descended, and the solid earth became
As nothing, but the King stood out in heaven,
Crown'd. And Leodogran awoke, and sent
Ulfius, and Brastias and Bedivere,
Back to the court of Arthur answering yea.

Then Arthur charged his warrior whom he loved
And honor'd most, Sir Lancelot, to ride forth
And bring the Queen;—and watch'd him from the gates:
And Lancelot past away among the flowers,
 (For then was latter April) and return'd
Among the flowers, in May, with Guinevere.
To whom arrived, by Dubric the high saint,
Chief of the church in Britain, and before

The stateliest of her altar-shrines, the King
That morn was married, while in stainless white,
The fair beginners of a nobler time,
And glorying in their vows and him, his knights
Stood round him, and rejoicing in his joy.
Far shone the fields of May thro' open door,
The sacred altar blossom'd white with May,
The Sun of May descended on their King,
They gazed on all earth's beauty in their Queen,
Roll'd incense, and there past along the hymns
A voice as of the waters, while the two
Sware at the shrine of Christ a deathless love:
And Arthur said, "Behold, thy doom is mine.
Let chance what will, I love thee to the death!"
To whom the Queen replied with drooping eyes,
"King and my lord, I love thee to the death!"
And holy Dubric spread his hands and spake,
"Reign ye, and live and love, and make the world
Other, and may thy Queen be one with thee,
And all this Order of thy Table Round
Fulfil the boundless purpose of their King!"

So Dubric said; but when they left the shrine
Great Lords from Rome before the portal stood,
In scornful stillness gazing as they past;
Then while they paced a city all on fire
With sun and cloth of gold, the trumpets blew,
And Arthur's knighthood sang before the King:—

"Blow trumpet, for the world is white with May;
Blow trumpet, the long night hath roll'd away!
Blow thro' the living world—'Let the King reign.'

"Shall Rome or Heathen rule in Arthur's realm?
Flash brand and lance, fall battleaxe upon helm,
Fall battleaxe, and flash brand! Let the King reign.

"Strike for the King and live! his knights have heard
That God hath told the King a secret word.
Fall battleaxe, and flash brand! Let the King reign.

"Blow trumpet! he will lift us from the dust.
Blow trumpet! live the strength and die the lust!
Clang battleaxe, and clash brand! Let the King reign.

"Strike for the King and die! and if thou diest,
The King is King, and ever wills the highest.
Clang battleaxe, and clash brand! Let the King reign.

"Blow, for our Sun is mighty in his May!
Blow, for our Sun is mightier day by day!
Clang battleaxe, and clash brand! Let the King reign.

"The King will follow Christ, and we the King
In whom high God hath breathed a secret thing.
Fall battleaxe, and flash brand! Let the King reign."

So sang the knighthood, moving to their hall.
There at the banquet those great Lords from Rome,
The slowly-fading mistress of the world,
Strode in, and claim'd their tribute as of yore.
But Arthur spake, "Behold, for these have sworn
To wage my wars, and worship me their King;
The old order changeth, yielding place to new;
And we that fight for our fair father Christ,
Seeing that ye be grown too weak and old
To drive the heathen from your Roman wall,
No tribute will we pay": so those great lords
Drew back in wrath, and Arthur strove with Rome.

And Arthur and his knighthood for a space
Were all one will, and thro' that strength the King
Drew in the petty princedoms under him,
Fought, and in twelve great battles overcame
The heathen hordes, and made a realm and reign'd.

THE VILLAGE WIFE
or, the Entail

I

'Ouse-keeper sent tha my lass, fur New Squire coom'd last night.
Butter an' heggs—yis—yis. I'll goä wi' tha back: all right;
Butter I warrants be prime, an' I warrants the heggs be as well,
Hafe a pint o' milk runs out when ya breäks the shell.

II

Sit thysen down fur a bit: hev a glass o' cowslip wine!
I liked the owd Squire an' 'is gells as thaw they was gells o' mine,
Fur then we was all es one, the Squire an' 'is darters an' me,
Hall but Miss Annie, the heldest, I niver not took to she:
But Nelly, the last of the cletch[1] I liked 'er the fust on 'em all,
Fur hoffens we talkt o' my darter es died o' the fever at fall:
An' I thowt 'twur the will o' the Lord, but Miss Annie she said it wur draäins,
Fur she hedn't naw coomfut in 'er, an' arn'd naw thanks fur 'er paäins.
Eh! thebbe all wi' the Lord my childer, I han't gotten none!
Sa new Squire's coom'd wi' 'is taäil in 'is 'and, an' owd Squire's gone.

III

Fur 'staäte be i' taäil, my lass: tha dosn' knaw what that be?
But I knaws the law, I does, for the lawyer ha towd it me.
"When theer's naw 'eäd to a 'Ouse by the fault o' that ere maäle—
The gells they counts fur nowt, and the next un he taäkes the taäil."

IV

What be the next un like? can tha tell ony harm on 'im lass?—
Naay sit down—naw 'urry—sa cowd!—hev another glass!
Straänge an' cowd fur the time! we may happen a fall o' snaw—
Not es I cares fur to hear ony harm, but I likes to knaw.
An' I 'oaps es 'e beänt boooklarn'd: but 'e dosn' not coom fro' the shere;

---

[1] A brood of chickens.

We' anew o' that wi' the Squire, an' we haätes boooklarnin' ere.

V

Fur Squire wur a Varsity scholard, an' niver lookt arter the land—
Whoäts or turmuts or taätes—e' 'ed hallus a booök i' 'is 'and,
Hallus aloän wi' 'is boooks, thaw nigh upo' seventy year.
An' boooks? whats' boooks? thou knaws thebbe neyther 'ere nor theer.

VI

An' the gells, they hadn't naw taäils, an' the lawyer he towd it me
That 'is taäil were soä tied up es he couldn't cut down a tree!
"Drat the trees," says I, to be sewer I haätes 'em, my lass,
Fur we puts the muck o' the land an' they sucks the muck fro' the grass.

VII

An' Squire wur hallus a-smilin', an' gied to the tramps goin' by—
An' all o' the wust i' the parish—wi' hoffens a drop in 'is eye.
An' ivry darter o' Squire's hed her awn ridin-erse to 'ersen,
An' they rampaged about wi' their grooms, an' was 'untin' arter the men,
An' hallus a-dallackt[1] an' dizen'd out, an' a-buyin' new cloäthes,
While 'e sit like a graät glimmer-gowk[2] wi' 'is glasses athurt 'is noäse,
An' 'is noäse sa grufted wi' snuff as it couldn't be scroob'd awaäy,
Fur atween 'is reädin' an' writin' 'e snifft up a box in a daäy,
An' 'e niver runn'd arter the fox, nor arter the birds wi' 'is gun,
An' 'e niver not shot one 'are, but 'e leäved it to Charlie 'is son,
An' 'e niver not fish'd 'is awn ponds, but Charlie 'e cotch'd the pike,
For 'e warn't not burn to the land, an' 'e didn't take kind to it like;

---

[1] Overdressed in gay colors.
[2] Owl.

THE VILLAGE WIFE 303

But I eärs es 'e'd gie fur a howry[1] owd book thutty pound an' moor,
An' 'e'd wrote an owd book, his awn sen, sa I knaw'd es 'e'd coom to be poor;
An' 'e gied—I be fear'd to tell tha 'ow much—fur an owd scratted stoän,
An' 'e digg'd up a loomp i' the land an' 'e got a brown pot an' a boän,
An' 'e bowt owd money, es wouldn't goä, wi' good gowd o' the Queen,
An' 'e bowt little statutes all-naäkt an' which was a shaame to be seen;
But 'e niver looökt ower a bill, nor 'e niver not seed to owt,
An' 'e niver knawd nowt but boöoks, an' boöoks, as thou knaws, beänt nowt.

VIII

But owd Squire's laädy es long es she lived she kep 'em all clear,
Thaw es long es she lived I never hed none of 'er darters 'ere;
But arter she died we was all es one, the childer an' me,
An' sarvints runn'd in an' out, an' offens we hed 'em to tea.
Lawk! 'ow I laugh'd when the lasses 'ud talk o' their Missis's waäys,
An' the Missisis talk'd o' the lasses.—I'll tell tha some o' these daäys.
Hoänly Miss Annie were saw stuck oop, like 'er mother afoor—
'Er an' 'er blessed darter—they niver derken'd my door.

IX

An' Squire 'e smiled an' 'e smiled till 'e'd gotten a fright at last,
An' 'e calls fur 'is son, fur the 'turney's letters they foller'd sa fast;
But Squire wur afear'd o' 'is son, an' 'e says to 'im, meek as a mouse,
"Lad, thou mun cut off thy taäil, or the gells 'ull goä to the 'Ouse,
Fur I finds es I be that i' debt, es I 'oäps es thou'll 'elp me a bit,
An' if thou'll 'gree to cut off thy taäil I may saäve mysen yit."

---

[1] Filthy.

X

But Charlie 'e sets back 'is ears, 'an 'e sweärs, an' 'e says to im "Noä.
I've gotten the 'staäte by the taäil an' be dang'd if I iver let goä!
Coom! coom! feyther," 'e says, "why shouldn't thy booöks be sowd?
I hears es soom o' thy booöks mebbe worth their weight i' gowd."

XI

Heäps an' heäps o' booöks, I ha' see'd 'em, belong'd to the Squire,
But the lasses 'ed teärd out leaves i' the middle to kindle the fire;
Sa moäst on 'is owd big booöks fetch'd nigh to nowt at the saäle,
And Squire were at Charlie ageän to git 'im to cut off 'is taäil.

XII

Ya wouldn't find Charlie's likes—'e were that outdacious at oäm,
Not thaw ya went fur to raäke out Hell wi' a small-tooth coämb—
Droonk wi' the Quoloty's wine, an' droonk wi' the farmer's aäle,
Mad wi' the lasses an' all—an' 'e wouldn't cut off the taäil.

XIII

Thou's coom'd oop by the beck; and a thurn be a-grawin' theer,
I niver ha seed it sa white wi' the Maäy es I see'd it to-year—
Theerabouts Charlie joompt—and it gied me a scare tother night,
Fur I thowt it wur Charlie's ghoäst i' the derk, fur it looökt sa white.
"Billy," says 'e, "hev a joomp!"—thaw the banks o' the beck be sa high,
Fur he ca'd 'is 'erse Billy-rough-un, thaw niver a hair wur awry;
But Billy fell bakkuds o' Charlie, an' Charlie 'e brok 'is neck,
Sa theer wur a hend o' the taäil, fur 'e lost 'is taäil i' the beck.

XIV

Sa 'is taäil wur lost an' 'is boöoks wur gone an' 'is boy wur deäd,
An' Squire 'e smiled an' 'e smiled, but 'e niver not lift oop 'is 'eäd:
Hallus a soft un Squire! an' 'e smiled, fur 'e hedn't naw friend,
Sa feyther an' son was buried togither, an' this wur the hend.

XV

An' Parson as hesn't the call, nor the mooney, but hes the pride,
'E reäds of a sewer an' sartan 'oäp o' the tother side;
But I beänt that sewer es the Lord, howsiver they praäy'd an' praäy'd,
Lets them inter 'eaven eäsy es leäves their debts to be paäid.
Siver the mou'ds rattled down upo' poor owd Squire i' the wood,
An' I cried along wi' the gells, fur they weänt niver coom to naw good.

XVI

Fur Molly the long un she walkt awaäy wi' a hofficer lad,
An' nawbody 'eard on 'er sin, sa o' coorse she be gone to the bad!
An' Lucy wur laäme o' one leg, sweet'arts she niver 'ed none—
Straänge an' unheppen[1] Miss Lucy! we naämed her "Dot an' gaw one!"
An' Hetty wur weak i' the hatties, wi'out ony harm i' the legs,
An' the fever 'ed baäked Jinny's 'ead as bald as one o' them heggs,
An' Nelly wur up fro' the craädle as big i' the mouth as a cow,
An' saw she mun hammergrate,[2] lass, or she weänt git a maäte onyhow!
An' es for Miss Annie es call'd me afoor my awn foälks to my faäce
"A hignorant village wife as 'ud hev to be larn'd her awn plaäce,"
Hes for Miss Hannie the heldest hes now be a grawin sa howd,
I knaws that mooch o' sheä, es it beänt not fit to be towd!

[1] Ungainly, awkward.
[2] Emigrate.

XVII

Sa I didn't not taäke it kindly ov owd Miss Annie to saäy
Es I should be talkin ageän 'em, es soon es they went awaäy,
Fur, lawks! 'ow I cried when they went, an' our Nelly she gied me 'er 'and,
Fur I'd ha done owt for the Squire an' 'is gells es belong'd to the land;
Boooks, es I said afoor, thebbe neyther 'ere nor theer!
But I sarved 'em wi' butter an' heggs fur huppuds o' twenty year.

XVIII

An' they hallus paäid what I hax'd, sa I hallus deal'd wi' the Hall,
An' they knaw'd what butter wur, an' they knaw'd what a hegg wur an' all;
Hugger-mugger they lived, but they wasn't that eäsy to pleäse,
Till I gied 'em Hinjian curn, an' they laäid big heggs es tha seeas;
An' I niver puts saäme[1] i' *my* butter, they does it at Willis's farm,
Taäste another drop o' the wine—tweänt do tha na harm.

XIX

Sa new Squire's coom'd wi' 'is taäil in 'is 'and, an' owd Squire's gone;
I heard 'im a roomlin' by, but arter my nightcap wur on;
Sa I han't clapt eyes on 'im yit, fur he coom'd last night sa laäte—
Pluksh!!![2] the hens i' the peäs! why didn't tha hesp tha gaäte?

[1] Lard.
[2] A cry accompanied by a clapping of hands to scare trespassing fowl.